Parent
School

Parent School

Simple Lessons From the Leading Experts on Being a Mom & Dad

Compiled and Edited by

Jerry and Lorin Biederman

Foreword by Penelope Leach, Ph.D.

M. Evans and Company, Inc.
New York

M. Evans and Company, Inc.
216 East 49th Street
New York, New York 10017

Library of Congress Cataloging-in-Publication Data

Parent School: Simple lessons from the leading experts on being a Mom and Dad/compiled by Jerry and Lorin Biederman; foreword by Penelope Leach.
    p.cm.
    Includes index
    ISBN 0-87131-958-6
    1. Parenting. 2. Child rearing. I. Biederman, Jerry. II. Biederman, Lorin Michelle, 1964-

HQ755.8.P373 2001
649'.1—dc21

2001040755

Printed in the United States of America

9 8 7 6 5 4 3 2 1

This book is dedicated to our children, Jennifer Nicole and David Harrison, who have been patient, wise, gentle, and loving teachers and who continue to fill our lives with wonder.

Curriculum

Foreword, *Penelope Leach, Ph.D.* xv

Acknowledgments xvii

Orientation xix

Parenting 101

LESSON 1

Tending Your Child's Soul, Michael Gurian 2

LESSON 2

Getting Behind the Eyes of Your Child,

William Sears, M.D., and Martha Sears, R.N. 6

LESSON 3

The Seven Best Things Good Parents Can Do,

John C. Friel, Ph.D., and Linda D. Friel, M.A. 8

LESSON 4

The Joys and Challenges of Parenting:

What We Have Learned from Raising Our Ten Sons,

Catherine Musco Garcia-Prats and Joseph Garcia-Prats, M.D. 13

LESSON 5

Am I Doing it Right? What Makes You a Good Parent

Mary Snyder 19

LESSON 6

Four Thoughts for Parents from the *Tao Te Ching*,

William Martin 22

LESSON 7

Dr. Mom's Greatest Lesson for Parents,

Marianne Neifert, M.D. 27

LESSON 8

The Seven Keys to Good Parenting, Lawrence Kutner, Ph.D. 31

LESSON 9

    Raising Good Kids in a Troubled World, Ross Campbell, M.D.   34

LESSON 10

    Lessons in Taming the Dragon, Meg Eastman, Ph.D.   39

LESSON 11

    Sex and Parenthood, Valerie Davis Raskin, M.D.   43

Health and Nutrition

LESSON 12

    Engage and Participate in Your Child's Health Care,
    Steven P. Shelov, M.D., M.A.   48

LESSON 13

    Sleep Pretty Baby:
    The Importance of Sleep in Your Child's Life, Inda Shaenen   51

LESSON 14

    How to Handle Homesickness, Christopher Thurber, Ph.D.   55

LESSON 15

    The Mastery of Intimate Conversations with Your Child,
    Jessica Gillooly, Ph.D.   61

LESSON 16

    Sex Differences in Health, Susan Gilbert   65

LESSON 17

    Avoiding a Weight Problem in Your Child,
    Irving Penn, M.D., J.D.   70

In the Beginning

LESSON 18

    The First Signs of Intelligent Life:
    Awaken Your Baby's Inner Resources, Joseph Garcia, Ed.D.   76

LESSON 19

    The Importance of Early Childhood Parenting,
    Burton L. White   80

LESSON 20

    My Own Best Mom, Julia Indichova   82

Mommy and Me

LESSON 21

What You Didn't Expect When You Were Expecting,
Karen Kleiman, M.S.W.   86

LESSON 22

Redefining the "Good" Mother, Chris Fletcher   90

LESSON 23

Four Ground Rules for Life as an At-Home Mother,
Darcie Sanders and Martha M. Bullen   93

LESSON 24

A Letter to Your Child, Bettie B. Youngs, Ph.D.   98

Rules of Discipline

LESSON 25

Listen, John Gray, Ph.D.   106

LESSON 26

The New Protective Parent: Striking a Healthy Balance,
Paula Statman, M.S.W.   114

LESSON 27

Eighteen Ways to Avoid Power Struggles, Jane Nelsen, Ed.D.   119

LESSON 28

Dare to Dine Out, Roslyn Duffy   124

LESSON 29

"It's Mine!"—How to Teach Sharing,
Mark L. Brenner, MFCC   129

LESSON 30

The Best Discipline is Strict Discipline, John Rosemond   132

LESSON 31

Learn to Give Praise and Positive Attention,
James Windell, M.A.   136

LESSON 32

The Wonderful World of Wits-End Parenting,
Charles Fay, Ph.D.   141

LESSON 33

Raising Responsible Kids, Darrell J. Burnett, Ph.D.   147

LESSON 34

Practical Tools to Discipline Effectively,
William P. Garvey, Ph.D.   154

LESSON 35

Waist-High Fences: An Approach to Discipline,
Marilyn E. Gootman   160

LESSON 36

Who's in Charge at Your House? Managing Kids'
Testing and Manipulation, Thomas W. Phelan, Ph.D.   164

LESSON 37

You Can't Make Me—But I Can Be Persuaded!
Cynthia Ulrich Tobias, M.A.   172

LESSON 38

Face Reality, Valerie Wiener, M.A., M.A.   179

LESSON 39

Turning Conflict into Cooperation, Becky A. Bailey, Ph.D.   181

LESSON 40

Keeping Your Teen from Remaining a Tribe Apart,
Patricia Hersch   189

LESSON 41

Better to Prepare or to Punish?, Paula Statman, M.S.W.   195

LESSON 42

Excerpts from Rebel Without a Car, Fred Mednick, Ed.D.   197

Lessons in Learning: Educating Our Next Generation

LESSON 43

Learning Really Is Fun!
Naomi E. Singer and Matthew J. Miller   204

LESSON 44

What Is Smart? Understanding and Nurturing the
Multiple Intelligences in Your Child, Laurel Schmidt   210

LESSON 45

Children and Books, Trish Kuffner   216

LESSON 46

A Father's Place Is in the School, Aaron Kipnis, Ph.D.   222

Secrets to Self-Esteem

LESSON 47

"Teaseproof" Your Kids, Jim Fay   228

LESSON 48

Helping Your Child Develop Meaningful Self-Esteem,
Maureen Stout, Ph.D.   233

LESSON 49

Help Children Learn to Believe in Themselves,
Michele Borba, Ed.D.   238

LESSON 50

Teaching Self-Reliance, Rae Turnbull   242

LESSON 51

"My Child is Being Teased! How Can I Get This to Stop?"
Excerpt from Good Friends Are Hard to Find,
Fred Frankel, Ph.D.   247

Family Values

LESSON 52

What Really Matters, Alvin Rosenfeld, M.D., and Nicole Wise   254

LESSON 53

Ten Ways to Show Gratitude Within the Family,
Mimi Doe, M.Ed.   261

LESSON 54

Excerpt from How to Talk to Your Kids About Really
Important Things, Charles E. Schaefer, Ph.D.,
and Theresa Foy DiGeronimo, M.Ed.   263

LESSON 55

Encourage Your Loved Ones, Judy Ford, M.S.W.   266

LESSON 56

"What Do You Say?" Sandra E. Lamb   268

LESSON 57

Little Things Long Remembered, or Filling Your Child's
Memory Bank, Susan Newman, Ph.D.   271

LESSON 58

Raising a Giving Child, Jackie Waldman   274

LESSON 59

Building Empathy in the Preschool Years,
Myrna B. Shure, Ph.D.   277

LESSON 60

Always Make the Highest Choice, Judy Ford, LCSW   282

Parenting Kids with Labels

LESSON 61

Great Expectations: The Only Child, Susan Newman, Ph.D.   286

LESSON 62

Understanding and Coping with ADD/ADHD,
David Nylund   291

LESSON 63

A Wonderful Parent, Karen Seroussi   297

LESSON 64

The Anxious Child,
John S. Dacey, Ph.D., and Lisa B. Fiore, Ph.D.   302

"D" Is for Divorce

LESSON 65

Helping Your Children Cope with Divorce,
Edward Teyber, Ph.D.   308

LESSON 66

I'm a Bonus Mom, Jann Blackstone-Ford, M.A.   314

Fun and Games

LESSON 67

The Wonder of Play, Cheryl L. Erwin, M.A., MFT   320

LESSON 68

Creating Creative Kids: Turning Boredom into Brightness,
Charles Fay, Ph.D.   323

LESSON 69

The Importance of Humor in Parenting,
Joseph Anthony Michelli, Ph.D.   332

LESSON 70

Kids and Sports: What's a Parent to Do?
Darrell J. Burnett, Ph.D.   335

LESSON 71

Raise a Child Who "Plays Smart," Susan K. Perry, Ph.D.   341

LESSON 72

Help! I Have a Toddler! Trish Kuffner   344

LESSON 73

Quality Time—Anytime! How to Make the Most of
Every Moment with Your Child, Penny Warner   354

Tips and Tricks
You Can Really Use

LESSON 74

Tools for the Trade, Lisa Whelchel   358

LESSON 75

Drive Time: Excerpt from Survival Tips for Working Moms,   363
Linda Goodman Pillsbury

LESSON 76

Positive Discipline Techniques, Nancy Samalin, M.S.   367

LESSON 77

Enjoy the Ride, Maureen A. O'Brien, Ph.D.   369

LESSON 78

Tips We've Learned While Attending *Parent School*,
Jerry and Lorin Biederman   372

Parent School Faculty   *381*
Index   *413*
About the Editors   *421*
Extra Credit   *423*
Extra Curricular Activities   *424*

"I have always looked on child rearing not only as a work of love and duty, but as a profession that was fully as interesting and challenging as any honorable profession in the world, and one that demanded the best that I could bring to it."

—*Rose Kennedy*

Foreword

Penelope Leach, Ph.D.

Concern for children's care and upbringing is more widespread now than ever before. Parents find themselves observed and advised, exhorted and criticized, not only by individuals with a particular personal or professional interest in what they do, such as grandparents and pediatricians, but also by policy- and opinion makers in government, civil institutions, media and industry. The White House hosts conferences on brain development in the early years; Britain's Labour party bases its push for a second term on improvements in child care; industry invents a "tween" market to fit between children and teens; and mass media rely on parental guilt and anxiety to ensure an audience for stories about the work–home or mother–father balance and about child neglect or abuse.

Inevitably there has been an explosion of books about parenting, and because there is so little spare space on the bookstores' child care shelves, each new one seems designed and marketed to make a place for itself by shouldering others off. But while extreme positions on controversial issues—spanking, spoiling, schooling—attract media attention and shelf space, they seldom make a positive contribution to the growing body of knowledge available to parents. Parent education, like any other kind, should evolve. New information demands that old knowledge be continually reshaped, but seldom that it be dismissed.

For parents, this plethora of information and opinion often spells confusion rather than knowledge or support. If their lives are currently dominated by a 2-year-old who says no to everything, a book on taming toddlers seems irresistible. But its implications for how they should parent their (constantly) nursing newborn are uncomfortable, and something else they have read suggests that the negativism of one child and the nursing of the other may be linked. Parenting demands a long timescale and a broad perspective. Even when life seems dominated by one issue—a potty, a pacifier, a feared teacher—a single-issue book cannot provide lasting help. In order to make good decisions for themselves, parents need to know if there's a consensus view of these (and a million other) issues among responsible professionals. And they need to find one or two such professionals who address any or all specific issues with a consistent voice—a voice whose tone, and style, and sense of humor seem to support their own feelings about their children and themselves as parents so that even tough messages are easy to listen to.

Parent School meets these needs. Many leading authorities on parenting and child-care have set out what they consider to be their most valuable tips or pieces of information or advice for parents. These experts come from various professions and have different angles; they cover every age group from birth through adolescence, and they focus on a vast range of troublesome topics in each. Yet although their specific messages vary and sometimes disagree, the book as a whole is pervaded by a remarkable consensus. Nobody—not even the toughest disciplinarian—thinks it's okay to spank. Nobody—not even the most convinced behaviorist—thinks leaving babies alone to cry it out is the best way to deal with sleeping problems.

A parent who reads all these self-selected highlights of parent educators' work will find that the differences between their voices emerge as forcefully as differences and similarities in their views or recommendations. The voice that appeals in the brief entries in this book will probably also be comfortable and helpful at the greater length of its own books. With each contributor's own works listed and described, *Parent School* can serve as a critical catalog to guide parents through those packed shelves to the books that are most likely to fill their particular needs.

Acknowledgments

We would like to thank our family—especially our *own* parents—and our friends whose love, devotion, faith, and support lights our way. Sometimes special people in our lives can take on the role of a parent, so we'd like to acknowledge our Uncle Jules and Auntie Bonnie for their love and guidance. We are also indebted to our babysitters—Heather, Stephanie, Andy, Erin and Jenny—who are always there when we need them (like every Saturday night). To all of our neighbors—especially Mike, Karyn, Kayla, Noa, Lori, and Marty—you are our village. A special thank you to our agent, B.J. Robbins; our publisher, George C. de Kay; our managing editor, Rik Schell; our editor, PJ Dempsey; our copyeditor, Mary Dorian; our publicist, Amy E. Koch; as well as Harry McCullough, Evan Johnston, and Marc Baller at M. Evans for bringing this book to life (childbirth should be so easy). We are most grateful to each of the authors who so generously contributed their expert advice and their precious time to the making of *Parent School*. It has been a pleasure working with and getting to know all of you. Your unwavering dedication to children and parents has been and will continue to be an invaluable benefit to our society.

Orientation

If most parents had their wish, babies would come with instructions and parenting *Cliffs Notes* would be issued on every birthday.

Parents are pretty much left to fend for themselves when it comes to learning everything from the pros and cons of pacifiers to the do's and don'ts of disciplining (not to mention diapering). Self-esteem is left to chance, family values are hit and miss, and schooling is politics as usual. Is facing common parenting issues such as postpartum depression, ADD, and divorce really supposed to be instinctual? After all, they don't teach *mommying* and *daddying* in school.

With every stage—from excessive drooling to home schooling, from sleepless nights to teenage fights—there's always a need to know how to be a good parent.

The good news is—there's no shortage of information out there. The bad news is—there's *so much* information that it's hard to know where to turn to get the very best, and it's impossible for most parents to find enough time to sift through it all.

Chefs go to chef school and hairdressers go to beauty school. There are schools for beginning drivers, new dog owners, cake decorators, wine tasters . . . you name it. So, why not a school for parents?

After all, good parents are one of the four fundamentals needed for the raising of good kids—along with air, food, and water. The very future of our society (not to mention the sanity in our homes) relies on the quality of the next generation.

While these days the responsibility of raising children is often passed off to others (child care centers, nannies, teachers, television, etc.), clearly it is parents who hold the key to success.

Orientation

As new parents, we recently found ourselves in need of some important advice. We were enjoying our time with our sweet, affectionate, and well-behaved 20-month-old daughter, Jennifer. Expecting another child in less than a month, we began to wonder how this new child would affect our relationships. How could we make sure that Jennifer's life wouldn't be turned around by the presence of another child in the house? Could we stop the seed of sibling rivalry before it even had a chance to be planted?

Since we were both second-born children in our respective families, we were anxious to understand what a first-born child goes through—from being the center of attention to becoming one of the kids. How would this affect her personality? How could we make this transition smooth for her?

We were in need of yet another parenting book.

With each new challenge, we found ourselves making the familiar trip to the neighborhood bookstore. The parenting/child care section was just big enough to be paralyzing. Our eyes would glaze over while scanning the shelves—back and forth, up and down—looking for *the* book and author who spoke to us. We would take books off the shelves, haphazardly search through the pages, and then put them back. Sometimes we would walk out with way too many books, and other times, frustrated, with none at all. What we really needed was a quick guided tour of each book.

It occurred to us that what we could use was a condensed course in parenting. What if there was a book that had the best advice from today's top parenting authors all rolled into one?

Hence, *Parent School* was born.

We began by writing to authors of parenting books, and we simply asked each one to answer the same question: *What is your greatest lesson for parents?*

The response was remarkable. It was exciting to be receiving personal letters, e-mails, and even phone calls every day from the acclaimed authors whose names had become so recognizable from bookstore shelves, bestseller lists, parenting web sites, and popular TV talk shows.

Here, the most respected and renowned parenting experts have joined our *Parent School* faculty for the purpose of giving readers the most important lessons in parenting.

Surprisingly, many shared that they had never been asked this simple and significant question before. Time and again, we were told it was both challenging and fun for them to have to choose—from their myriad of teachings—the one greatest gift they had to offer.

Included in this book are inspired contributions on every subject of importance to parents, including the best ways to discipline your child; how to nurture self-esteem; making the most of your pediatrician's visit; the art of listening to your child; understanding postpartum depression; dealing with divorce; the ADD epidemic; building family values; the importance of play; making the most of education; and many more.

Compiling the parenting lessons for this book enabled us to learn valuable and helpful information that we were able to start using *right away*, because each lesson is short, to the point, and easy to read. *Parent School* was truly written for the mom and dad who haven't time to read much more than the dosage on the bottle of Children's Tylenol. It's amazing how much you can learn—between feedings, diapering, piggyback rides, and making yet another peanut butter and jelly sandwich—just flipping through the following pages.

Parent School has taught us lessons that we use every day and can pass along to other parents in our lives. These gems have touched and moved us. We now have the tools in our back pockets that will make us better parents. Not only are we more educated, but we feel more enlightened, philosophical, and inspired, too. We were also exposed to some issues and information that we didn't even know we needed to know until it was unexpectedly spoon-fed to us as a contributing doctor's most passionate advice.

Depending on your child's age, you will find some of the information useful today, while you will want to refer to other information in the future as your child enters the different stages of growing up.

These days, when we go to the bookstore, we have a good idea of who's who and we have developed our own list of must-reads! After attending *Parent School*, you will, too.

Each time you come across a lesson that is especially pertinent, we encourage you to pursue it further by reading the author's complete works (biographical information for all contributors is in the back of this book). *Parent School* is not intended to provide fast-food answers to parents' questions. Rather, it offers gourmet appetizers, and readers are encouraged to go out and get the main course from those authors who match their tastes.

We wish you luck and joy in your parenthood journey. As any seasoned parent will tell you, it is never-ending. This book was created to assist in your pursuit of higher education, and to give you the core knowledge to make the bumps smoother and the joy greater. The greatest part of being a *Parent School* student is that *this* school is one where graduation day happily never comes. A good parent is always learning more and growing along with the kids.

Hear the bell? *Parent School* is in session . . .

—*Jerry and Lorin Biederman*

Parenting 101

"Most important was to bring up the oldest one the way you want them all to go. If the oldest one comes in and says good night to his parents or says his prayers in the morning, the younger ones think that's the thing to do and they will do it."
—*Rose Kennedy, mother of President John F. Kennedy*

"Parents who are lucky in their children usually have children who are lucky in their parents."
—*Anonymous*

Tending Your Child's Soul

Michael Gurian
Author of *The Good Son, The Wonder of Boys* and *A Fine Young Man*

When Gail and I lived in Turkey, we spent a lot of time in villages in the eastern part of the country. We had no children, and I recall one Kurdish woman with seven children saying to Gail, "What is wrong with you? Why don't you have children?" To this woman, being 30 and having no children meant a serious flaw in Gail (or in her husband); it meant a life of little meaning and no real path to happiness. Without children, life just did not matter that much. When Gail and I engaged in long conversations with this woman, her mother, her sister, and many others in the village, including her husband and his male relatives at the *chai* house, there was no breaking down their certainty that children were the reason adults were alive. Many times during these conversations, Gail and I heard the old Turkish saying, "You are not an adult until you have had a child."

Brought up in both Asia and America, I have found myself straddling both Eastern and Western ideas of parenting. Any generalization about West and East would be a gross one, so I will only say that in my personal experience there is, in America, a degree of child loneliness and parental confusion that I have not quite found anywhere else. For three of my books, I studied thirty cultures and could not find a single one where children are more profoundly lonely than in America. Simultaneously, our adults seem the loneliest, too. In my studies, I found that American parents were the least likely to say that once they had a child, all personal ambition had to be sacrificed for the good of the child.

> *Everyone, even if they never sire children, is still a parent—the greatest reason for living is to ensure the happy, ethical future of the next generation.*

American parents were the most likely to want to absorb their child into their busy lives and the least likely to say they would give up their busy lives for their child.

I cannot pretend to tell other parents what the greatest lesson of their lives will be. I can say, however, that my own greatest lesson has been this: The child is the reason I'm alive. There is no other comparable, ontological reason for a human being to be alive than to care for his, her or the world's children. And everyone, even if they never sire children, is still a parent—the greatest reason for living is to ensure the happy, ethical future of the next generation.

This is simple wisdom, of course. Ozgul, the village woman, was trying to tell us this in her own provocative way. My own father, when I was 7 and we were returning to America from India, talked fondly of the many people who helped him and my mother raise me there. "Aiya," he said, referring to the woman who helped the most, "knows something basic, and she knows it from the heart: Our children give us our limits, but they also set us free." I did not understand what he meant; he had a penchant for talking to me as if I were already an adult. Now, however, long a father myself, I understand this point. My children have certainly reigned me in, tamed me, pushed me into corners, trapped me in my own inadequacies; but they have also been the most fruitful and freeing encounter in my life.

After writing nine books in the field of parenting and self-help, and reading perhaps thousands along the way, I realize that none, including my own, have adequately spoken to me about why I became a parent. In America, we have given many of our children perhaps the most luxurious childhood anywhere on earth, and certainly the most extended adolescence. But are we accomplishing all of this for the child? Is the child the center of our human existence? Has each of us adequately asked this question: *What is the meaning of each child's existence?*

For me, asking that question is the reason for my life; I hope I am answering it through experience and duty and the actions of parenting. I hope each of us who cares for children will inspire others with a real passion for parenting, like the kind Ozgul and her family felt. In the midst of nearly impoverished conditions, her passion grew from simple equations of meaning. While the modern intellectual in me judges her, saying, "Of course, she'll say this. She is oppressed and has no other substantial way of developing self-worth except by having a lot of children," the historical human in me knows that although, to some extent this judgment may be true, there's much more going on. From within her culture, somewhat alien to my America, she speaks a universal truth. It is not her culture but mine that wrestles so gravely these days with a banquet of choices but a poverty of meaning.

I hope each of us who cares for children will inspire others with a real passion for parenting.

Ozgul has inspired me to make sure that any candidate I vote for, any television program I let my kids watch, any conversation I have in their presence and any community or experience I expose them to overtly displays its care for the child. In my daily morning meditation, I repeat the words, "Thank you for my children and all the children of the earth. May I be today the parent they need me to be. May my meaning today grow from my care of children."

Often I do badly at the task of being a soul tender, but often I do well. And at least when I do my evening prayers, I have a daily chart of meaning to review. This gives me a sense of why I lived this day. Perhaps not for everyone, but at least for me, it is important to know why I have been alive—alive in the substantial way that this universe lets me live. My greatest debt to nature will certainly go, on my deathbed, to the gift of the child, who crosses all cultural boundaries, and, in the end, truly makes us adult, alive, loving, and of real purpose to life itself.

Getting Behind the Eyes of Your Child

William Sears, M.D., and Martha Sears, R.N.

Authors of *The Pregnancy Book, The Birth Book, The Baby Book, The Discipline Book, Parenting The Fussy Baby, The A.D.D. Book, The Family Health and Nutrition Book,* and *The Breastfeeding Book*

In parenting our eight children, an early lesson we learned is that when we were uncertain how to react to our children, we would get behind their eyes and imagine situations from their viewpoint. For example, our sixth child, Matthew, was a very focused toddler. When he was engrossed in play, he had a hard time switching from his agenda to ours. If we would insensitively interrupt his play because we needed to go or were late for an appointment, he would justifiably pitch a fit. Instead, we got behind his eyes and saw things from his viewpoint, and this encouraged us to develop more creative discipline strategies. Realizing that he was in a state of hyperfocus, we gave him time to sign out before we left: "Matthew, say bye-bye to the boys, bye-bye to the girls, bye-bye to the toys . . . " This helped Matthew easily transition from his agenda to ours.

We also used the getting-behind-the-eyes-of-a-child approach when deciding where it was best for our infants to sleep. First, we believe that there is no right or wrong place for an infant to sleep—it's where all family members get the best night's sleep, and that may be a different arrangement at various stages of a child's development. In deciding whether it was wise for our infant to sleep in our bed or in a crib, we got behind the eyes of our baby. We asked ourselves, "If we were an infant, would we rather sleep alone in a dark room—behind bars—or nestled securely close to parents?" Once we looked at it this way, the choice for co-sleeping versus solo sleeping was an obvious one.

One of the most important lessons we learned is that we have to put our time in at one end of a child's life or another, and it's best to put time in those early years.

One of the most important lessons we learned is that we have to put our time in at one end of a child's life or another, and it's best to put time in those early years with a high-touch, high-responsive style of parenting we term *attachment parenting*. We believe that the time a baby spends in-arms, at mother's breast, and in your bed is a relatively short time in the total life of a child—but the memories of love and availability last a lifetime.

Remember to get behind the eyes of your children and see how they are looking at the world. It will give you a whole new perspective.

⮐ **Lesson 3** ⮐
Age: All

The Seven Best Things
Good Parents Can Do

John C. Friel, Ph.D.
and Linda D. Friel, MA

Authors of *The 7 Worst Things Good Parents Do*

W e have been working with families in our private psychology practice for 20 years. For the past decade, we have seen a consistent, gradual decline in the emotional health of families and children in America, which we attribute to the following trends:

One is the increasing disconnection and fragmentation that is happening in families. Another—a corollary to the first—is the abdication of the leadership role by many parents. The third is the overdoing of the self-esteem movement.

To put this in simpler language, we believe that kids are more violent, more depressed, and more alienated because (1) Dad and Mom aren't around enough; (2) when they *are* around, they spoil, smother,

8

indulge, and baby their children in a damaging attempt to make up for not being around enough; and (3) many of us have lost sight of the fact that becoming competent is the only way a child will have true self-esteem.

This combination of emotional neglect and babying is harmful enough, but when you add the crippling effects of over praising children without helping them to actually become competent at something, the effects are deadly.

Based on the most disturbing trends that we have witnessed over the past decade, we set out to identify and then provide some helpful solutions to seven of these more troubling trends. As you read through this *Parent School* lesson, try to see how parents who are leaders, rather than tyrants or pals, will have the fewest problems in each area.

1. *Don't Baby Your Children.* When we remove the struggle from our children's paths, all we do is doom them to a life of misery, disappointment, and emotional paralysis. Struggle is good. Challenge is what makes life worthwhile. Doing everything for kids so that they don't have to experience difficulty is not a gift—it's a form of severe neglect. So let your child fall down and pick herself up (unless, of course, it's a serious fall). Don't pay off your teenager's credit-card debt. Let him figure out that his actions have consequences, and that his decisions make a difference in his life. Love isn't babying, and babying isn't love.

2. *Put Your Marriage First.* Children desperately need us to take care of our marriages. In a National Institute of Mental Health study, parents of healthy young adults said that child-focused families were not good and did not make for healthy children or adults. Keep it balanced. Our little ones need us a lot. Raising infants and toddlers is a huge job. Nurturing your marriage during these early years may mean having 15 minutes of absolutely sacred alone time with your mate every night, a date every week to 10 days, and at least one overnight trip per year. Do something just for your marriage on a regular basis. Kids look at these moments as magic—they love to see Mom and Dad get dressed up and go out on a date.

3. *Limit Activities.* Forty years ago, children had time to breathe. They had time to have relationships and to eat dinner with their families. They had time to dream and plan, to play and regenerate, to connect and reflect. Today they don't, and the consequences are ominous— depression, poor relationships, alienation from family, addiction. And the solution is relatively simple. Parents need to step in and say, "We love you. We see you burning out. We don't need you to be over- scheduled to prove to the neighbors that we're just as successful as they are. Your being overscheduled and burned out just proves that we are not being leaders. So, we're going to pull you out of one activ- ity. Which one should it be?" See. It's still possible for parents to raise their children.

4. *Don't Ignore Your Emotional or Spiritual Life.* Being spiritual means being able to acknowledge that there are things in life that are beyond our control. It means being able to look up at the night sky and feel infinitely small and at one with creation in the same instant. It is the ability to have awe and wonder about the universe, and to admit that we'll never know everything, and that as soon as we think we do, we're doomed. Being spiritual means being powerful by being able to admit mistakes and limitations, and also by letting go of our attempts to control the uncontrollable in creation. And it is also the ability to connect emotionally with each other. How can we possibly begin to be spiritual when our lives are so overscheduled that we don't have time to sit down and eat?

5. *Remember, You Are the Parent.* Our children need us to be their par- ents, not their friends. When you try to be your child's best friend, you are robbing him of a parent. What's worse, you are seducing him into a role that will make it next to impossible for him to have a suc- cessful love relationship when he gets into adulthood. If you had a painful childhood, take some time to work through that pain so that you don't have to act it out in your relationship with your own chil- dren. Trying to heal our own childhood wounds by overdoing it with our kids is, unfortunately, just as bad as if we did to them what was

done to us. It always backfires. Be your child's parent. He needs his own friends, and you need yours.

6. *Control the Amount of Structure.* Children depend on us to structure their lives for them when they're little so that they can internalize this and do it for themselves when they're older. However, too much structure as well as too little structure can do a lot of damage to a child. The right amount is golden. Have a few rules that you enforce consistently, such as a very regular bedtime that is allowed to flex only four to six times a year, maximum; a couple of chores that are reasonable for your child's age; and one or two more. What's much more important than what your rules are is if you are strong and whole enough to enforce them consistently—it's the day-to-day follow-through that separates the great parents from the mediocre ones. And by all means, be a role model for civility, restraint, and balanced impulse control. If you engage in road rage or temper tantrums around your kids, expect them to learn that from you.

7. *Don't Expect Your Child To Fulfill Your Dreams.* Our children are genetically different from each other and us. One of them might be an extrovert, the other an introvert. Introversion-extroversion is 80 percent biological, so our job as parents is to help our children develop their unique talents and strengths so that they can adapt to a rapidly changing world. Our job as parents is not to try to mold our children into our own image, or worse, to mold them into something about which we feel an unresolved sense of failure. If your child is genetically, biologically set up to be the next Picasso, but you have some unconscious agenda that she should become the next Einstein, then you will doom her to a life of failure and frustration as you doom yourself to a life of bitterness and disappointment. Again, be a leader. It pays off in the end. The more we work with parents, families, and teachers, the more we have become convinced that parents need to be encouraged, guided, and taught that they are the architects and leaders of the family; and that when it comes to core health or dysfunction, no other influence comes close to affecting children as much as parents—not video games, television,

school, or even peers. The real challenge for parents who are serious about improving themselves and their families, of course, is that there are no glamorous quick fixes, no brief seminars, and no single book that will make a dent in the troubles of a particular family system. Parents need to learn that one small change held consistently for 6 to 12 months will ultimately produce more system-wide improvement than a host of resolutions and rules that are instituted simultaneously and then reinforced haphazardly.

While it may seem that being a parent today is 100 times harder than it was 50 years ago, the truth is that it's just different. Kids will always be kids. Teens will always be teens. History very clearly shows that the lot of parents and children has improved dramatically over the past 2,000 years. It will always be a challenge to raise children. It always has been!

The Joys and Challenges of Parenting:

What We Have Learned from Raising Our Ten Sons

Catherine Musco Garcia-Prats and Joseph Garcia-Prats, M.D.

Authors of *Good Families Don't Just Happen: What We Learned from Raising Our Ten Sons and How It Can Work for You*

Parenting is one of the greatest responsibilities bestowed upon anyone. How humbling to be entrusted by God to foster the physical, emotional, spiritual, and intellectual development of another individual.

Parenting takes effort and hard work if one is to reap the joyful rewards of a loving family. Our *Parent School* lesson comes from our experience of raising ten sons who presently range from 6 to 24 years of age. We learned firsthand how the investment of our time, energy, and money in our sons has been returned to us 100-fold.

Every day we face so many decisions and choices that affect our children. Some choices are as simple (although many people wouldn't consider them simple) as what to prepare for supper or who's taking which son where. Some are more difficult, such as how to balance the financial demands of a large family or which schools will provide our sons with the best educational environment appropriate for their abilities and talents, from pre-school through college.

Choices are part and parcel of family life. It is up to us as parents to make choices and set examples that will enable our children to grow up to be the loving, caring, responsible, respectful, well-educated, and faith-filled individuals we want them to be. We must also teach them that their self-worth and success will be measured in such nonmonetary terms as who they are, what they do with the gifts within, and how they live their lives. This is contrary to how society defines success and self-worth.

> *Our children need to feel our love from the moment they wake up in the morning until they fall asleep at night.*

What choices must we make as parents to enable our children to reach their full potential? We must choose to love our children, respect our children, make them a priority in our lives, and share our faith and beliefs with them.

1. *Choose to love your children.* Eric Fromm in *The Art of Loving* tells us, "Love is not just a strong feeling—it is a judgement, it is a promise." If we believe that statement, then loving our children is a decision and a promise. Waking up each morning, we could throw up our hands and lament about having ten sons and all the work associated with taking care of them. Instead, we choose to wake up and thank God for the gifts of our ten sons. We then ask for guidance during

the day as we face the many tasks we know we have scheduled and all the unexpected situations that may develop.

Our children need to feel our love from the moment they wake up in the morning until they fall asleep at night. Our children need to witness our love in the way we approach the responsibilities of the day. If we are constantly complaining about the work we have to do, we send a message to our children that they are a burden in our lives instead of showing them they are our gifts and treasures. We believe "the feet find the road easy when the heart walks with them." Our example demonstrates to our children the joy of life, especially family life, by our attitude and actions.

2. *Choose to respect your children.* If we want our children to learn respect, we must exemplify respect in the way we speak to each other and in the way we treat each other as husband and wife. It is not only the words that matter. Please, thank you, and other words and acts of kindness and appreciation demonstrate a respectful relationship. Are our words and our actions kind or unkind, positive or negative, respectful or disrespectful?

In addition, we must respect each other's individuality: our strengths, our weaknesses, our abilities, and our personalities. We must then treat our children with the same level of respect: in the way we speak to them, in the way we treat them, and in the way we recognize and appreciate their individuality. Then we expect our sons to demonstrate this same level of respect to each other. Each family member must feel loved and secure in his own home. If siblings are not respectful to each other in the way they treat each other, in the way they talk to each other, and in the way they respect each other's individuality, then a child will not feel that love and security in his own home.

Respecting each family member's individuality is essential in a loving home. All of our sons have unique gifts, abilities, and personalities. A few of the boys are intellectually gifted, a few are athletically gifted, a few are socially gifted, and a few are artistically and creatively gifted. Not one of them is gifted in all areas. Our challenge as parents is to recognize and appreciate each child for the gifts he possesses. We

15

encourage and guide them in their strengths and weaknesses, thereby enabling each one to reach his full potential. We want our sons to understand they are loved for who they are. We keep our expectations realistic and age appropriate so that they feel good about who they are and so that they are not trying to be the other brother. We thus minimize sibling rivalry when each child knows and understands he is loved and respected for his uniqueness.

3. *Choose to make your children a priority in your lives.* We determine how much time we spend with our boys. We believe that quality time is any time we are with our sons—diapering, bathing, reviewing homework, peeling potatoes, riding in the car—not just some designated time in our day or week. Children know they are a priority in our lives by our interactions with them. We choose, for example, to shut the television off in the evenings and spend that time reading with our children.

Parenting isn't easy. We know and understand it's challenging—we had five teenagers at once. We know it's demanding—we had children in diapers for 20 consecutive years. We know it's constant—the twenty loads of laundry a week, multiple trips to the grocery store (the boys drink 5 gallons of milk a day when they are all home), doctor, dental, and orthodontic appointments, soccer practices, homework, bills, and so forth. And no two days are the same, and no two children are exactly alike. We cannot decide, though, to fulfill our parental responsibilities one day and not the next. Our children need our constant love and attention.

We observe too frequently how parents allow the stresses and demands of every day life to interfere with the enjoyment of their children. Or we observe parents setting priorities that do not include their children. They act as if work, social functions, and the accumulations of wealth and things were more important than time spent with family.

Family values are words used frequently today. We need to examine our values and decide what is important to us. Are we chasing the American dream, which is defined in materialistic terms? Or do we set the example and show our children that their self-worth and success, as well as ours, is measured by who we are, what we do with the gifts God has given us, and how we live our lives.

We must stand up and make the choices and live the values that will enable our children to understand what is important in life. Our sons may not drive their own cars, or wear the latest name-brand clothes, but they are well fed and well educated; moreover, they treasure each other as much as we treasure them. They know and understand that what we have is more rewarding and more long-lasting than any "thing."

4. *Choose to share your faith with your children.* We find that our faith is an invaluable source of strength, inspiration, and guidance in our parenting efforts. If we want our children to embrace our faith, we must show them how faith is relevant in their lives. We believe one's faith is lived day in and day out rather than something done for just an hour or two once a week. A child's first impression of God usually stems from his experiences with his parents. Are we good examples of God's love and laws?

We minimize sibling rivalry when each child knows and understands he is loved and respected.

We must accept the responsibility of teaching our children what is right and wrong, appropriate and inappropriate, good and bad. We strongly believe children want and need guidelines; and they need us, their parents, to establish and enforce them. If you love your children, do what you know is best for them, not what is easy. Remember: NO is often a loving word.

We must start at an early age and continue to reinforce our values every day of the year. We assure you that children do not wake up on their thirteenth birthday and decide to be loving, responsible, respectful, and faith-filled individuals. The learning begins from the moment they are born and is a continual process that we show them is throughout life. Leo Buscaglia tells us, "Be what you want your children to be and watch them grow."

The years do fly—although some days do not seem to fly by fast enough. As our older two sons are entering new phases of their lives, we look at them and remember them as our youngest two sons are today. We can still picture them racing their big wheels up and down the sidewalk while wearing their beloved orange Astros baseball caps.

Love, respect, appreciate, and enjoy your children. We know parenting is challenging and demanding, but when done well and with love, there is no greater reward for ourselves and for society.

Am I Doing It Right?

What Makes You a Good Parent

Mary Snyder
Author of *You CAN Afford to Stay Home with Your Kids*

What makes you a good parent? Time, or rather the passage of time, is the number one answer in my book. I am sure I will seem like a much better mother 10 or even 20 years from now when my daughters are grown and out of the house. I will either look like a much better mom or I will be the blame for everything bad that has happened in their lives. I don't see much of a middle ground. I ask myself daily if I am doing a good job and my daily response is "I sure hope so."

How can we ever know if what we are doing is right or even good enough? Do I spend enough time with my kids? I hope so. Do I ask too much from them? I hope not. Do they respect me? They had better or hone their acting skills and learn to fake it.

When I first became a parent, I panicked over every little incident. After almost 15 years of parenting, I only panic if large amounts of blood are involved. Seriously, I have learned to pick my moments of panic, as every parent should, or else you will spend the majority of your parenting days panicking over one thing or another. Being a parent does become easier with time. You learn to get a handle on it, but the one thing that continues to confound me is how my actions will impact my children's adult lives.

I often wonder if screaming "pick up your clothes" will condemn my daughters to a lifetime of living knee deep in dirty laundry. Or even worse, years on a therapist's couch only to call me when they are 30 years old to announce that I am the reason they can't do laundry.

I wonder if I spend enough time with my kids. I have been a parent long enough to learn this: When I am ready to spend "quality" time with my kids, they are not interested. Quality time is something that was created to help overly busy parents feel better about spending only a couple of short hours a day with their kids. Look for quality in the simple, mundane chores of life—the squeals of excitement from your toddler as he tries to catch a butterfly; the joy in the eyes of your child when she sees her first rainbow; the look of pride on the face of your child when he hits his first home run. This is quality time, and you can't plan it, force it, or prepare for it—it just happens.

I wonder about the impact I have on my girls' lives, and I wonder if my mother worried about such things or if my grandmother ever worried as much as I do. I doubt it. Mothers once had a defined role, as did the kids. No one worried much about our self-esteem or whether we would be emotionally damaged because we had to clean house every Saturday. I think my generation grew up just fine. Of course, we had our share of nut cases, but doesn't every generation. And I don't remember my parents being overly concerned about my self-esteem. They were more concerned that I learned good manners, did well in school, and said "sir," "ma'am," "please," and "thank you." All these things I learned, and they have done me well along my path of growth and self esteem.

As parents in today's world, we are inundated with information overload. Pick up a crying baby. Don't pick up a crying baby. Work full-time and your kids will be more self-sufficient. Stay home full time and your kids will be more secure. Let your kids experience failure—it builds character. Help your kids excel at all they do—it builds self-confidence. What is a parent to believe? For every study done that proves one theory of parenting, there is another study that disproves the same theory.

Every child is different just as every parent is. What works for one child will not work for another. Parenting isn't about following the rules or adhering to a set of guidelines. Parenting is about following your heart and your head. I never want to see my daughters fail, but I know that without failure they will never understand the true victory of success. I never want to see my daughters' struggle, but I know without struggle there is never a sense of accomplishment. I never want to see my daughters cry over a broken relationship, but without those tears true understanding never comes.

I will let my daughters experience failure and my heart will ache. I will watch my child struggle to master a task that I could easily do for her and my heart will ache. I will listen as my daughter tells me of her emotional trials and my heart will ache. But when she achieves the goals she struggled so hard to master, when she excels where she once failed, and when she grows wiser through her emotional trials, my heart will soar, for I have watched her grow and mature. I will see the beginnings of the woman she will one day become—smart, accomplished, and caring.

I think, as a parent, I should not worry too much about my daughters' self-esteem, and I should worry more about their self-respect. I want to raise my daughters to have fun, to laugh, to love, to give, to care, to learn, to respect, and above all, to live—and live well. This is the essence of self-esteem.

Parenting is about time—the time to help our children learn and grow. We can't do it for them, although it would be easier, but we can be there to love them through the trials, the failures, and the struggles. We can be there to cheer them on when they achieve those goals—this is true self-esteem. This is love.

Four Thoughts for Parents from the Tao Te Ching

William Martin
Author of The Parent's Tao Te Ching

In my book, *The Parent's Tao Te Ching*, I explore the wisdom of an ancient Chinese classic and apply its teachings to the task of parenting in our modern world.

The original *Tao Te Ching* was written in China around 600 B.C. One of the ways its title may be translated is "The Book of the Way Things Naturally Work." It is composed of 81 short chapters of advice that are drawn from attentive and detailed observations of the natural world. It is sometimes inspiring, sometimes obscure, and always thought-provoking. Its applications to parenting are numerous and profound.

For my *Parent School* lesson, I would like to share four concepts that I see reflected in the *Tao Te Ching*. These are not rules or infallible guidelines to follow. They are observations designed to stimulate your own inner knowing. Within you lies all you need to know to be a compassionate, peaceful parent. Look carefully.

Flexibility Is Life, Rigidity Is Death

There is a lovely park near our home in Chico, California, which is filled with huge old oaks as well as many other varieties of trees. When we walk through the park after a storm, the trails are littered with huge branches of these massive oaks. Sometimes an entire tree will fall victim to the winds. Yet the smaller, more supple trees that bend and sway in the wind remain intact.

So let it be with your parenting. Don't make every difference of opinion or conflict of needs into a battle that must be won or lost. Don't be afraid to open your mind to each new situation. Don't be afraid to change your mind if you wish. The consistency your children need is not the rigid inflexibility of opinions and rules that never bend or change. The consistency they need is the unchanging foundation of compassionate understanding.

Approaching each situation with compassion and flexibility does not mean that you allow your children to run roughshod over your needs and guidelines. Notice after a storm that the flexible trees have remained firmly rooted. They have danced and bent in the wind but have not lost their footing. They are alive and undamaged by the storms. Oak trees have many wonderful qualities, but amidst the winds of parenting it is better to dance like a willow than stand like an oak.

QUESTION: Is there a current situation with your children where you have been standing like an oak? Is it possible to dance like a willow just a bit?

Children Have a Natural Virtue

It is the basic nature of a young plant to push its way up through the earth, to sink its roots deep in nourishing soil, and to stretch its arms upward to the sun. In the same manner, it is the basic nature of our children to emerge from the womb, to draw nurture and love from family and community, and to reach upward to life in trust, courage, and compassion.

The restraints and boundaries we provide for our children are important to their emotional and physical safety. They are like the supports given a young tree to help it during its formative years. But these supports do not replace the young tree's innate capacity for perfect growth. In fact, if the supports are not carefully used and removed when no longer needed, they will actually stunt and deform the growth of the mature tree. This is a subtle difference in perspective but can make a great deal of difference in your life with your children.

You do not have to force your children to learn virtue, to be loving, to enjoy creative work, or to act responsibly. These qualities are natural for them. It is our culture that quickly indoctrinates them with such unnatural qualities as fear, egocentrism, competition, acquisitiveness, and greed. Let the restraints and boundaries you set be for the purpose of encouraging natural growth and reducing the effects of unnatural qualities. You don't need to teach the tree to grow. You only need to support it and nurture it. Your children have within them all the seeds of virtue. You only have to support and nurture them.

Question: Instead of always being alert for signs of rebellion and dishonesty, can you watch carefully and see the seeds of virtue and love? Is there a way you can nurture these seeds once you see them?

Failure is Necessary

Life is so very complicated and we ourselves have made so many of what seem to be unwise choices that we understandably want to spare our children the agonies of mistakes and failures. Yet our understandable desire for their success often cripples our children instead of helping them.

My father wanted me to have a life full of success and safety. He therefore constantly pushed me to achieve good grades and make responsible choices. I could play the school game and was able to produce the grades. But I eventually became so worried about doing the responsible thing that fear became the dominant feature of my life. I made choices based not on a trust in my basic strength but on a fear of failure. I have spent many years unlearning this fear.

It is much better to welcome the failures of your children early on. Nothing increases self-confidence like a good failure. The child who fails and is helped to learn from it in a nonblameful, nonpunishing manner is blessed indeed. Such a child learns that failure is not evil or shameful but a natural part of the successful life. This child learns courage and self-confidence. This child learns not to fearfully avoid failure but that he or she can handle failure and profit from it. This child learns to look directly at failure and say, "I'm still okay!"

Question: Is there a recent failure in your child's life that you can, by your attitude, use to bring confidence and strength to your child? (Remember to avoid blame and shame.)

Nurture Without Conditions

The life-giving water in the Sacramento River flowing near my home brings nourishment to everything it touches without asking for gratitude or return. The warmth of the sun generously soaks into every atom of our earthly life with no consideration of our worthiness. The earth produces all manner of life-sustaining food and never asks whether we deserve to partake.

Some would say that if we imitate such graciousness we will spoil our children. Nonsense! Graciousness never spoils. Unconditional love never harms a child. It is conditional love that spoils. It is conditional love that creates approval seeking. It is conditional love that creates a sense of entitlement to good things because they are somehow "earned" and "deserved." Unconditional love creates a sense of security that enables true courage and compassionate living.

Certainly boundaries and rules must be a part of family life. Use them as guidelines and use them mindfully. But never withhold love as a method of discipline. Such behavior is unnatural and contrary to the way the universe works. Sadly, our culture, often uses this horrendous manipulation as a method of control. Thus, we have created generations of approval-seeking, fearful people. It is from this fearful foundation that the violent acting-out behavior emerges that we all abhor.

Give with compassion and generosity to your children not because of their apparent worthiness but because of your own gracious nature. Behave this way not to control or manipulate, not to coerce gratitude or love, but because it is your great joy to do so. This will provide a model that your children will eventually follow. Don't be afraid to trust your compassionate nature.

Question: Are there ways in which you unconsciously withhold love and nurture because you are afraid to be too lenient? Can you find a way to maintain your position of discipline without withholding love?

∾ *Lesson 7* ∾
Age: All

Dr. Mom's Greatest Lesson for Parents

Marianne Neifert, M.D.
Author of *Dr. Mom: A Guide to Baby and Child Care,*
Dr. Mom's Parenting Guide: Commonsense Guidance for the Life of Your Child,
and *Dr. Mom's Guide to Breastfeeding*

When I was invited to share with readers my greatest parenting lesson, numerous possibilities quickly emerged. I could easily focus on the challenge of helping our children develop high self-esteem and a strong sense of self-worth. Certainly children have an essential need to feel lovable and capable; to have the assurance of their intrinsic worth and importance, along with the conviction that they are competent to handle life's challenges. Unconditional love is the cornerstone on which self-esteem is built, and the family is the first setting where a child experiences this love with no strings attached. The most effective way a parent conveys unconditional love for his or her child is by giving liberal one-on-one focused attention—the best quality time of all.

A great parenting lesson is found in the magical gift of being fully engaged with your child. It is the reason kids spell love: *t-i-m-e*.

I could just as eagerly counsel mothers and fathers to rank their parenting commitment above other seemingly urgent, but far less important, demands of today's hectic, fast-paced world. I've learned that effective parenting involves continually reassessing our priorities and choosing to say no to perfectly good—even glamorous—opportunities in order to say yes to our children's compelling needs. There's a profound parenting lesson in the realization that the passage of time diminishes the importance of our workplace achievements while magnifying the significance of our intimate relationships.

The most effective way a parent conveys unconditional love for their child is by giving liberal one-on-one focused attention.

I could excitedly share with parents a great lesson about the labor of love called discipline, by which children learn to handle difficult feelings, distinguish right from wrong, make good decisions, and develop responsibility and self-control. An enduring, supportive parent–child relationship creates a spirit of cooperation and learning that promotes desired behavior. Never forget that you and your child are on the same team, and immediately disengage from power struggles with your child. Remember that your own positive role model, frequent praise for desired behavior, and consistent enforcement of rules and limits are the best ways to motivate and instruct your child. Effective correcting of misbehavior is a creative process that requires choosing a suitable response from a variety of effective options without dealing a blow to either your child's self-esteem or your parent–child relationship.

I could happily share the lesson that parenting is the ultimate leadership role in which we groom our children for eventual independence and self-sufficiency. Effective parents help children understand that they are responsible for the choices they make, for the consequences of their actions, and for their state of happiness. We can promote a sense of competency and self-reliance in our child by offering age-appropriate choices and responsibilities, promoting healthy risk taking, encouraging perseverance, rewarding personal accomplishment, and teaching problem-solving skills. We can teach our children to appreciate the outcome of their actions by weighing the probable consequences of various choices before selecting and implementing the best option and help them learn to use mistakes as the basis for making better decisions in the future.

I could share with parents an important lesson about how familiar routines and family traditions can offer children a measure of security and predictability that promotes a comforting sense of acceptance and belonging. Daily routines, weekly activities, annual rituals, and special celebrations provide essential structure and reassurance that reduce childhood uncertainty and anxiety and increase a youngster's perception of control. Traditions are the social glue that bonds one generation to another, generates many of the "anchor" memories in a family's history, and creates a sense of family continuity and cultural heritage.

I could remind parents that we nurture our children from our own emotional overflow. Parents need permission to periodically refuel their energies and renew their perspective in order to provide a healthy model of self-care. Self-neglect can leave parents physically and emotionally depleted and make them less effective in the parenting role. A valuable lesson is the recognition that the ultimate form of giving is to be a gracious recipient of necessary help and care from others.

I would rank as the greatest parenting lesson of all the essential need to nurture our child's precious inner spirituality.

Yet, above all these thoughtful insights, I would rank as the greatest parenting lesson of all the essential need to nurture our child's precious inner spirituality. As our children's most influential teachers, role models, and mentors, I believe we are called to not only promote their intellectual, physical, and emotional development, but to cultivate their natural interest in God and help them embark on an exciting faith journey. All the daunting responsibilities of parenthood seem easier when we turn to a higher power to reinforce our human inadequacies.

I take great consolation in knowing that, even when my imperfect love lets my children down, they can always count on the dependability of God's incomprehensible love. When my own example disappoints, I am confident in God's perfect model that provides my children with an immutable moral compass and timeless values. When my children struggle in a complex and confusing world, spiritual beliefs provide a constant anchor, a comforting sense of security, and a meaningful way to live. When life brings inevitable setbacks, sorrows, and heartache, the belief that God is involved in our lives and cares deeply about our pain brings comfort, hope, and healing. God's gift to humankind of the free will to choose to acknowledge His sovereignty and obey His ordinances teaches children about the consequences of their choices and actions, as they reap what they sow. Faith traditions and a community of believers provide parents and children with a faith family that creates a shared heritage and a sense of belonging. Children experience compassion and empathy as they respond in action to God's gracious love by extending care and kindness in service to others.

All parents want to give their children the things they treasure most in life. For me, it is the priceless gift of God's love, example, guidance, comfort, and strength from which all other blessings flow. Thus, after much deliberation, the greatest parenting lesson I want to offer is this: Do not neglect the spiritual training of your child. When I contrast the incredible responsibilities of parenthood with my own limitations, I take enormous comfort in knowing that each of my children is created and uniquely loved by God, for a special purpose, and each is eternally under His protection and care. What more could a parent ask?

The Seven Keys to Good Parenting

Laurence Kutner, Ph.D.

Author of *Parent & Child: Getting Through to Each Other, Pregnancy and Your Baby's First Year, Toddlers and Preschoolers, Your School-Age Child,* and *Making Sense of Your Teenager*

1. Control

Understand what you can and what you cannot control. For example, you can control when your child goes to bed. You cannot control when your child goes to sleep. Often, parents become most frustrated when they're struggling to take charge of things they simply cannot control. Equally important, pay attention to and reward the behaviors your child cannot, not the ones he cannot. For example, your child can control how much and how well he studies for school. Your child cannot control his grades. Reward the studying behavior, not the grades.

2. Normal Behavior

Learn about the natural history of childhood: those behaviors that are normal and appropriate at different stages of development. For example, we would expect a 2-year-old to become more defiant than a 1-year-old. Those parents who have the least understanding of what behaviors are normal among children of different ages are often the ones who are the most frustrated with both their children and themselves.

3. Stages of Development

Pay attention to the developmental links between different stages. I often tell the parents of toddlers not to think of their children as big babies but rather as short teenagers. They're struggling with a lot of the same issues: independence, self-reliance, and distancing themselves from their parents.

4. Treat the Age

Let your children know that you can see how they're maturing. This way they're more likely to rise to your level of expectation. Nothing irritates a 13-year-old more than being treated like an 11-year-old.

5. Being Good Should Be Rewarded

Pay more attention to the behaviors you want than to the behaviors you don't want. In other words, catch your child being good—and pay extra attention to her when she is. This is a much more powerful approach to discipline than punishing for bad behavior.

6. Discipline Is Different from Punishment

The word *discipline* comes from the same Latin root as the word *disciple*. It has to do with teaching. Whenever you discipline your child, you're teaching that child something. However, it may not be the message you wish to teach. For example, if you haul off and hit a child for misbehaving, you're teaching that child that it's appropriate for big people to control little people with physical violence.

7. Admit Your Mistakes

Make lots of mistakes. We often learn the most—and the most important lessons—when we have to recover from our mistakes. Admit your mistakes freely. Apologize to your children when it's appropriate. That gives them permission to apologize to you when they've done something inappropriate and removes the pressure on them to deny that they've made mistakes.

Raising Good Kids in a Troubled World

Ross Campbell, M.D.

Author of *How to Really Love Your Child* and
How to Really Love Your Teenager

B eing a parent has become one of the most difficult professions in the world, especially in our present-day culture. However, even though the statistics are alarming and discouraging, a wise parent can experience the joy of seeing his or her own child develop into a wonderful, wholesome, healthy adult. This is not easy, of course, but almost anyone can accomplish this critical, rewarding adventure.

The key to successful parenting today is to understand the four types of needs, which every child has. I call these the foundation stones of effective parenting. Few children today are fortunate enough to have these needs sufficiently met. This is the primary reason so many of our precious ones are not doing well today. We parents have a wonderful opportunity to assure the future well-being of our children, by making sure all four foundation stones are set. This will assure our children's progress both now and in the future.

Your consistent expression of love needs to take very specific forms that adapt to the age and developing personality of your child. That expression, which forms the basis of effective parenting, consists of these four foundation stones:

1. Meeting the emotional and nurturance needs of your child

2. Giving loving training and discipline to your child

3. Providing physical and emotional protection for your child

4. Teaching and modeling anger management for your child

Most parents do well with one or two of the foundation stones, but most parents are not managing the others. The critical fact is that *all* of the child's four basic needs must be met. *All* of the four foundation stones must be accomplished or the child will be unable to develop to be his or her best. In essentially every troubled situation, the child's problems were either caused by or aggravated by failing to fulfill one of the foundation stones.

Yet most parents truly believe that they are doing everything possible for their child. But the truth is that very few parents are even aware of all that is within their power to enable their child to be and to become his or her best. *Please do not misunderstand what I am trying to say. I am not saying that all problems are the fault of the parents.* In fact, more and more of our children's problems are due to cultural factors, which are anti-parent as well as anti-child. For us to do all within our power for the sake of our children, we must make

Few parents are even aware of all that is within their power to enable their child to become his or her best.

sure that we are meeting *all* of their needs. This means using all four foundation stones.

The First Foundation Stone:
Meeting the Emotional and Nurturance Needs for Your Child

Most children do not feel adequately loved by their parents even though most parents deeply love their children. This is because children are *behaviorally* motivated, whereas adults, especially as we become parents, are *verbally* motivated. To transmit our heartfelt love to their hearts, we must do it on their terms—behaviorally. Of course, telling children we love them is important and we should certainly do this; however, simply telling the child we love her is not sufficient in transmitting our love from our hearts to hers. We must primarily transmit our love behaviorally, by use of such means as physical contact, eye contact, and focused attention.

The Second Foundation Stone:
The Giving of Loving Training and Discipline to Your Child

Here again, there is great confusion among parents. Many parents use punishment as the primary way to discipline or train their children. There are many far more effective ways to train your child in positive ways that elicit a child's obedience and respect for the parent.

In addition, parents must understand three basic facts about children before they can begin to discipline a child effectively. Without these prerequisites, their training or discipline will bring about strong anti-authority—including anti-parent—passive-aggressive attitudes. These three prerequisites are:

1. The difference between discipline and punishment
2. How a child loves (quite differently from how a mature adult loves)

3. The correct questions to ask ourselves to determine the best response to a child's misbehavior

The Third Foundation Stone:
Providing Physical and Emotional Protection for Your Child

This requirement to successfully raise a healthy child has taken on increasing significance in our rapidly changing culture. In the not-so-distant past, most influences upon our dear children were wholesome, healthy, and trustworthy. Just look at the sitcoms as recently as ten years ago. Most of them were not only safe from unwholesome, evil messages, but usually contained moral, ethical themes. Now look at most of the messages available to—and often directed to—our children and teenagers. I don't have to tell you of the unhealthy, often evil messages. This is true not only in most movies and television programs but also on the Internet. Parents must effectively learn to combat these heinous influences on their young ones.

The Fourth Foundation Stone:
Teaching and Modeling Anger Management to Your Child

This is what I believe to be the most difficult part of parenting today. Because our culture is changing so rapidly, it was only recently that a parent could leave the training of anger management to the environment and influences of peers and authority figures. This is why parents do not realize that it is one of their most critical responsibilities. How many parents have been taught how to handle their own anger maturely? I have not met one yet. Few are addressing this devastating problem. The increasing violence in our children and youths is only the tip of the iceberg. Immature ways of handling anger is without a doubt the primary lifetime threat in the child's life. Handling anger is the greatest determinant of your child's character, integrity, and the overall outcome of the quality of his or her life. In today's world, only the parent is in the position to train the child and teenager to handle anger maturely.

Immature ways of handling anger is without a doubt the primary life-time threat in the child's life.

All this may sound overwhelming, but let me assure you, dear parent, that you can do it. Any caring parent can provide the child with the four foundation stones needed for a child's success.

I trust that this brief lesson will whet your appetite to learn more about applying these principles so that you will have the tools you need. Thus, your child will grow to be his or her best, and you can have the confidence of being the parent you wish to be.

❧ *Lesson 10* ❧
Age: Infants to Teens

Lessons in Taming the Dragon

Meg Eastman, Ph.D.
Author of *Taming the Dragon in Your Child:*
Solutions for Breaking the Cycle of Family Anger

The dragon of anger lurks within us all. In this age of violence, parents are eager to promote a path of peace for their children. Overwhelmed and overstimulated by media violence, aggression in the school, and toys and video games that model fighting, parents can feel hopeless and wonder what they can do to promote healthy ways of handling anger in their child.

Parents are often unsure about how to deal effectively with anger in the family. On the one hand, we often are afraid of bottling up our child's anger for fear of damaging them through repression. On the other hand, we do not want to encourage physical outbursts and verbal outcries. We become afraid that our child will never learn to handle anger effectively.

> *As a parent, when you become upset, it is important to express in very simple terms that you are frustrated, hurt, or angry.*

Successful parents will teach their children the tools of peacemaking on a daily basis from infancy through adolescence. The peacemaking starts within us and becomes how we model and encourage our child to handle frustrations and disappointments in the small day-to-day difficulties of life.

Let there be peace and let it begin with me. As parents, we often become so preoccupied with being the voice of authority and with the demands and frustrations of our own lives, that we can be very harsh and demanding with our children. Normal struggles and upheavals become opportunities for crisis and conflict. We yell and scream things at our children that we swore we never would, and feel embarrassed by our lashing out.

Following are five steps to successfully taming your dragon within:

1. *The teaching parent will be a peaceful model in the day-to-day frustrations of life.* As a parent, when you become upset, it is important to express in very simple terms that you are frustrated, hurt, or angry. We can identify the mental and physical cues that we are upset, we can physically calm down, and we can mentally regain control. By our model, we teach our child that part of growing up is to learn when our feeling temperature rises and to learn to regain physical and emotional control. We can then work with others to meet their needs and solve the problem.

2. *When we are calm we can be soothing and help our child be in control.* Once you have gained your composure, the next step is to coach your child to physically get in control. Infants and toddlers need immediate consoling and physical soothing. Children can benefit from our validating their frustrations and emotions while we provide

40

the soothing and comforting. Older children can begin to provide self-soothing and self-comforting with our coaching and direction.

Emotional self-control is modeled and taught in a reciprocal dance between parent and child. We must resist the power struggle to gain authority, discipline immediately, or enforce our way through lectures. We must believe in the importance of calming the emotional arousal first. No amount of wonderful, emotional communication or productive problem solving can occur when our physical arousal is too high.

3. *Timing is everything.* First, you and your child need to soothe and regain a sense of physical and emotional composure no matter how long it takes. Then disciplinary strategies, emotional communication, and problem solving can be effective.

It is important that we differentiate problems that really require discussion and solutions from the day-to-day "have to's" that require structure, routine, and emotional support. We often become authoritarian regarding the day-to-day "have to's," when primarily what we need to do is provide coaching in how children can cope with the boredom, frustration, and fatigue required for daily chores and homework. Children will resist our forced authority, but they will be very receptive to our empathy. We can coach children to use rhythms, routines, nurturing rituals, and positive affirmations. When the work is done, we can enjoy the pride of accomplishment.

> Successful parents will teach their children the tools of peacemaking on a daily basis from infancy through adolescence.

4. *Trust.* It is important that emotional self-control will create an atmosphere in which our children can become respectful, planful, and responsible.

5. *Let it go.* Once calming has occurred and the problem has been resolved, let it go. Discipline can most effectively focus on apology, restitution, and making amends. Then we can forgive and truly move forward. The goal is to learn from our mistakes that we are human and can deal with the next frustration that life brings.

Nurture yourselves, be proud of your accomplishments, don't expect perfection, forgive, and move on. Remember that anger, hurt, and frustration are a normal part of daily life. If you are experiencing overload in your family, make sure that you have plenty of nurturing rituals to soothe the dragon of stress and to ensure the emotional connection between you and your child.

More information can be found in my book. If you still feel the dragon is controlling you and overtaking your family, or that your child is becoming increasingly violent, it is important to seek professional help.

❧ *Lesson 11* ❧

Sex and Parenthood

Valerie Davis Raskin, M.D.
Author of *Great Sex for Moms:*
Ten Steps to Nurturing Passion While Raising Kids

The lesson I'd like to share with parents is this: Don't put your romantic relationship on hold. Stop waiting until the kids are in college to have sex again. Don't buy into the myth that perfect parents have no needs of their own. Don't accept trading the pleasure of couplehood for the pleasure of parenthood.

It's perfectly natural that becoming parents stresses a couple's sexual relationship. New mothers generally shudder when their obstetricians tell them it's okay to have sex again, and new fathers may feel shut out of the mother–baby dyad. Sleep-deprived parents looking forward to the preschool years may discover to their surprise that exhaustion is still a factor, as many parents fall asleep shortly before their tired 4-year-old finally nods off.

During the school-aged years, kids usually sleep through the night, but life can be even more hectic. Moms may return to part- or full-time work, and who feels like making love after an afternoon of shuttling Suzy to soccer and Jack to piano lessons, overseeing homework, and pulling dinner together? The teen years? Who can find the privacy? The same adolescents who can't hear you when you beg them to come down for dinner seem to have radar tuned into what's going on in your bedroom.

Sex and parenthood don't have to be mutually exclusive. If you are waiting for the perfect timing, waiting for the embers to burst into flame on their own, consider this an opportunity. Just as parenthood challenges you to grow in other ways, so, too, can parenthood push your sexual relationship into a new phase, one characterized by mindfulness.

Stop waiting until the kids are in college to have sex again.

Becoming mindful about your sexuality takes courage, commitment, and good communication. Start by talking about the problem with your spouse, understanding that the sexual blahs are a common but not inevitable part of parenthood. Stop blaming yourself for never being in the mood; stop blaming your spouse for wanting more sex.

Start by addressing a libido mismatch, in which one partner (most commonly the wife) has far less sex drive than the other partner. Sexual energy is derived from overall energy, and chances are that if you're too tired for most things, you're too tired for sex. Take an honest inventory of how household tasks are allocated among parents, and consider whether there's a reason why one partner is always too tired for sex! If that doesn't help, pick a day, and send the low-sex-drive spouse off for a libido-boosting minivacation. For example, let Dad take full responsibility for the kids and the household while Mom shops at Victoria's Secret, spends the afternoon at a romantic and sexy R-rated movie, and soaks in a hot tub reading a trashy romance novel while the kids go to sleep.

Making time for making love can be accomplished at any stage of parenthood. Recognize that it's okay to have sex at odd hours of the day. During the child's infant stages, parents can plan to leave the baby at the grandparents and rush back home to an afternoon in bed. Hire a teenager to take your preschoolers to the latest Disney movie and spend the time making love. Parents of school-age kids and teenagers can sneak a vacation day and spend it together at home while the unsuspecting children are at school.

Becoming mindful as a sexual couple means being brave. Expand your horizons just to the limit of your comfort zone. Try writing sex e-mails to each other, make love by candlelight, whisper memories of the first time you made love as pillow talk, make out in the car, experiment with massage oils, giggle together over an outrageous *Cosmopolitan* magazine article, or make sexy phone calls to one another. Best of all, tell your partner what feels good, and ask your partner what she or he likes best.

It isn't reasonable to expect that busy, tired parents have mind-blowing sex all the time. Even if most of the time sex is, well, sort of routine, highly predictable, and rather rushed, sporadic bouts of mindful, interesting, and spicy sex go a long way to keep parents connected, body and soul.

Health and Nutrition

"Don't take too seriously all that the neighbors say. Don't be overawed by what the experts say. Don't be afraid to trust your own common sense. Bringing up your child won't be a complicated job if you take it easy, trust your own instincts, and follow the directions that your doctor gives you."

—*Benjamin Spock, M.D., and Michael B. Rothenberg, M.D. from* Dr. Spock's Baby and Child Care

Engage & Participate in Your Child's Health Care

Steven P. Shelov, M.D., M.A.

Author of *Caring for Your Baby and Young Child: Birth to Age 5*

There are really two major lessons for parents that are interdependent. The first, you know your child better than anyone, and what you have to say is vitally important to any health care professional. A person who disregards your point of view, your experience, your hunches, or your observation should not be a source of advice.

Second, when seeking health information about your child or a condition you suspect, depend on proven, reliable sources. Throughout the book that I edit for the American Academy of Pediatrics (AAP) titled *Caring for Your Baby and Young Child: Birth–Five*, we often complete our statements of advice or guidance with the line, "If you have any further questions or seek more information, or just don't know what to do, call your pediatrician." That statement is not just to create more business—pediatricians already have plenty, as you know. It is meant to reinforce the principle that your child's pediatrician *is* the most knowledgeable and reliable source of information *and* knows your child *almost* as well as you do.

The reason that the AAP's child care book has been so successful (almost 3 million copies in print) is that the sources of the information within it *are* the most up to date and accurate available.

Parents often struggle with whether to be more aggressive in asking questions for fear that the question is a stupid one. The fact is there are no "stupid" questions. Pediatricians realize that parents have a wide range of experience, have past knowledge, and sometimes feel confident in their abilities or are anxious and overwhelmed. The education of the pediatrician throughout the 3 years of residency repeatedly emphasizes the broad range of parental abilities and knowledge. The more you ask, the more you will know, and the more you know, the easier will be the job of the pediatrician. Hopefully, the result will be that your child's health and well-being are maximized.

> *The more you ask, the more you will know, and the more you know, the easier will be the job of the pediatrician.*

Another thing that parents often don't realize is that pediatricians are not just interested in the hard medical stuff. Raising a child has many dimensions to it, and often the concerns are not about infections, skin problems, asthma, or some other physical problem. The concerns may be about your baby's crying, your child's bed-wetting, fighting between your two older children, twins' adjustment to going off to school, or other behavioral topics. These are all well within the pediatrician's training and expertise. If answered properly, the pediatrician will often ask back to you, "What do *you* think is going on?" This response is not a cop-out. It simply reinforces the first lesson above—that you know your child best and probably have a good idea about what may be wrong and what might be done in response. Once you offer your thoughts, you will often find the pediatrician's response to augment your own thoughts, add additional information from his or her own experience, and create a true dialogue about the questions you have raised.

You should not be surprised if the pediatrician suggests some additional reading or information to expand further on the issues you raised at the office visit. You should be sure to follow up on that advice. Often you will not be able to get *all* of the answers you need in the face-to-face contact in the office, especially with the time pressure of current pediatric offices. Take the advice of seeking further information seriously and you won't regret it. You will find that as your ability to add to your own knowledge is expanded, your interactions with your child's doctor will ultimately be more satisfying.

Trust yourself, value what you know and what you have experienced, and trust your pediatrician and the sources of information he or she may recommend. Engage and participate. Don't be afraid of being assertive. Remember that the ultimate concern is your child's health, which both you and your pediatrician have as your mutual goal.

Lesson 13
Age: All

Sleep Pretty Baby
The Importance of Sleep in Your Child's Life

Inda Shaenen
Author of *The 7 O'Clock Bedtime*

You feed your children a balanced and nourishing diet. You provide them with weather-appropriate clothing. You shelter them in a home that protects them from rain and snow. You encourage them to exercise their bodies in order to stay healthy. You warn them about the risks of abusing drugs, alcohol, and tobacco. You love them and provide them with an education so that they may grow into compassionate, intelligent, productive adults. So what's missing?

Sleep. Children need to sleep. Sleep is a primal need, a physiological and biological necessity. In order for children to learn, grow, play, reason, and mature into healthy human beings, they must spend a certain nonnegotiable and age-specific amount of time asleep. Recognize and respect this need and you will find the whole process of childrearing to be that much easier. Here's why. When you know that your infant must take a morning nap, it's easy to say no to a 10 A.M. play group. When you know that your preschooler requires an after-lunch nap of 1 or 2 hours, it's easy to decline an invitation to an afternoon pool party. When you know that your 6-year-old has to be in bed at 7 P.M. in order to get the 11 hours of sleep he needs, it's easy not to sign him up for tee ball teams that meet in the early evening. When you know that your 9-year-old needs to have a calm and peaceful hour or two before going to bed at 8 P.M., it's easy to say no to a trip to the mall after dinner. Saying no is ususally easy when you feel that you are acting in the best interests of your child—interests that cannot be compromised without also compromising your child's health, well-being, and future development.

Imagine coming home to find that your babysitter threw away the sandwich and milk you laid out for lunch and instead served your child six chocolate bars, a bag of potato chips, and a bottle of cola. You would be outraged, and rightfully so. But it is no less outrageous to make commitments and arrangements that cut into what ought to be sleep time. The results of current studies leave no doubt as to the consequences of compromising sleep. Mood and temperament deteriorate first. A chronically underrested child is emotionally brittle and less resilient. Tired children overreact to their environment and are easily frustrated. Some children will become depressed. Next appear neuropsychological complications, including deficiencies in short-term memory, in the ability to react appropriately to situations and to reflect on behavior, and in the capacity to organize thoughts and materials. All of these faculties are compromised in children who are deprived of sleep over time.

So how much is enough? While individual patterns vary, sleep scientists have determined a rough estimate of what most children require. Newborns and very young infants remain awake for only an hour or two at a time. Older infants can stay awake for up to 2 to 3 hours before they need to nap or go to sleep for the night. Between ages 1 and 2, a baby needs 14 hours of sleep, which includes one or two naps during the day. At age 2, a toddler needs 11 to 12 hours of sleep at night, plus a midday nap of 1 to 2 hours. Three-year-olds require 12 to 12½ hours of sleep in every 24-hour period. (If they nap, a couple of these hours can be logged in during the day.) At age 4, children need

11½ to 12 hours of sleep. Children at 5 require 11 hours of sleep. Six-year-olds need 10¾ to 11 hours of sleep. At age 7, children require ten and a half to eleven hours of sleep. Eight-year-olds require 10¼ to 10¾ hours of sleep. At age 9, children need 10 to 10⅓ hours of sleep. Prepubescent 10-year-olds need 9¾ to 10 hours of sleep. And from puberty through adulthood, people generally require about 9¼ hours of sleep each night. Pediatric sleep specialists can help you determine how much sleep is right for your own child.

Once you have determined how much sleep your child requires, try to hold bedtime steady at the appointed hour. If your child needs to go to bed at 8 P.M., then he ought to go to bed at this time every single night of the week, including weekends. Also, try to sustain a regular prebedtime order of activity. After dinner, move right into washing up, reading books, singing lullabies, and kissing goodnight. Exceptions to the daily routine will come up from time to time—illness, travel, vacations at home, and visitors all throw a wrench into the schedule. Nevertheless, always try to return to routine as soon as the special days are over.

Do not feel guilty about putting your children to bed. At first you may be discouraged by the compromises you need to make in order to stick to a scheduled bedtime. In many instances, such compromises may well situate you and your family outside of the mainstream culture. But have faith! By establishing a regular daily routine that allows your children to get enough sleep, you will return your family's life to a humane rhythm. The current busyness of childhood is bad for children and trying for parents. There is no need to fly from activity to activity all day long and into the night. What children need is time every day to play freely without adult guidance and structure. Find places where your children can play safely—the playground, the backyard, the park—and supervise them from a distance as they create a magical realm of their own.

One warning: Do not imagine that you will be creating perfect children and a perfect family. There are no such things. Nor should there be. Just as an all-sunny life would be an inhuman life, so a bedtime without a pang of regret at the loss of another day would be an inhuman bedtime. Bedtime can be loving, happy, peaceful, and sacred; but it always marks a bittersweet separation and an end. If you accept even this much, you will be that much more patient with your child's resistance to going to sleep.

The most important lesson in parenting—one that you, as a parent, teach yourself over and over again, every single day—is where to draw those lines in the sand and how to maintain them. Your child wants something; you want something else. How do you get past the apparent impasse and negotiate the solution? In general, draw your line only where the stakes are high. Bottom-line rules:

• Your child may not hurt himself or others, either physically or emotionally.

• Your child may not destroy valuable property.

Now fit sleep into this paradigm. Getting enough sleep is obviously a matter of health and vitality. Compromise sleep and you hurt your child. Ergo, bedtime is one of your lines in the sand. Hold it with love, with good cheer, and with authority. Your happy, balanced, rested, playful, and loving child will be living proof every day that you are doing the right thing.

How to Handle Homesickness

Christopher A. Thurber, Ph.D.

Author of *The Summer Camp Handbook: Everything You Need to Find, Choose, and Get Ready for Overnight Camp—and Skip the Homesickness!*

Nurturing a child's independence is one of the most powerful and, at times, painful things a mother or father can do. Parents give birth to children, hold them physically and emotionally close throughout their development, and then need to let them go. Not forever, of course, but for a time . . . and at different times across the life span. How parents manage those times will, in both subtle and obvious ways, influence the child's attachments later in life. How parents nurture independence and help a child prepare for separations will shape the child's attitudes about close relationships. Interpersonal bonds can be strengthened or weakened by separations because children are exquisitely sensitive to the tone and tempo of time apart from their caregivers. For this reason, the greatest lesson I have for parents concerns the time they spend apart from their children.

Over the past 7 years, my colleagues and I have researched the phenomenon of homesickness. We define homesickness as the distress or impairment caused by an actual or anticipated separation from home and note that homesickness is characterized by acute longing and preoccupying thoughts of home and attachment objects. Sounds complicated, but it's not. Quite simply, being in an unfamiliar environment can be uncomfortable. Therefore, it's natural to think about home and the things you hold dear. So natural, in fact, that our studies have shown 95 percent of boys and girls between the ages of 8 and 16 experience some degree of homesickness on a least one day of a two-week stay at overnight summer camp. Some children miss their parents the most; others miss junk food or television the most; still others miss their siblings or a favorite stuffed animal. Almost all children (and most adults!) miss something about home when they are away. Homesickness is normal.

With the prospect of leaving home also comes parental anxiety, which is also normal. Parents wonder: Will my child be okay without me? Will she make friends? Who will comfort her when she's feeling blue? Obviously, no one knows your child as well as you do, but even without you there, your youngster can probably manage. Millions do.

Indeed, nearly seven million children attend overnight summer camp each year in the United States alone. That's a lot of marshmallows and bug juice. Naturally, many of these children experience homesickness. But there is a silver lining: These children also learn ways to cope with their feelings of homesickness. Such emotion regulation is a coping skill that will serve them well for the rest of their lives. These children will also leave camp with an unparalleled sense of accomplishment. Their self-esteem will have made a quantum leap. Such authentic feelings of "I can do it" come not from vapid praise but from real achievement in a challenging context.

Unfortunately, well-meaning parents sometimes undermine this remarkable growth experience. As anxiety mounts with the approaching camp season, parents often make "pick-up" deals with their children. "If you feel homesick at camp," they explain, "I'll come pick you up." Such deals destabilize a child's burgeoning independence. They give children a mental crutch and they paralyze the camp staff.

The subtext of the message "If you feel homesick at camp, I'll come pick you up" is: *I lack so much confidence in your ability to cope with this separation, my child, that I think the only way to resolve this situation is for me to rescue you.* Of course, as we know, most children are, with the occasional help of the camp staff, exceptionally skilled at learning to cope with feelings of homesickness. We also know that the rewards of completing an entire week or two or ten away from home are extraordinary. The message "If you feel homesick at camp, I'll come pick you up" also contains a false pretense. It's really not *if you feel homesick* but rather *when you feel homesick.* Remember, 95 percent of children have these feelings. Children who are not informed that feelings of homesickness are common end up feeling homesick *and* abnormal—a combination that can cause anxiety to snowball.

Of course, there is something else going on here. Parents who make these pick-up deals are erecting a safety net for their own fears. Ironically, it all becomes a self-fulfilling prophecy. According to our research, one of the hallmarks of homesickness is *preoccupying* thoughts of home and attachment objects. Thus, children need something about which to be preoccupied. Pick-up deals give them that something on a silver platter. They think, *My parents are worried about me. They don't think I can make it. If I feel homesick, it's gonna be bad . . . so bad that my parents will have to come get me.* Even if children don't think these exact thoughts, pick-up deals give them something to fixate on and they neglect drawing on their own coping skills. Why should they make efforts to cope? Their mom or dad has given them an easy out.

Imagine the common summertime scenario of a young, teary-eyed camper approaching her cabin leader after dinner on the second day of camp. Having been trained to expect some homesickness from her campers, the leader invites the camper to sit with her and talk. "I want to go home," the camper sobs.

"You sound homesick," says the leader. "That can hurt inside," she adds empathetically. "Tell me all the things you think or do to help make things better," she instructs, probing for all the ways the child has tried to cope so far. The camper's reply stops the conversation short.

"My mom said that if I felt homesick, she would come and get me."

I know from experience that trying to convince a homesick camper to stay at camp once a pick-up deal is in place is about as easy as turning straw into gold. After learning about a pick-up deal, our cabin leader doesn't have much choice. She needs to contact the child's parents and find out whether it is true. And if it is, parents are faced with two equally unsatisfactory choices. They can either (1) stick to their promise and come pick the child up or (2) renege and force the child to stay. Option 1 preserves trust but risks making the child feel like a failure. Option 2 erodes the child's trust in the parents and risks making her feel helpless and abandoned.

So, how can parents best respond to a child's frank question, "Dad, will you come pick me up if I get really homesick and hate camp?" The best answer is something like, "You sound a little nervous about going to camp. But I think you're really going to love it. It's normal to feel nervous before you go. Plus, even if you do have some homesick feelings at camp, you'll know what to think and do to make things better. We're going to learn some strategies that help a lot with homesickness. So, even though you might have some homesick feelings, I think you're going to have a great time at camp."

There is one caveat: Camp is not a jail. Every once in a great while, the best thing for a child is to return home early. Naturally, skilled cabin leaders first work hard with such children to help them cope. Yet, if the child's distress is severe and lasts more than a few days, staff should recognize that sometimes the benefits of going home outweigh the benefits of staying at camp.

Because decisions about shortening a child's stay at camp are complex, parents and camp staff need to make the decision together. However, such cases of severe, chronic homesickness are rare. Only about one in fourteen children experiences a level of homesickness that is associated with severe symptoms of depression and anxiety, and, at the camps where I have conducted research, fewer than one child in one hundred needs to return home early because of intense homesickness.

What are the best ways to cope with homesickness? There are basically two kinds of strategies: things you do and things you think. The most effective things that children *do* to help minimize feelings of homesickness are staying busy, talking with friends and trusted adults, and doing something to feel closer to home, such as writing a letter. The most effective *thinking* strategies include looking on the bright side, putting time in perspective (realizing that a few weeks at camp is not very long compared to how many weeks old you are), and keeping track of the camp stay on a calendar.

Working with your child to develop these and other coping strategies *before* camp starts will dramatically enhance his time away from home. Have a candid conversation about homesickness and use some practice time away from home, such as a weekend at a friend's house, as a testing ground for his adjustment and coping. Simulate how you will keep in touch during the actual separation by having your child write a postcard. When he returns home, debrief the experience and decide together whether the time is right for a longer separation. In any event, always involve your child in the decision to spend time away from home.

> The most effective things that children DO to help minimize feelings of homesickness are staying busy, talking with friends and trusted adults, and doing something to feel closer to home, such as writing a letter.

Finally, remember that when a child grows in independence, this does not mean that she is growing apart from her parents, as many moms and dads fear. Instead, she is growing confident in her ability to manage new situations and regulate her own emotions. These are two life skills that parents are in a unique position to endow. But wait! There's more: If the time apart was thoughtfully undertaken, the child is likely to grow closer to her parents. As one 12-year-old boy told me during my initial summer of research, "Sometimes homesickness can feel bad, but actually be ... good. It helps form that bond between parents and children. I find without a little homesickness, you're not as close to your parents because you don't appreciate them as much."

The Mastery of Intimate Conversations with Your Children

Jessica Gillooly

Author of *Before She Gets Her Period:*
Talking with Your Daughter About Menstruation

Intimate conversations are different from all other conversations that you have with your children. Conducting intimate conversations with your children is a skill that you have to work to develop with time and practice. You must persist by initiating these conversations with your children throughout adolescence, because as they get older and more independent they will resist your input more and more. With consistency on your part, not only will you get better at discussing intimate issues but so will your child. The development of these skills leads to openness, which in turn leads to trust and mutual understanding.

After interviewing and reading hundreds of firsthand intimate stories written by young girls (aged 8 to 17) and adult women and men (aged 18 to 60s) about their physical, sexual, and emotional maturation, the one consistent request among all groups was that they wanted their parents to talk with them more often and with more depth about intimate issues. As they aged, they were thankful to their parents for persistently, sometimes doggedly, continuing to talk even when the children did not want to hear or be bothered with the parents' efforts at intimate conversations.

> **Your child really wants you to talk with him or her about sexual maturation.**

If you are a parent of a preadolescent or adolescent, you may find it hard to believe that your child really wants you to talk with him or her about sexual maturation, but it is true. It is also true that you most likely will not hear the thanks for your efforts until you are both older. I promise you, however, that the thank you will be sweet and well worth all your efforts.

As a marriage and family therapist for over 20 years, I have seen innumerable parents who are exhausted and ready to give up on their preadolescents and adolescents. However, children this age need your guidance as much as when they were younger, and they need your wisdom at this time of their lives more than ever.

All youths this age realize they do not know everything about most important things, but they still try to show you that they are in fact knowledgeable—more knowledgeable than they were even a year, a month, a day, or a minute ago. Sometimes they are so adamant in their insistence on knowing everything (or at least knowing more than we do) that we want to give up the struggle to actively discuss intimate topics. Adolescents crave parental involvement and sensitive intimate guidance in their lives. They just cannot tell you how much they needed your guidance until years later.

When I first starting interviewing young girls in preparation for my book *Before She Gets Her Period*, they were reluctant to share their menstruation stories, but with a little encouragement they told me their intimate feelings of beginning their periods. To my surprise, the stories of girls and women of all ages had one common theme: They all needed more information about menstruation before they began their first periods. Even girls who acted as if they did not want or need conversations about their approaching menstruation in fact later realized how valuable these conversations were. The more accurate the information they obtained, the fewer fears and anxieties they experienced.

Also, the girls and boys who I interviewed or whose stories I read realized that they needed conversations about maturing and about their changing bodies long before their parents realized that they did—or at least before the parents broached the topic with them.

Presently the average age for breast development in young girls is between 8 and 9 years of age, and the average age of onset of puberty or sexual maturity is currently thought to be between 9 and 15 years of age for both girls and boys. Therefore, if parents are to be active participants in their children's lives, they must begin intimate discussions about changing, maturing bodies when their children are still quite young.

Older adolescents and young adults recognized that they needed repeated parental conversations to grasp the complicated physical, emotional, and sexual changes that were occurring. It is a real challenge to explain the complicated body changes to young children whose physical clocks have sped ahead of their cognitive and emotional clocks. Therefore, to be effective, keep your discussions short, but keep them coming. Conversations that are short and frequent, even if you do all the talking, are best for your children. I always tell the parents

If parents are to be active participants in their children's lives, they must begin intimate discussions about changing, maturing bodies when their children are still quite young.

who work with me to remember how many times they talked to their children about something as simple as brushing their teeth. Sexual development and understanding deserves as much time as dental health and hygiene.

The young adults who I interviewed were clear that if their parents talked to them about changing secondary sex characteristics, sexual maturation for both girls and boys, and emotional swings, they felt more open with their parents. They were receptive to their parents' later intimate conversations concerning such topics as dating, falling in love, being hurt by love, and expressing one's sexuality.

Through all the interviews and personal accounts of sexual maturation, many young people told me that they desperately wanted to hear their parents' own stories of growing up. Sharing your stories of how you felt at their age, who you talked to, who educated you, how you learned about menstruation and the sexual development of both sexes, and how your own parents and relatives acted are all important connecting pieces of information. Of course, you choose when and where to share the intimate details of your life and how much you want to share. But remember, if you cannot share aspects of your struggles, frustrations, mistakes, and misunderstandings, then it is not likely that your children will choose to share their intimate struggles with you.

The last point I gathered from the stories and interviews is that there can be a lot of laughter in the sharing between parents and children. Laughter is a good icebreaker and laughing at yourself is important for your children. Growing up physically, sexually, and emotionally is full of many good times, in addition to the struggles. Your children will remember your shared stories and experiences, and will thank you in the future for talking with them and educating them.

Sex Differences in Health

Susan Gilbert

Author of *A Field Guide to Boys and Girls*

It's no news that some health problems are more common in boys and that others are more common in girls. Eating disorders are largely female illnesses, for example, whereas attention-deficit hyperactivity disorder is more prevalent in males. But lately doctors have found that other conditions, long thought to know no gender, affect boys and girls in different numbers or in different ways. Parents who know about sex differences in health can use this information to help protect their sons and daughters.

To be sure, many of the gender inequities in health are genetic and therefore can't be prevented—yet—although the human genome research could change that. But there are several conditions that you can do something about now.

Accidents

Far more boys than girls are hurt as a result of accidents. Among 5 to 12-year-olds, the accidental injury rate is twice as high for boys as it is for girls. It's not that boys are clumsier. Boys get injured more because practically from the time they can walk they take more risks: reaching for a hot coffee cup, climbing onto the kitchen counters, jumping off the top of the slide, and bike riding without a helmet.

Helping your son think twice before taking risks can help keep him out of the emergency room. But how do you do this? The just-say-no approach alone doesn't work, experts say. Better to help your boy experience the potential consequences of his recklessness. Here's what worked in an experiment with elementary school students in Toronto: A researcher had them pretend that they broke an arm in an accident. They had to do things like zip and unzip their backpacks and get on their jackets with just one hand. The students realized just how much harder their lives would be and how much they would have to rely on others for help. Suddenly, being a daredevil didn't seem so appealing. Four months after the study ended, the kids were engaging in less risky behavior than they were before it started.

Sports Injuries

Even when they play the same sports as boys, girls get more injuries on the field and court. The greatest difference is in knee injuries, which are about four times as common in girls as in boys. An important reason is that girls get inadequate training, leaving their muscles significantly weaker than boys' muscles. When strength training is improved for girls, their rate of knee injuries goes down. For example, by age 8, girls can benefit from doing push-ups and other resistance exercises. Beginning at age 12, they should do weight training. Such conditioning is especially important for basketball, softball, volleyball, and soccer. It also helps when girls are taught to run and land from a jump in a slightly crouched position, which takes some pressure off their knees. If your daughter's coach isn't aware of the special needs of female athletes, bring him or her up to date.

Adult-Onset Diabetes

This disorder was long thought to be just what its name suggests—an illness that hits in adulthood. But in the past several years, doctors have been surprised to see many children as young as age 7 with adult-onset diabetes, which is diagnosed by abnormally high levels of blood sugar. Most of these children are girls.

The surge in adult-onset, or type II, diabetes parallels the surge in the rate of obesity in children, and obesity is more common in girls. Obesity helps cause diabetes by interfering with the body's mechanism for controlling blood sugar. One of the main reasons that girls are more likely to be obese is that they're less active than boys. So, doctors think that fewer girls would be obese—and develop diabetes—if parents redoubled their efforts to turn off the TV and get their daughters outside playing sports, biking, swimming, or running around the park.

Depression

A female problem? Not quite. The gender difference in depression is one of timing: During the teen years, it's twice as common among girls, but among younger children it's more common among boys.

The reasons for these differences are complex, but they may be due partly to key differences in the ways in which society encourages boys and girls to behave. Many boys have trouble showing emotion because they think they've got to act tough—something that's especially hard to do when they're very young. So they deny or play down their feelings, even when something bad happens. But psychologists think that bottling up their feelings can lead to depression.

Girls, in contrast, go too far in the opposite direction. As they approach adolescence, they spend more time ruminating on negative events or sadness. Other females—their friends, their mothers—tend to encourage them to vent their feelings. But the habit of ruminating is a risk factor for depression.

Some experts on depression now think that boys would be better off if they learned to open up more and girls if they opened up less. Parents can help by making more time in the day to talk with their sons and being prepared to drop what they're doing when their sons are ready to talk about what's on their minds. For girls, the goal is to discourage rumination. This doesn't mean cutting your daughter off when she wants to pour her heart out, but rather helping her come up with ways to deal with whatever is bothering her.

Eating Disorders

Between 85 percent and 95 percent of people with anorexia and bulimia are girls and women. Though eating disorders usually develop during the teenage years, they're showing up more often in girls as young as age 7. To help prevent them, experts suggest starting early, when your daughter is still in preschool. Avoid talking about dieting in front of your daughter. Girls whose mothers complain about their own weight problem are more likely than other girls to worry about their weight and eventually start dieting, which is a risk factor for developing an eating disorder.

But, surprisingly, an overarching desire to be thin isn't the only cause of eating disorders or even the main cause, experts now say. Being a perfectionist is the strongest predictor of who will develop an eating disorder—stronger even than being female. How, then, can you support your daughter's high standards at school, in sports, and in other activities without the unhealthy consequences? There's no easy answer, but one constructive step is to look for signs that she's stressed out from too many activities. For some children, the pressure of going from violin lessons to ballet to softball practice is too much to bear. One of the ways girls crumble under the pressure is to develop abnormal eating habits, possibly in a desperate attempt to gain control over their lives. If girls kicked back and had a little more downtime, some experts think that fewer of them would have eating disorders.

There are many other health conditions with sex differences. They are a varied lot that includes sensitivity to pain and difficulty in quitting smoking, as well as autoimmune diseases, asthma, anxiety, and certain cancers. The field of gender-based medicine is in its infancy, but one goal is to find gender-specific ways to prevent and even treat these health conditions. When that day comes, checking the male or female box on a medical form may be more than a formality; it could mean better health all around.

Avoiding a Weight Problem in Your Child

Irving Penn, M.D., J.D.
Author of *The Penn Program: for Weight Control*

Have you ever seen a fat lion or an overweight zebra? Or a healthy fish that eats until it explodes? I doubt it. That's because when most beings are born they have the innate ability to eat only when they are hungry and stop when they have had enough fuel.

What parents need to remember is that no one, not even a child's own mother, can know how much that child needs to eat. When your baby cries and you know she wants food, you feed her until she stops eating. When a healthy newborn doesn't want any more breast milk or formula, she will let you know.

Once an infant begins to eat food, we must continue to listen to him. Have faith that he knows when to eat and how much is good for him. This is a scary concept. Suppose your 2-year-old wants a grilled cheese sandwich for breakfast? Well, what's wrong with that? It's not conventional? Mmm. Let's see. It has bread, which we could call toast, and cheese, which we would put in a breakfast omelet. So, what's wrong with that grilled cheese sandwich? Nothing.

When she is still young, you want your child to learn to enjoy fruits and vegetables—a good idea. So what do you do? You present your child with segments of oranges or slices of apples—pieces that the child can handle rather than struggling with a whole fruit. But more important is that you test it first. A child starts out enjoying foods that tend to be sweet. If you start her on a food that is somewhat sour or tart, it could turn her off and start her out not wanting to ever eat that food again. That is why it is so important for the parent to eat a child's new food first. If the apple, for example, is not a particularly sweet one,

> *A child starts out enjoying foods that tend to be sweet.*

then the parent may discard it before the child takes a bite. But if the first taste is sweet and the child sees the parent eat and enjoy it, you can well imagine how she will follow. As the child matures, she learns there are different tastes to the same or different fruits and an aversion tends not to develop nearly as easily.

So Mom introduces the child to as many different foods as she can, and even with a bit of sweetening added if Mom thinks it will help. It is important to remember that children tend to imitate the parents.

As the child grows, you will begin to learn which foods he enjoys eating.

And what if that child eats only a few bites, then says, "All done." He *is* all done. If you tell him, "Just a few more bites, Honey," he will force down food he doesn't need and his body will eventually lose that innate ability to stop when it has had enough fuel. Instead, the body will begin to store food as fuel that it doesn't need. Hence, the overweight child.

Think of the body as you would a car. We have a gas tank for fuel. Suppose every time that tank was close to empty, we filled it. Great. We could continue to function until we ran out of fuel again. Now, suppose we overfilled it, and every time we did, the car automatically created a reserve. So, if we overfilled it every time it needed fuel and didn't use all of the fuel including the reserve, imagine the number of reserve tanks it would have created.

We, as parents, believe we know what's best for our children. Of course we do. We know that we should hold hands while crossing the street. We know that no child should be left near a swimming pool unattended. After all, the most important part of being a parent is to make sure our child is safe. When it comes to food, though, we must give some of the control back to the child. We must have faith that her body knows what it needs to function.

When it comes to food, we must give some of the control back to the child.

It is important to expose your child to different kinds of foods. Your child may learn that she does not like spinach but loves broccoli. Perhaps her body may be able to digest and distribute the nutrients in that broccoli better than the spinach, so she feels more comfortable after eating that particular food. And don't worry so much about the vegetables. If your child wrinkles her nose at all vegetables and you're worried she's not getting enough nutrients, there are a plethora of vitamins you can give her.

As a child gets older and starts asking for a particular food, the parent will decide whether the child gets it. Now, if your 4-year-old daughter is asking for cookies (which, when broken down into ingredients, are quite healthy), you can give her a cookie or you can give her choices. "How about some grapes?" You'd be surprised how many times your child will say, "okay." The trick is to listen to what your child is requesting and remember that she hasn't been exposed to all the choices that are available.

Many moms believe a fruit is always healthier than a cookie. Why is that? If you break the fruit down, it is mainly sugar and water. Fruit juice is rapidly absorbed into the bloodstream, which is no problem for a normal, healthy child. And because so many calories are absorbed so quickly, some are stored in the liver for future use. The sugar in the cookie, however, is absorbed more slowly because the body is busy distributing the other macronutrients present. I do not believe there is a problem with a child getting sugar from fruit, but I also do not believe there is a problem with a child getting sugar and other nutrients from a cookie.

Carbohydrates, or sugars, are the driving force behind a child's growth and development, and protein and fat to a much lesser extent. That doesn't mean the child should sit around eating spoonfuls of sugar. However, carbohydrates—sugar, starches, whatever you want to call them—are found in many, many foods and rather than just eating a spoonful of sugar, it is healthier to eat a food such as a cookie with sugar in combination with other nutrients. I also do not suggest eliminating all candy from a child's diet. Restricting food such as candy only causes the child to want it more and then he may overeat when he is allowed sweets because he is not sure when he will get to eat that yummy food again.

Many parents believe in no sugar because it's bad for the teeth. It is bad if the sugary substance is left on the teeth. That's why teaching youngsters to brush twice a day and rinse their mouth or drink water after eating sugary foods helps a great deal.

It is not the KIND of food that is important; it is the QUANTITY of the food.

The purpose of all of this is to stress that there are few foods that should be restricted or that are unhealthy. It is not the *kind* of food that is important; it is the *quantity* of the food. If you can retrain yourself to think of no food as bad, but instead think of what is in that food and the quantities of the different ingredients, then you will be better able to assess what your child needs.

Now for something completely unconventional—the mealtime habit. Your child comes to you at around 5 P.M. and tells you he's hungry. You say, "We're having dinner in an hour. I don't want you to spoil your appetite." Once again, you are suppressing his innate ability to know when he is hungry. Let him eat a few slices of apple if he wants. If dinnertime arrives and your child eats only a few bites, grin and bear it. We mustn't be selfish and think, *I slaved over this meal and my kid's not even eating it.* Instead, we must once again believe that his body, to function effectively, is telling him what it needs.

I have yet to see an overweight child or adult whose parents didn't make her take even one more bite or eat their vegetables (just more calories if their body didn't need those vegetables), or wait for dinner until she was so hungry that she ate more than her body needed. As you are well aware, it is the extra food that puts the extra weight on children as well as adults. Extra calories from that extra food are what make a child chubby or fat. It does not improve the child's health, strength, or self-esteem.

What if your child appears too thin to you? Be patient, go along with the child's wishes, and you will see a healthy and happier child.

What if you protest that you are only encouraging your child to eat more healthy foods? Carbohydrates, fats, and proteins—the macronutrients—are what put weight on everybody. Vitamins and minerals do not add weight but are certainly important for a healthy body. Encouraging your child to eat more of any type of food is not the way to do it. From infancy to old age, if you wish to take in extra vitamins and minerals—whether you need them or not—you do not do it with food, as I mentioned; you do it with supplements (pills) and bypass the macronutrients that your body doesn't need.

I know these concepts are somewhat unconventional. I also know that watching and studying overweight patients for more than 30 years has proven to me the information I just gave to you.

Here's another benefit to following the Penn Program: There is less conflict involved in our daily experiences when we give some of the control over foods back to our children. Conflict is something we could all use a little less of in our parenting experience.

In the Beginning

"When you're the parents of a new child, all the craving and desire you've ever felt for sex is transferred over to sleep. It's like somebody sneaked into your brain, found the wires going to the sex button and the sleep button, and just switched them."

–Paul Reiser, from Babyhood

The First Signs of Intelligent Life:

Awaken Your Baby's Inner Resources

Joseph Garcia, Ed.D.

Author of *Sign with your Baby*

My contribution to *Parent School* is based on my research and observations and is flavored with my excitement and passion for helping parents be the best any child could want. One question that directed my research while studying early childhood development was *When do individuals first identify and draw on their inner resources to solve problems and meet life's challenges?*

I believe that communication is one of the first challenges young children encounter. When children begin to communicate, they start a complex and aggressive journey in problem solving. The journey is complex in that children attempt to arrange in their minds the order of the world around them. They encode and decode sights and sounds into memories and then link combinations of experiences into the sequences that will help guide them through life. The journey is aggressive in that in order to understand and react to situations using communication, children must observe and aggressively experiment with life to gain knowledge and confidence.

Once an individual is faced with a challenge and triumphs over it, the next challenge is less frightening. Once an individual draws on his inner resources and finds success, he is better able to draw on those resources again and again, and overcome more and more challenges.

In my research, I was looking at ways to help very young children discover and use their inner resources. I wanted to find out how parents could help this self-discovery process. The method I came up with—my lesson to parents—is this: By using manual gestures or signs in tandem with spoken language, parents can engage their babies in reciprocal communication. Babies have control over their hands long before they develop the fine motor skills required for speech. I learned that children as young as 6 to 8 months have adequate cognition, memory, and dexterity to effectively use their hands to communicate.

Studies suggest that frustration can be both positive and negative in a child's development. A little ignites curiosity. A lot can shut everything down. Some of the frustration children feel is initiated by their lack of ability to solve a particular problem. Examples of problems are children not being able to reach something, eat when hungry, drink when thirsty, play with a toy they want, or explain to the parent that they feel discomfort. Consider the tremendous relief and personal satisfaction an infant must feel when her first attempt to express her needs is successfully received by the parent. Compare this to the frustrating months infants spend unable to express themselves. Communication can reduce the time spent in frustration and disappointment. That precious time could be better used for discovery and growth.

My method does not require that parents learn an entirely new language. Rather, by using a few simple gestures, we as parents can make a big difference in empowering and meeting the needs of our young children. When we provide our children with a communicative modality such as signs many months before they can talk, children begin recognizing the gestural patterns and can reproduce these movements to rep-

> *Using signs, our preverbal infants will have more opportunity to solve problems and discover their inner resources.*

resent their needs and thoughts. Using signs, our preverbal infants will have more opportunity to solve problems and discover their inner resources.

This manual communication process provides several further benefits. My observations and other research have concluded that signing with preverbal infants accelerates verbal language acquisition, increases a child's interest in books, and strengthens the parent–child bond. Research also indicates that signing with preverbal infants is associated with an increase in IQ scores with those infants later in life. However, I do not want parents to see using signs as a way to develop genius children. In my opinion, the increase in learning is largely due to more interaction and engagement. Those parents who sign with their children feel more responsive to their infants' developmental needs. Many caregivers have remarked that using signs changed the way they parented.

As you embark on the thoroughly wonderful experience of having communication with your prespeech infant, these important rules should be followed:

1. Never ask a child to sign outside of the experiential context.

2. Don't ask your child to show off her signing abilities to others.

3. Don't compare your child to other children.

4. Don't show disappointment if your child chooses not to sign in a particular situation.

5. Don't make signing with your baby a lesson, but use signs in your daily life as an augmentation to your speech.

6. Reward your child's attempts to communicate so that he receives love and acceptance when he makes those first attempts to connect with you.

7. Try not to overanticipate and overrespond to your child's needs. Otherwise, your infant may seldom have need-driven opportunities to communicate. I'm not advocating neglect; I'm simply encouraging you to allow a few seconds or moments for your child to search for and discover her internal resources.

By establishing reciprocal communication with preverbal infants, we empower our children at a critical age. We help them awaken their understanding so that they can begin to steer their lives and not passively wait for life to steer them. This is why I developed the "Sign with Your Baby" system. The challenge we as parents have is to help our children awaken their internal resources as early as possible. Then, over the years, our children's confidence will grow and their life's challenges may not seem so overwhelming.

Importance of Early Childhood Parenting

Dr. Burton L. White

Author of *The New First Three Years of Life: The Completely Revised and Updated Edition of the Parenting Classic,* and *Raising a Happy Unspoiled Child: How Parents Can Help Their Baby Develop into a Secure and Well-Adjusted Child*

The most important thing parents ought to know is that nothing in life is more important than helping their children to a great start in life by giving them the best experiences they can during the children's first few years. They should also know that information created since the mid-1960s can help them achieve that goal, but there is far more misinformation available than sound information. They have to figure out which is which.

The single most important ingredient in effective early experience is time spent with at least one adult who is passionately in love with the child. The two most likely people who qualify are the child's parents. My recommendation, based on over 40 years of study of good development in children is as follows: During a child's first 7 months, give or take a week or two, one of the two key people should be nearby most of the time. From 7 to 30 months, one or the other of those two people should be nearby for the majority of the child's waking hours.

It should be noted that I do not recommend full-time parenting during the 7 to 30-month period. The pressure on a parent from the physical dangers to the child becomes high during the 8-to 20-month period due to the usual strong urge of such children to climb as high as they can. Psychological pressures exacerbate the stress substantially during the 15-to 24-month period when normal children begin to struggle for power with their parents.

Finally, if parents want more than one child, they would be well advised to space their children at least 3 years apart regardless of what the biological clock is telling them.

Lesson 20
Age: All

My Own Best Mom

Julia Indichova
Author of *Inconceivable: A Woman's Triumph Over Despair and Statistics*

On a Tuesday afternoon in April 1992, I was sitting in my kitchen waiting for the results of my FSH test. It was supposed to indicate whether my husband, Ed, and I would be able to have another child. Though my daughter, Ellena, was just over a year old and we'd only been trying for a few months, at 42 my biological clock demanded immediate action.

"The FSH [follicle-stimulating hormone] helps the follicles in your ovaries to develop into eggs," explained my gynecologist. "When the level is over 20, your ovaries are not working as well as they should be." My FSH turned out to be the same as my age.

The fertility specialist to whom the gynecologist referred me, struck the first blow. "I'm sorry," said his receptionist. "Dr. R will not accept you as a patient. Your FSH is too high. He doesn't think he could help you." A decent man, he was saving me money. But all I heard was it was so bad that he didn't even want to try.

The five reproductive endocrinologists who did agree to see me displayed charts and diagrams with statistics. They showed me how I clearly didn't have a chance. "No," they intoned, "there is no documented case of anyone conceiving with these numbers."

Lying in bed at night, I fluctuated between despair and guilt. How could I have been so arrogant and ignored my age? "Besides, what is your problem?" asked a familiar voice in my head. "You dare lament with all those childless couples out there? To clamor for seconds before everyone gets their turn?"

Turned down by mainstream medicine, I decided to look for answers elsewhere. My first stop through the maze of alternative healers was a Native American medicine man, who opened his consultation by asking if I was having intercourse with my husband, and then proceeded to press down on my chest bones while recounting numerous stories of success. Before my departure, he discreetly motioned toward a small ceramic bowl where I was to leave my $150 in cash.

I tried homeopathy with its tiny white sugary pellets that melted under my tongue, and a month later decided to move on to Chinese medicine. The four acupuncturists I consulted commanded me to lie on narrow massage tables while they turned my body into a rare breed of porcupine, with needles pointing in every direction. They prescribed little black-and-white pellets in plastic bags, large quantities of herb-laced chicken soup, and dhuri fruit, which smelled like the aged cheese my father used to bring out when he wanted to hasten the departure of our guests.

They also recommended jumping rope "to shake up the organs," daily hot and cold showers, and making love on bright red sheets. I did it all, but my mind remained tightly clenched. Part of me was sitting on the sidelines, sneering, as if to say, "You don't really expect me to believe in all this stuff, do you?"

A year later, I was still not pregnant, and the pile of unpaid bills warned me from any further pursuit of a miracle cure. One day, as I skimmed through a diet book a friend had recommended, it occurred to me that becoming healthier could, perhaps, rejuvenate my wilting ovaries. Improving my diet was something I had always intended to do. Someday. Now I imagined my baby leaning over the clouds, dimpled hands cupped around its mouth, yelling: "Go, Mom, go! You can do it!"

Even if I don't get pregnant, I thought, at least I'll have the healthiest body I ever had.

For the first time since the diagnosis, I did not look for an expert's validation. With hardly a whimper, I bade good-bye to my afternoon cappuccino and chocolate cake, and ushered in a diet of greens, tempeh, brown rice, and fresh fruits and vegetables. Two months later, my body responded with the disappearance of my sinus headaches and a 13 point drop in my FSH. Inspired, I started a daily yoga practice and imagery exercises, visualizing healthy vibrant eggs floating into my uterus.

One day, as I skimmed through a diet book . . . it occurred to me that becoming healthier could, perhaps, rejuvenate my wilting ovaries

Eight months after the adjustments in my diet and lifestyle, the voice of the nurse on the other end of the phone announced my reward. "Oh, yes, Julia. Your test came back positive. Congratulations! You're pregnant!"

My younger daughter, Adira, is almost 8 years old. She makes her own vegetable juice and reads the ingredient labels on the cereal boxes at. I thank her every day not only for the astounding gift of her presence but for the gifts she brought with her. Though I was unaware of it at the time, this pilgrimage was more about learning how to be my own best mother than about getting pregnant My longing for a second child was also a longing for the abandoned child inside me calling to be heard.

For many of the millions of women and men caught up in the baby search, medical intervention may be the only path to parenthood. For me, my inability to conceive turned out to be the most powerful opportunity of my 43 years. It was the first time in my life I dared to follow through on all the healthy impulses that urged me to keep going; to pursue an idea simply because it made sense to me, even if no one else agreed with me. My desire for a baby was stronger than my self-doubt and my fear of change. After a lifetime of abdicating all decision making to experts, I finally became my own authority.

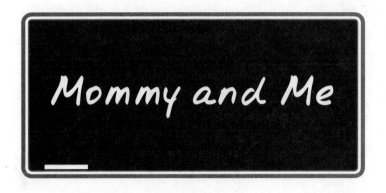

Mommy and Me

"My mother loved children—she would have given anything if I had been one."

—*Groucho Marx*

What You Didn't Expect When You Were Expecting

Karen Kleiman, M.S.W.

Co-author of *This Isn't What I Expected: Overcoming Postpartum Depression*

When we talk about having a baby, we often hear how exhilarating it can be. We hear about the promise of personal fulfillment and the brilliant glow that accompanies the miracle of life. We hear stories of abounding joy and delight as mothers seemingly glide through the various phases and tasks by which they are confronted. We are told we will beam when we're pregnant, we will bond instantly when we hold our baby for the very first time, and we will evolve naturally and gracefully through this transition into motherhood.

We all hope it will be like this when we have our baby.

The picture, however, is not always so perfect. Of course, we also hear about the many loads of laundry we will do with our eyes shut from exhaustion and how many showers we'll take in 30 seconds flat with the door open while our baby screams for attention. And though, to some extent, we are geared to compromise our previous lifestyle, most women find themselves inadequately prepared for the unpredictable adventure they have embarked upon.

We live in a culture that romanticizes motherhood. Even today—when we find ourselves surrounded by enlightened and progressive thinkers—the myth of the perfect mother persists. That is, the good mother is, with absolute commitment, self-sacrificing and nurturing. She provides unconditional devotion to her family and is motivated by endless self-denial that will ultimately fortify her children's emotional well-being.

All of this sounds good on paper.

A woman may hear how motherhood will change her life forever. Indeed. But what is often not said is that some of these changes will be profoundly disquieting, often launching her into a crisis, the likes of which she has never known.

What does a mother do with the burden of ambivalence she feels toward the baby she has longed for?

How does she reconcile her desire to be the best mother she can be with her yearning for the life she had before her baby?

To whom does she dare admit her secret wish that she never had this baby?

How can she sleep at night as she tries to balance the unsettling thoughts that constantly race through her mind and the imposing guilt that follows?

Can she be a good mother if she struggles, at times, with abrupt feelings of discontent, resentment, and anger toward her baby?

How does she resist the temptation to surrender to the loss of control and the assault to her self-esteem and identity?

Will she ever, again, reclaim her feelings of sexuality and passion for her former self?

Is this what being a mother is all about, or will she ever truly feel like herself again?

Our mothers didn't tell us about these changes and the losses that can take place after we have a baby. The medical community doesn't tell us. Often, our friends and family don't tell us. Yet, if we look very closely and listen very carefully, we can see the labored smile that marks the face of a mother lost in the challenge of her lifetime.

Sometimes being a mother doesn't feel good.

It is the story of a woman who looks very good on the outside—one who tries desperately to maintain the illusion that everything is fine, that this is, in fact, as easy and as pleasurable as it appears to be for every other mother to whom she compares herself. It is also the story of a woman who doesn't know where to go when she needs to say out loud that being a mother doesn't always feel so good. Just when she expects this to be the best time of her life, she is often left feeling as if she is doing something wrong, she's just not good at this; Perhaps she was not cut out to be a mother?

Sometimes, it's easy to claim rights to the hardships of motherhood. It is easy for most mothers to identify with the dreadful sleep deprivation, the brutal colic wail, or the breakfast dishes from yesterday never quite finding their way to the kitchen sink. But when a woman endures the pain of disconnection from her baby, or fails to meet the expectations dictated by her critical mother, or can't face her own reflection in the mirror because she has lost touch with the soul within—it's hard for her to know where to turn.

And this leaves us with a simple thought: Sometimes being a mother doesn't feel good.

Let's face it—it's hard, it's constant, and the endless work is rarely something for which we are thanked or rewarded. Sometimes, even when we are doing our best, it doesn't feel like as if we're doing quite enough. Other times, no matter what we do or how hard we try, we are left feeling depleted, overwhelmed, angry, and exhausted. Clearly, some of that just goes with the territory. There are times, too, when depression sets in, complicating the picture. But whatever the context, it is urgent that we debunk the myth, which perpetuates the notion that the transition to motherhood comes easily and naturally to most women. We need to challenge the presumption that good mothers take better care of their children than they do of themselves. In doing so, we can begin to set the stage for women to be released from the expectation that they manage this mother role perfectly.

So what do we do? We need to modify the messages they hear. We need to tell them it's okay to make mistakes. We need to tell them it's okay to ask for help.

And we must remember that it is essential that we, as mothers, be selfish sometimes. We must put our needs at the top of our priority list, without feeling guilty. This is not easy to do. But it's important. We need to rest when we can. Eat well. Get some fresh air, reach out to our friends, avoid people and things that make us feel bad, set limits, or simply take a walk.

We need to nourish our spirits.

Only then will our children have an opportunity to truly experience us at our best, be enriched by our efforts, and thus derive the most benefit from what we have to offer.

Redefining the "Good" Mother

Chris Fletcher

Chris Fletcher's humorous essays on parenthood have appeared in the book *Tales from the Homefront* and in a number of parenting publications.

Halfway through undressing my second son for his 18-month-old checkup, I realized he hadn't had a bath the night before. Surprising? Not really—we often have nights when we end up skipping a bath. No big deal.

What was illuminating, however, was my reaction to this knowledge. I just said, "Oh. No bath. Well, I guess you'll look clean enough." And that was it.

If this had happened with my first child, I would not have reacted so casually. I would have been deeply ashamed of what I thought was my lack of parenting ability. Like so many first-time mothers, I was too caught up in the image I was presenting to others. With smug certainty I decreed that my son would never consume junk food or watch television, play with war toys, or wear anything but clothing made of natural fibers. It was vitally important to me that everyone—my mother, the pediatrician, strangers on the street—could tell just by looking at my child that I was a *good mother*.

So what happened? Why was I so meticulous with the first, so laissez-faire with the second? I know I'm not the only one. I have seen a similar relaxing of standards in other families. It seems that we move from "Nothing is too good for my princess" to "Well, it's not the greatest, but it'll do." From designer overalls and educational toys to garage sale jeans and cartoon videos. From homemade organic baby food to orange soda pop in a bottle at parties.

Is it possible that we love child number two less than child number one? No. Of this I am certain. A more likely reason is the rapid reduction in parental time and energy that accompanies numbers two, three, or more.

When there is only one child (and especially when that one still naps), there is time for such luxuries as making your own baby food and hand-knitting little bunny sweaters. And after that? Well, in my case, I have two preschoolers who believe that sleep is against their religion, and I work two mornings teaching nursery school and one full day at another job each week. Plus writing. Oh, and a bird whose cage is never clean, a husband who would like some adult companionship, and a house that seems to spend nights burping up new and creative messes. No, suffice it to say that the Rolling Stones were wrong—time is definitely not on our side.

I think we are looking at this issue from the wrong perspective. I propose that relaxing our standards is a sign of positive growth. There

> *There comes a point when we eventually learn to stop worrying about being seen as good parents, and choose instead to focus on being the parents that our kids truly need.*

comes a point when we eventually learn to stop worrying about being seen as good parents and choose instead to focus on being the parents that our kids truly need. We cease defining our parenting ability according to other adults and so-called experts, and start measuring it by how our kids are actually doing. Are they reasonably happy? Do we feel comfortable with who we are and how our family is holding together? Then we must be doing something right.

For just as children grow in confidence and competence, so do moms and dads. We cannot expect to be fully capable and assured parents the first few months—or even years—on the job. As with any new role, we must give ourselves time to gain experience, make a few stupid mistakes, and gradually find our comfort zone within the job description. We compromise, practice, and after enough time or enough kids, we come to believe that we are actually good at this. And, more important, we believe it with our hearts and not just our brains.

❧ *Lesson 23* ❧

Four Ground Rules for Life as an At-Home Mother

Darcie Sanders and Martha M. Bullen
Authors of *Staying Home: From Full-Time Professional to Full-Time Parent*

The Center for Research on Women at Wellesley College conducted an enlightening study on women's happiness. They found that the two primary components of satisfaction were mastery and pleasure. The Wellesley researchers defined mastery as what makes a woman feel good about herself as a valuable member of society and as a person in control of her own life. Pleasure was defined as that which makes her find enjoyment in life.

The findings have profound importance for anyone trying to achieve satisfaction.

For our *Parent School* lesson we would like to share the following new ground rules that people contemplating a radical change in lifestyle often need and apply them to the position of being an at-home mother.

Ground Rule Number 1:
Know What You Want Your Job to Be

What roles do you want your job as an at-home mother to encompass? Parent, teacher, cook, chief financial officer, laundress, doctor, educator, homemaker, playmate, homework supervisor, at-home entrepreneur, chauffeur, purchasing agent? As a mother at home, you're likely to take part in all these roles.

However, this doesn't mean that you should be locked into anyone else's expectations or stereotypes of what your job is. Not all women aspire to mastery in the same areas. Today's mother at home has the freedom and self-awareness to make her own choices about how she wants to spend her time.

For example, some mothers assign considerable importance to their role as educator, even to the point of taking responsibility for total home schooling. Some—though certainly not all—women derive personal pleasure from domestic activities. Others focus on community activism, personal growth, or an at-home business. Whatever aspects are most important to you, the point is that *you*—not some outmoded societal stereotype—should decide what you want your job to be. The happiest women we encountered shaped their role into one that fit comfortably with their own personality and aspirations.

> *The happiest women we encountered shaped their role into one that fit comfortably with their own personality and aspirations.*

Ground Rule Number 2:
Acknowledge Your Skills

Many women share the common fear that their skills, talents, or inter-ests will disappear when they leave the office. However, while new par-ents face an overwhelming learning curve regarding child care and their new lifestyle, it's important to realize that most of your skills can be transferred to your new life at home. Heidi Brennan, a founder of the national association Mothers at Home, told us that she sees moth-erhood as "the ultimate management challenge."

The next time someone asks you what you do all day, think about all of the professional skills you use during your typical 12-hour work-day. Strategies that will help you in your new profession include estab-lishing your priorities, knowing when to delegate, working within a budget, financial planning, negotiating, organizing your household, managing your time, and training and supervising your children.

Most of the mothers we surveyed agree that setting goals is one of the most important tools you can use to make your life more manage-able—with one caveat. Many women find that the often recommend-ed daily "to do" lists are actually very frustrating, since sick children or rebellious 2-year-olds may prevent you from accomplishing what you planned. By creating a more realistic weekly or monthly list of goals, you can make some visible progress without undermining yourself.

Ground Rule Number 3:
Validate Yourself

As an at-home mother, you need to find a way to meet your needs for positive feedback and self-respect by finding support. Unfortunately, your old office network of colleagues and friends may not be up to the task. For this reason, it definitely helps to find other women in your situation as quickly as possible. Mothers need encouragement from one another and someone to talk with about their day-to-day frustrations, joys, and challenges.

You can find your own support network by meeting other mothers at the park, joining a play group, or joining a local or national mother's group. Mothers and More (www.mothersandmore.org), based in Elmhurst, Illinois, is a supportive national organization for home-based moms.

Another strategy is to find a mentor. Sometimes even one other mother you can talk to can make all the difference in easing your transition to being at home. An experienced mother who has been at home for a while can be particularly helpful, since she can serve as a sounding board and a role model. A friend you can call at any time and ask, "Why won't this baby stop crying?" or "What do I do when she hits her brother?" is worth her weight in gold.

Ground Rule Number 4:
Consider Yourself a Feminist

Historically, the feminist movement has been accused of not respecting mothers at home. As Anna Quindlen noted in *Ms.* magazine, "There has always been a feeling on the part of moms that the Women's Movement has not taken them seriously, has in fact denigrated what they do, unless they do it in a Third World country or do it while running a Fortune 500 company and the New York marathon."

A significant portion of the women we surveyed said that they feel personally let down by the women's movement, and that the message feminists gave them while they were growing up was that staying home to raise children was a waste of a woman's life and education.

Can you be a full-time mother and a feminist, too? The answer is, "Yes, absolutely."

One mother in our survey commented, "I really feel the feminist movement is about supporting women's choices. For me to take time out and be with my kids does fulfill the ideals of feminism. It's okay to have time for work and at-home motherhood at different times in your life. You don't have to take sides."

If a woman chooses to use her talents in the domestic arena for herself and her family instead of in the office arena for someone else, feminism should affirm that choice.

One of the lessons feminism has taught us is that like any other worker, you are entitled to time off. Finding time for yourself can be difficult when your workplace and your relaxation place are one and the same. This is a problem mothers share with other people who work at home. When you sit down to read a book or strip down for a soak in the tub, or whatever it is you do to relax, you are surrounded by undone tasks and the pitter-patter of small emergencies on eager feet.

Whether your alternate caregiver is your spouse, a relative, a paid babysitter, or a colleague from your babysitting co-op, remember that you are entitled to your leisure time without guilt or interruption.

Considering yourself a feminist does not mean that the only achievements you can make are in the workforce. As Suzanne Chambers, a former advertising manager, put it, "I'm trying to raise my daughter as a feminist, something I wouldn't trust an outsider to do. I hope she will realize that my choice to be a professional mother is part of my feminist philosophy. I chose this job because I felt it was the most important job I could do in my life."

A Letter to Your Child

Bettie B. Youngs, Ph.D.
Author of *Gifts of the Heart, A String of Pearls, Taste Berry Tales*, and *Values From the Heartland.*

The best lesson I could ever pass on to parents is to write your child—each one—a letter explaining yourself.

I gave a letter to my child when she was 16. She so loved it that she carried it for nearly a year in the bottom of her backpack, then it was folded into her purse. Later that year, I decided to include it in a book I wrote.

I've written love letters to my child all of my life; at 19, she started doing them back. Over the years, they've become ways we share how we each grow as a result of being in each other's lives, but also ways we see the struggles of being in our respective roles (parent and child). So, it gives insight to each of us of the other's struggles in that role. This adds to our empathy for each other, which increases our understanding and admiration for each other, as well as gives insight to the work of being a child and the work of being a parent.

It is important for your child to know that you are human. And, being human, you have weaknesses as well as strengths. Children really need to know that you are doing the best you can through every step and that you expect no more from them. Sometimes spoken words are not as heard as the written word. Here is part of the letter I wrote to my daughter, which I published in my book *Values from the Heartland*:

Dear Jennifer,

I have so many shortcomings; I can hardly believe that God entrusted you to my care. To run an organization, yes. To help others sharpen intellectual prowess, yes. But to help an innocent little being, one as precious and magnificent—and complex—as you develop sound emotional health? I am so inadequate.

You came anyway.

You knew how busy I was. There are so many things for me to do and learn in this lifetime. I am compelled to fulfill my willful curiosity about life and its mysteries. I find it such a joyous adventure; the world is so big; my work so interesting; there is so much to do and so little time.

I have other excuses for not taking more time to show you the way. Are you a lesson? My lesson? Did you come to show me the way?

I have been fortunate in my life to have had so many exemplary teachers—all honorable, colorful, unforgettable, wonderful people who believed in me, opened doors for me, encouraged me, mentored me. Each has deeply influenced my life in many ways. But it was you, my daughter, who has been my greatest teacher; you have touched my heart and soul unlike anything I have known. It is from you that I have learned the most intense and extraordinary lessons. Parenting you, Jennifer, being your mother, has offered some of the most profound insights. It has been an impassioned exercise in perfecting my own nature, and often difficult precisely because of that. It has been joyous, yet arduous; and sometimes painful.

The awesome task of parenthood has helped me focus more clearly on the meaning of my own personal journey; this has kept me from sleepwalking through life. Seeking to understand can sometimes be uncomfortable work. Parenting you forces me to take stock of my values and to clean house on them—sometimes refining, sometimes overhauling, sometimes being challenged to become big enough to readily practice a value I endorse but don't always follow. The desire to be a good parent causes me to examine and reconcile duplicities, to take a stance on those things for which I can be counted upon. By virtue of needing to get organized and prioritize that which gives meaning—or causes turmoil—I live more fully than I might otherwise. Loving you as I do causes me to look beyond my own needs and to care deeply about yours. Caring and doing are different, though, and when I am unable to meet your needs, the pain is a searing one. Pain can be a catalyst for growth. Caretaking you, dear daughter, alters my feelings of aloneness. Sometimes this makes me feel burdened with a sense of responsibility; at other times I feel so lucky to be needed.

In the process of helping you climb the ladder of childhood and learn skills to surmount the challenges found each step of the way, I discover that teaching you how to pass the test of life quite often presents me with a learning curve, too. I've learned that I don't always have the answer key—but for certain, I wish I did.

In living with you, Jennifer, in loving you, in being a soulmate and helpmate as you learn and grow, you have taught me:

About Love:

By loving you, I taped into a reservoir of love, and find it bottomless. I didn't know I could love so much. Nor was I aware just how much this emotion would forever bond me to you, causing me to always be concerned about your well-being. I learn that love can be painful. I hurt when you hurt. Likewise, in those times when life rewards you and finds you worthy of its trophies, loving you as I do makes me cry in joy for your joy. I find, at times, that the line between caretaking and codependency is a fine one.

Happiness:

By myself with you, I've experienced the deepest level of happiness. I learn that giving really is more rewarding than receiving.

Empathy:

In seeking to understand you, I have had to put myself in your place and learn the meaning of unconditional caring. Sometimes my heart aches as I watch you struggle with a lesson or learn from a potent consequence. Always I have to hold myself back from intervening, because I want to rush to your side to help you, to prevent you from experiencing hurt, even though I know these lessons are yours from which to learn.

Patience:

Even with my guidance, you experience the world through your own eyes, in your own time, at your own pace. You just can't hurry some things. Time, it appears, is the essence of many a lesson. I have had to learn to be more patient than is my nature.

To Listen:

I am learning to decipher not only the various tones of your voice, but to read your feelings—often disguised in subtle behaviors—and to hear what you are really saying rather than what I want to hear. Many times these are different. Sometimes I am wrong.

To Be Responsible:

Because you are so precious to me, I accept the duties and obligations of being a parent and can be depended upon to fulfill them, even when at times I might prefer to be doing something else. You can count on me.

To Seek God:

The miracle of life and your birth became the catalyst for renewing and deepening my own faith. Daily challenges teach me to continually search out my heart and turn my eyes heavenward. Praying for the redemption of my soul and yours is priority over asking for abundance.

Your Needs:

By listening and observing, I am discovering what you need

from me and learning that sometimes these are different from my expectations. Daily I learn how different we are. And how alike.

The Fragility of Human Life:

Though this feeling began with my pregnancy, as soon as you were born I knew your life was mine to protect, and that I was committed to it at all costs. As I began to understand and value the fragility of human life, I began to take better care of my own health. Protecting your life is a compelling duty. I am often fearful. Such feelings pave the way to care about others whose lives are in jeopardy anywhere in the world—from evil, oppression, hurt, starvation, or war.

To Live Consciously:

Because I am being constantly observed by you, I must be aware of what I say, as well as what my actions convey. Setting a good example is an ever-present challenge. Sometimes this makes me feel caged and I must confront my selfishness; other times I am grateful for caring enough to grow. Confronting my own values up close is sometimes rewarding and at other times a bit unsettling.

Empathy for Other Parents:

I believe parenthood is a universal language connecting mothers and fathers everywhere. Once I sympathized with the parents of sick, crying, dying, injured, or missing children; now I feel with them. Parenthood has made me realize that other parents have the same joys and sorrows as do I. Sharing in this sister/brother/parenthood is very bonding. I feel closer—as though I "know" something about those who are parents.

To Grow, To Evolve:

I know that I am becoming a better, wiser, and more loving person than I might otherwise have been. And, of course, I also learn what I am not but wish I were.

To Set Priorities:

After I accepted that my days were not going to suddenly get longer simply to accommodate my expanded responsibilities, I resigned myself to the fact that my desire for perfection just had to go. I've learned that while some things must be done, other things are a matter of choice—even people. Those who stimulate and motivate, inspire or encourage me are crucial to my wellness; people who drain me and are not supportive, are jaded or negative or insist on seeing the cup half empty, must find friendship elsewhere.

That Parenting Is Forever:

When you were an infant, I looked forward to a time when you would be able to play independently, and when you could, you still looked around to see if I was there. When you were in grade school, your intellect was insatiable, and the need for instilling rules and guidelines to help you operate safely in the outer world was a must. Your abundant activities in junior high school required multiple bandages and a daily carpool; your quest and need to understand your feelings sometimes made me feel like a clinical psychologist (with you as my entire caseload).

Now that you are a young adult, you need to know your place in the world and to understand that the dynamics of relationships on an experiential basis occupy a good portion of your waking hours. Just as I worried when you were little that you might stick a finger in a light socket or be treated badly by another child, I worry now that you might leave a stove burner on (or an iron or hot rollers), or that you or another driver will exercise poor judgment while in a two-ton car. I want to protect you from being emotionally devastated in relationships even though you must learn such lessons firsthand.

Perhaps my concerns will go on for some time. Just yesterday my mother called and lovingly expressed her concerns for my safety on my upcoming trip abroad, though I have made the same journey nearly 20 times over the past 25 years.

To Forgive My Parents:

The constancy of parenting, the work, the responsibility, the ever-present concern of wondering if I am bringing out the best in you—helping you find and develop your abilities, talents, and goodness—is a lingering one. I often struggle with the juggle of being true to my own needs, yet being there for you. This duplicity is insightful and helps me to forgive my parents for the ways they didn't know me, but I expected them to, and for the experiences they didn't provide me, but I wished they had.

Parenthood has taught me that parenting is, by design, an exercise in completing one's own unfinished business of childhood. I've come to realize that children are little creatures who come to us with their own spiritual history, and as such, every child-and-parent relationship is unique. While parents can devise a master plan, each child comes with his or her own needs for caretaking, individual in the purpose to be lived out in an earthly lifetime. Understanding this helps me judge less, and honor more, the parental actions of my parents.

Daughter of mine, teacher of mine. Always you are on my mind. I am the possessor of a heart that loves you so much! When can I quit being a mother, a student? When can I stop caring so much?

Thank you, Jennifer, for choosing me to help you find your way in this world. I am so genuinely sorry for all the ways I have let you down, and for not always praying enough for insight and guidance. Though sometimes I thought I knew what to do or could figure it out, in some ways I didn't have a clue; sometimes it wasn't until afterward that I learned if what I did (or didn't do) was, or wasn't, good for you.

Interestingly, I tried to be the parent to you who, while I was growing up, I wanted my parents to be for me. Ironically, just as my parents weren't always the parents I wanted them to be, you, too, have found that I haven't always done what you wanted or been what you needed. Alas, the same snow that covers the ski slopes makes the roads to them impassable.

Thank you for choosing me anyway, for having the courage to take a chance on me. Though it was I who was your parent, it was you who were my teacher. You are the greatest lesson—and teacher—of all.

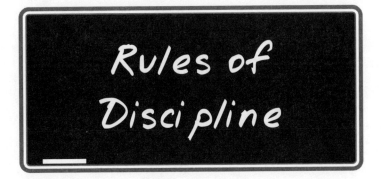

Rules of Discipline

"Don't be afraid to be boss. Children are constantly testing, attempting to see how much they can get away with—how far you will let them go—and they secretly hope you will not let them go too far."

—*Ann Landers*

❧ *Lesson 25* ❧
Age: Toddlers to Teens

Listen

John Gray, Ph.D.

Author of *Children Are from Heaven: Positive Parenting Skills for Raising Cooperative, Confident, and Compassionate Children*

For my greatest parenting lesson for *Parent School*, I'd like to take several ideas and squeeze them into one.

More than anything, what your children need to create cooperation in your family—what works more than anything else—is taking time to *listen* to your children, to hear where they're coming from.

Listen to them, but make sure they always follow your leadership. Listening doesn't mean caving in. It means hearing their perspective and making adjustments based upon that information, but never giving away your power as the parent to direct and lead your children.

Your children will talk to you if you minimize punishment and invite cooperation. Don't expect or demand obedience. Instead, invite cooperation and your children will follow your leadership.

Sometimes, when they're not getting their needs met, and they're

106

stressed and distressed, they won't cooperate. At those times, they may need a little incentive or reward (just as we, as adults, would want an incentive or reward if we were asked to work overtime).

When a child is asked to do something and he resists, assume that the child is only resisting because something else may be going on in his life. For instance, he didn't get enough sleep, he's hungry, he's not getting enough attention, or he's not being heard enough—some need is not being met. So you have to give a little extra.

Learn to reward your children appropriately by saying, "Negotiation is over. If you just put on your jacket, then I'll have more time, and later today I can take you to the park." Or, "If you just brush your teeth now, then I'll have more time, and we can read a story."

> **Children should never feel that they're in control.**

These are things you were already planning to do anyway, but you just point out to your child that if she eats up all the time arguing or resisting, then you won't have time to give her the things that she wants.

After the age of 13, material rewards are fine, because children have gone through a change. They have to learn to deal with money. The danger is that if parents reward their kids just to get them to do things they'll become overly materialistic. They won't do what the parent wants freely, from love. They'll say, "Well, what's in it for me?" and resist.

The truth is, if you're listening to your children and nurturing them, they won't need rewards all the time to be motivated.

Listen to them, create a sense of cooperation, and set strong limits. Children should never feel that they're in control. You should always have the option, and exercise this option, to say, "Negotiation is over. Now I want you to do this." I call that *commanding*. "Why? Because I'm the boss," and that's the only reason you give. Then you don't have to give arguments, you don't have to lecture, and you don't have to get upset. In a calm voice, you simply say, "Because I'm the boss, and this is what I want you to do." And you just repeat, "Right now. I want you to do it."

Now, if while you're listening during negotiation, your child makes a good point that changes your mind, say, "That's a good point. All right, we'll do it." There's no logic or reason to follow the old philosophy of *once you say do it, you stick to it.* That kind of rigidity teaches children to be rigid. What children need are flexible parents who are capable of realizing when they've made a mistake. It's enormously empowering to children. It's a huge gift to their self-esteem to recognize that Mom and Dad value what they have to offer. Mom and Dad make mistakes and self-correct. When a child gets that kind of message, then the child gets another important experience—Mom and Dad

> What children need are flexible parents who are capable of realizing when they've made a mistake. It's enormously empowering to children. It's a huge gift to their self-esteem.

make mistakes, and they're lovable. So, if I make mistakes, I'm also lovable. Rigid parents who can't ever make adjustments or change based upon feedback raise rigid children who can't adjust or change based upon feedback.

It's fine to be flexible in your position *until* you get to the place where you're not flexible, and then you say, "Negotiation is over. Now I want you to do this." At that point, it is damaging to continue conversation and give in. Once you pull in your command voice, you don't deviate; you just keep repeating, and repeating . . . even if you have to take 10 minutes doing it.

You don't argue. You just come back with "I want you to do it."
"Why?"
"I want you to do it."
"But I don't want to do it. You're awful."
"I want you to do it."

They can say anything, but you just persist and they will do it. And then they'll learn that when you say, "Negotiation is over," and you use your calm but firm voice (which you don't often use), they know they'd better do it.

When children is unwilling to cooperate, one of the causes could be that you've given too much power to them. The only logical reason for punishment is to teach somebody they did something wrong—and you use a bigger punishment to teach that person that he did something really, really wrong. That was needed and necessary in an age when people didn't know how to communicate—but not today.

> **When they see you taking command, they're more secure, and they come back with a willingness to cooperate.**

My dad used to say, when he'd occasionally spank us, "This hurts me more than it does you." He was following the old thought that you have to spank kids, somehow punish kids, in order for them to know that what they did was wrong. In those days, they didn't know what child development theories now prove—children can't learn that way. They only learn through imitation. Focusing on negative behavior only creates more negative behavior.

When you have to resort to punishment, it implies that you don't have the power without it. You give away your leadership when you have to threaten a child. I learned this before I had kids, when I was teaching classes for children who were already being punished to the maximum. They were grounded for life. Some were headed for jail.

With these kids, I couldn't say, "Look, if you don't do what I say, this is going to happen." They didn't care about anything I could say.

So, I had to learn this new technique of *commanding* and they all responded. I learned it from tiger trainers. Children want *leadership*. They want power, too, but when they see you taking command, when you know how to take back the power, they're more secure, and they come back with a willingness to cooperate.

I can talk to my kids in a way that they recognize something's wrong and I don't have to shame them for it at all. I forgive them for everything. There's no punishment. And they're very cooperative as a result—they want to follow my leadership.

You can begin making this change—using these lessons—now, regardless of your child's age, if you work on your *communication skills*. Without communication skills, perhaps we will resort to cave-man tactic, which is, "If you hurt me, the only way I can let you know what you did so that you'll change is to hurt you back." And you say, "That's how it feels!" That's caveman tactic. That's what you do when you don't have another way.

I've taught my seminars in prisons. Criminals have been punished more than anyone. Punishment is not a bad thing, but something that promotes a lack of cooperation.

The greater extent to which someone has been punished in life, the more criminal the behavior is. The less punished someone is, the less criminal he is. Unless, of course, the exception to that rule applies—you don't punish a child, but you don't parent a child, either.

You have to parent a child, which means *being in charge*. If you can be in charge without having to punish your children, you'll have the most successful and cooperative children.

When I interview very successful people, I ask about their child-hood. "Did you get punished much?"

"No."

"Did your parents punish you at all?"

They say, "Well, a little bit here and there, but I was a pretty good kid. They didn't need to."

"Why were you a pretty good kid?"

I answer that question: *Because your parents were able to nurture your needs.*

If you nurture children's needs, they cooperate. When children

> *If you can be in charge without having to punish your children, you'll have the most successful and cooperative children.*

don't get their needs nurtured, they stop cooperating.

But we live very stressful lives. You can't always meet your children's needs, and most people aren't even trained in how to meet their children's needs. So, your children are going to resist, and, when they resist, you have to think *What do they need?* Then, give them what they need and they will cooperate. They need your *leadership* and your *discipline*, but they don't need punishment.

My message is still "Spare the rod, spoil the child." But don't take it literally. If you don't have strong leadership, your child will be spoiled. Even people who justify spanking and punishing with that old phrase don't use the phrase the way it was used 2,000 years ago. The phrase came from the Roman Empire, where the law was that parents could legally kill their children if the children didn't obey. It was common practice that when a child was rebellious, the child was beaten to death. *Spare the rod, spoil the child* justified all childhood abuse; it would serve as an example to terrify the other children into obedient, mindless kids. This, in the long run, made them subservient to abusive leadership.

Sometimes things have to go to the maximum before we can see the problem. Go back to pre-Hitler Germany and you can see the result of punishing kids and not giving them permission to resist or challenge authority. They had to be mindlessly obedient to whatever their parents said to them, to whatever an adult said to them. What happened was that they grew up and they had no sense of self, no sense of will. When somebody commanded them, they just followed, as opposed to being able to have their own feelings and their own way of thinking.

In our society, we've gone to the max with child-centered parenting and seen how it spoils kids.

When young children are upset, parents often want to jump in and solve the problem. Just as men do that with women, both mothers and fathers do it with their kids. They either try to talk the children out of their feelings, or tell the children what they can do so that things won't be so upsetting—rescuing the children.

Parents can't bare to see their children cry or be unhappy: "Oh, don't worry about that. I'll go take you to do something and make you happy."

Children need to experience that life doesn't always make you

> This is a very important lesson to give to children. They don't always get what they want and they can still be happy with what they have.

happy and that you need to cry. They need to be upset—that's a part of life. They need to know that they can be upset about circumstances and then let go of those feelings without changing anything in the outer world.

This is a very important lesson to give to children. They don't always get what they want, and they can still be happy with what they have. At the same time, they need to have permission to ask for more and want more; however, it doesn't mean you always give it to them. But they're not wrong for wanting more.

Respect is really the key, and you can't respect your children unless you understand how they're different from you. Otherwise, you'll give them what *you* want instead of what they need.

In my book *Children Are from Heaven*, I point out the four temperaments: active, sensitive, responsive, and receptive.

Let's say I'm a *sensitive* parent. That's my temperament. And my child is *active*. Active kids don't need to look at their feelings. They need a lot of responsibilities. Active children need a lot of acknowledgment and a lot of forgiveness for mistakes. So, when my child has a setback, as a sensitive parent I'll want to focus on how my child feels. I may look at my active kid and worry, *Oh my God, my child has no feelings*, but she gets her compassion and feelings from being acknowledged and appreciated. When she feel successful, she becomes more compassionate. Likewise, sensitive children need to be heard. If I'm an active parent with a sensitive child, I'm just going to say, "Hey, just get up and do it. Let's go off and do something else." That child will just feel worse and worse. If I'm a different temperament, I'll tend to give the child what *I* want and not even suspect what she wants.

So, parents have to be educated on the different temperaments in children in order to give the respect children deserve. I think most parents do their best to respect their children. They just have to discover the way to sense that child's needs and learn the lesson of listening.

The New Protective Parent:

Striking a Healthy Balance

Paula Statman, M.S.W.

Author of *On the Safe Side*, retitled *Raising, Careful,*
Confident Kids in a Crazy World and *Life on a Balance Beam*

W hat does protecting children mean? Does it mean constantly being with them to keep them out of harm's way? If that's what you believe, you've probably learned that it's not possible beyond a certain age. And yet, the wish to keep our children safe is very strong. Some parents react by overprotecting their children, while others grant too much freedom, holding on to the illusion that nothing's going to happen to their children. Both extremes result in children being more vulnerable—just the opposite of what parents are trying to accomplish.

Overprotected children, for example, are not allowed to develop their own instincts and judgment, so they don't develop the skills to recognize unsafe or suspicious situations. They never develop a "sixth sense" about people or their surroundings. Overprotected children doubt their abilities and judgment, and depend too heavily on adults for guidance and information. As a result, they are more susceptible to overtures from both well-intentioned and not-so-well-intentioned people.

Parents overprotect children partly out of their own need to feel in control and, in some cases, out of their need to feel powerful. Often this pattern of overprotecting starts when their children are becoming more independent. To ward off the feeling that they are no longer the center of their children's lives, or to quiet their fears about their children making more independent decisions, parents unwittingly undermine children's self-esteem and increase their feeling of helplessness. Helplessness and low self-esteem will not protect a child in a potentially dangerous situation. In fact, these are the very qualities that contribute to children being victimized.

In too many instances, I know of young people who rebel against too-restrictive rules to prove that their parents' fears are unfounded. None of us wants to make our children feel so incompetent that they would try something foolish to prove us wrong, yet offering more protection than children really need can trigger this kind of risky behavior. If, in order to feel more powerful or important, you disqualify your child's ability to use critical thinking and make good choices, you may be setting the stage for him to become a teenager who acts out.

> *In order to support their journey from dependent children to competent adults, we must give them some room to grow up and away from us.*

As our children move toward adulthood, like it or not, we will have less and less influence on them. That's because as they grow their world expands to include new people with many different views and ideas. They must find out who they are, separate and apart from us. And, in order to support their journey from dependent children to competent adults, we must give them some room to grow up and away from us. By preparing children to be more independent and by allowing them to have the hundreds of chances they will need to practice their independence, we are doing our jobs as parents.

Now let's look at the flip side of overprotection: allowing children too much freedom, assigning them too much responsibility, and exposing them to too much too soon. Unlike parents who overprotect their children, highly permissive parents tend to be unrealistic about their children's ability to learn from trial and error.

I recall the news story of a woman whose baby drowned while her 9-year-old son was babysitting. The boy, who had been left in charge while the mother was at work, was giving the baby a bath. According to the report, the mother was on a waiting list for child care, and had routinely left her young son and baby with relatives while she worked and went to school. It was unclear why she didn't drop off her children at a relative's home that day and instead chose to leave the 9-year-old in charge.

This tragedy and many other less dramatic incidents illustrate that a child's ability to handle responsibility should be evaluated separately from—not in conjunction with—a parent's needs. "Just this once" kind of thinking is risky and often leads to failure. In some cases, it can be disastrous.

When one 4-year-old kept begging his mother to be allowed to walk down to a neighbor's to play, she gave in. Tragically, that was the last time she ever saw him. It's been my experience that a lot of parents, including myself, find it hard to say no when our children are whining, throwing a tantrum, pleading, or being just plain cute. It's important to remember that kids spend a great deal of time and energy on finding ways to get us to say yes. It's their right as children to do so. But it's our right and responsibility to be strong enough to say "No!"

Imagine the potential danger of allowing a small child who can't tell the difference between red pills and cinnamon candies to have access to a medicine cabinet because he "knows not to put things in his mouth."

Remember the national scandal caused by the couple who left their two children, both under the age of 12, at home while they went on vacation? They later lost custody of their children.

Errors in judgment like these are all too common. All of the decisions discussed above were filled with rationalizations or misinformation. The parent with the open medicine cabinet believed her preschooler had the discipline and understanding of a much older child. The mother of the 4-year-old believed her son would be safe since the neighbor lived "just down the block." And the rationalizations of the couple who abandoned their children constituted neglect and child endangerment. While these cases may seem extreme, they make a point about what goes into our decisions to either protect or expose our children to potential danger.

To keep our children safe, we must recognize when to:

1. Protect them from the situation because it is beyond their abilities

2. Prepare them for the situation because it is something they can learn about and will need to handle, or

3. Practice with them because they are not yet competent to handle the situation without supervision

In order to know which tactic to use, you must know something about your child and her abilities. You don't get that kind of information from a book. You get it from being a good observer, from noticing your child's strengths and weaknesses, and from keeping track of her progress over time.

What Gets in the Way

Let's look at some of the views we may carry into parenthood that can get in the way of protecting our children. Sometimes parents feel that the sooner they expose their children to adult experiences the better off they'll be. With this kind of thinking, there's the risk of overexposure—that is, telling children and showing children too much about adult life too soon. Overexposing children to adult matters can be overwhelm-

Overexposing children to adult matters can be overwhelming for them.

ing for them. Without the intellectual or emotional maturity to effectively deal with what they are seeing or hearing, they can become stressed or traumatized.

Parents who grew up in dysfunctional families often have distorted ideas about child-rearing practices. When their beliefs about child rearing are based on having had to grow up too fast, there's the risk of "parentifying" children, meaning that parents—unwittingly, in most cases—turn their children into miniature grown-ups. Without being aware of it, they may actively interfere with their children's need to function as children.

I have seen many adults over the years who, as children, took care of younger siblings because of a parent's illness, death, or incapacity. Their carefree days of childhood were cut short and replaced by years of being responsible for others long before they could adequately care for themselves. At the same time that these parents make a conscious effort to give their children a real childhood, they still grieve over the childhood they never had.

I see adult children of alcoholic parents who expect their children to "overfunction" just as they had to in order for their families to survive. Parents unknowingly burden their children with their troubles, sorrows, and pain. Family crises, drug and alcohol problems, and a pervasive lack of emotional security threaten to overwhelm their children. In some cases, these parents must also break the cycle of physical abuse they grew up with. Because of strong ambivalent feelings about exposing—rather than protecting—their children, adult children of alcoholics must work harder to create an appropriate psychological and emotional environment. The unconscious need to give their children "exactly what they got" can sometimes get in the way.

If these issues are getting in the way of your being the kind of parent you want to be, then I urge you to get help. Entering therapy yourself or with your family is good insurance against your personal history repeating itself.

Eighteen Ways to Avoid Power Struggles

Jane Nelsen, Ed.D.

Author of *Positive Discipline for Preschoolers* and *Positive Discipline: A–Z*

*I*t takes two to create a power struggle. I have never seen a power-drunk child without a power-drunk adult close by.

Too many parents do not think about the long-range results of what they do. They don't consider what their children are thinking, feeling, and deciding about themselves and about what to do in the future. Punishment may work to stop the behavior for the moment, but many children spend time-outs or time being grounded making decisions about themselves that range from "I'm not good enough" to "I'll get even later." Certainly, these are not good long-range results.

Parents often cry, "I've tried everything." However, when they list what they have tried, all they mention are punishments such as lectures, negative time-out, removal of privileges, and, too often, spanking. Punishment does not produce healthy long-range outcomes. Punishment

Power struggles create distance and hostility instead of closeness and trust.

usually increases power struggles.

Power struggles create distance and hostility instead of closeness and trust. Distance and hostility create resentment, resistance, rebellion, or compliance with a lowered sense of self-worth. Closeness and trust create a safe learning environment. You have a positive influence only in an atmosphere of closeness and trust where there is no fear of blame, shame, or pain.

Adults need to remove themselves from the power struggle without winning or giving in. How? The following nonpunitive suggestions in this *Parent School* lesson teach children important life skills including self-discipline, responsibility, cooperation, and problem solving—instead of "approval junkie" compliance or rebellion. They create a win/win environment:

1. *Hold family meetings.* Put problems on the family meeting agenda and let the kids brainstorm for solutions. Kids are more likely to cooperate when they are involved in the process. (Begin every meeting with compliments.)

2. *Get children involved in the creation of routines (morning, chores, bedtime).* During a family meeting, let them list what needs to be done and cut pictures from magazines to represent each item in order. Then, instead of lectures and power struggles, let the routine chart become "the boss." Simply ask, "What is next on your routine chart?"

3. *Ask "what" and "how" questions.* "How will we eat if you don't set the table?" "What is next on our routine chart?" "What was our agreement about what happens to toys that aren't picked up?" "What happened?" "How do you feel about what happened?" "What ideas do you have to solve the problem?" (This does not work at the time of conflict, nor does it work unless you are truly curious about what your child has to say.)

4. *Decide in advance what you will do.* "I will read a story after teeth are brushed." "I will cook only in a clean kitchen." "I will drive only when seat belts are buckled." "I will pull over to the side of the road when the children are fighting."

5. *Follow through.* The key to this one (and all of the following) is *kindness and firmness at the same time.* Pull over to the side of the road when children fight—without saying a word. Take children to the car when they are misbehaving in the grocery store, and sit quietly (no words) until they are ready to try again. Children learn more from kind and firm actions than from words.

6. *Give positive time-outs.* Create a "nurturing" (not punitive) time-out area with your children. Then ask, "Would it help you to go to our time-out area?" If they say, "No," ask, "Would you like me to go with you?" If they still refuse, model the value by saying, "Then I think I'll go." Teaching the value of positive time-out is a wonderful life skill. Follow-up (problem solving or making amends) is more effective when children feel better, not when they feel worse. "What" and "how" questions (number 3) can help children explore the consequences of their choices when done in a friendly manner.

7. *Distraction for young children and lots of supervision.* Children are often punished for doing what they are developmentally programmed to do—explore. Tell children what they can do instead of slapping hands for what they can't do. (Read *Positive Discipline for Preschoolers* to understand developmental appropriateness.)

8. *Use ten words or less. One is best.* Toys. Towels (that may have been left on the bathroom floor). Homework. (Sometimes these words need to be repeated several times.) Avoid, however, the lectures that usually surround the words.

9. *Don't use words.* Use pantomime, charades, or notes. Try a hug to create closeness and trust—then do something else. As parenting

expert Rudolf Dreikurs, M.D. used to say, "Shut your mouth and act." Take a child by the hand and gently take her where she needs to be.

10. *Non-verbal signals:* These should be planned in advance with the child—an empty plate turned over at the dinner table as a reminder of chores that need to be completed before dinner; a sheet over the television as a reminder that homework needs to be done first or that things need to be picked up in the common areas of the house.

11. *Use reflective listening:* Stop talking and listen. Reflect back what you heard to see if you are getting it.

12. *Use active listening:* Try to understand not only what your child is saying but what she *means.* Use your intuition and knowledge. When a child is acting angry, you might have a hunch that hurt feelings are at the core. "Sounds like you might be feeling hurt." If you are right, the child will feel understood and will feel relief.

13. *Offer limited choices:* "Do you want to do your homework before dinner or after dinner?" "Do you want to set the table or clean up after dinner?" "Do you want to hop like a bunny or slither like a snake while picking up your toys?"

14. *Tell the truth about your part in the power struggle:* "I have been too bossy." "I don't blame you for resisting." "I can't make you, but I really need your help."

15. *Make a "wheel of choice" together:* Draw a big circle and divide it into wedges. Brainstorm lots of solutions to problems. Draw illustrations for each solution. During a conflict, invite your child to pick something from the wheel.

16. *Take time for training and then don't do things for children that they can do for themselves:* Two-year-old children can dress themselves. Don't rob them of believing they are capable.

17. *Use your sense of humor:* "Here comes the tickle monster to get little children who don't pick up their toys." This creates closeness and trust, and can be followed by one of the above.

18. *Spend special time:* Schedule regular time with each child. In addition, while tucking children in bed, ask, "What was the saddest thing that happened today?" and "What was the happiest thing that happened today?" After listening to each, share *your* saddest and happiest times of the day.

19. *Bonus—Hugs! Hugs! Hugs!* A hug is often enough to change the behavior—theirs and yours.

Dare to Dine Out

Roslyn Duffy

Coauthor of *The Parent's Report Card* and *Positive Discipline*
for Preschoolers, Positive Discipline: the First Three Years

L ast week I had an experience I thought would be perfect to share as
a *Parent School* lesson. My sister-in-law took our family out to
brunch at an elegant restaurant. Our whole family consists of my husband, our 3-year-old daughter, 10-month-old baby, and me. Disaster
does not begin to describe the ordeal.

Our 3-year-old spent her time trying to hide under the tablecloth
and tickle people's feet—darting off between tables and nearly tripping
a waiter carrying a tray full of drinks.

I won't even mention what the baby did, but it involved me spending most of the meal in the ladies room, which was not equipped for
babies. I figured we wouldn't be eating out for at least the next 20 years.

A preschooler, lots of adult observers, and a lack of child-friendly
options add up to disaster. One of the hardest things for most adults is
figuring out how to discipline a child in public. We want to be regard-
ed by the rest of the world as rational, civilized people and caring par-

ents. Dealing with a wily youngster amidst the hotel's crystal glassware does not bring out the best of these traits in most of us.

There are many "shoulds" reverberating in parents' heads. They sound like this: "You should be a better parent." "You should be able to control the behavior of a 3-year-old." (Ha!) "You should not let your child get away with that kind of behavior." Let's just tell the "should" types to pipe down for a moment. In this *Parent School* lesson, instead of the "shoulds" we can proceed to the three Ps: *prevent, prepare,* and *practice.*

Prevent

The best discipline is often prevention. Take a good look at your dining partners. Does your 3-year-old have a fondness for elegant canapés? Is she content to sit quietly at a table for up to an hour? Is she adept with forks, glassware, and lace-edged napkins?

Probably not.

How well does your 10-month-old control his bodily functions? Does he usually require a bath after mealtime? Is his bowel timed to go off right after eating?

After taking inventory of the "raw material" represented by your proposed eating companions, decide what type of dining-out experience is most suitable. Chances are, the elegant hotel brunch will not top the list.

Prevent disaster by making your expectations fit the ability level of your children.

Prevent disaster by making your expectations fit the ability level of your children. If the brunch is a must, get a sitter for the children. If being together as a family is the true focus, suggest a trip to a more low-key setting that provides child-friendly activities such as coloring materials, high chairs, and changing areas in the bathroom. If getting in and out quickly is the goal, choose a cafeteria-style restaurant where there will be plenty of choices and no waiting.

If your child cannot handle the necessary decorum needed for any restaurant, don't go. Order take-out food and enjoy it around the family table.

Prepare

You have evaluated the needs, abilities, and expectations of the upcoming dining event. You are excelling at prevention by planning things well. Now, let's be sure to include the children in the equation.

Sit down with your little ones in advance and talk over the plans. Of course, the baby can't share in this discussion, but from 2½ on, young children can be involved in preparations for outings. Start by asking your child what sorts of things people do in a restaurant. Answers you can suggest, if your child does not include them, are: sit in chairs, use forks and spoons for eating, and use napkins to wipe hands. (This does not assume that home meals are eaten at a trough; it just gives children an opportunity to visualize the whole picture.)

Sit down with your little ones in advance and talk over the plans.

Ask your child what behavior is not acceptable in a restaurant. Cover topics such as: no running inside, salt and pepper must be kept in their shakers, only quiet voices are used inside, and no climbing over seats.

I am sure you can think of additional things to add to both of these lists—just be sure to give your child every opportunity to name them himself rather than turn this into a lecture of do's and don'ts. The more your child is involved in the conversation, the better he will visualize and act upon these plans.

Practice

Practice includes two parts. The first part is to give children time to practice dining skills in simple and undemanding settings. As their skills develop, up the difficulty level slightly. This may mean starting at fast-food places with an occasional foray into the local family diner and a grand celebration at a place that actually uses a tablecloth, albeit a plastic-coated one. You probably won't reach the hotel brunch level for quite a while.

The second part is to practice what you preach. This is the hard part. You have practiced prevention by scaling your expectations to your child's needs and abilities. You have prepared thoroughly and have involved your child in planning. You are now sitting at Dolly's Delightful Diner when little Anna jumps up and hurtles across the room to begin making faces at the older couple eating two booths away. Now what?

You told your child what you planned to do. Now, don't say it—do it.

Time for practice. Back there in the planning session, one of the things that needs to be included is a clear understanding of what you (the adult) intend to do if certain behaviors occur while in the restaurant. It might sound like this: "If there is a problem and you do not stay at the table with us, then I will take you out to the car and we'll wait there until you are ready to go back in and try again."

Many parents actually say something along these lines, but then ruin it when the situation occurs by saying things like: "Remember what I said about staying in your seat?" Or, "You'd better get back in your seat before I count to three . . . One . . . Two . . . Two-and-a-half . . ." Or, "If you don't get back in your seat, we're going to have to go out to the car . . ."

You told your child what you planned to do. Now, don't say it—do it. Calmly walk over to him and offer to let him hold your hand or have you carry him to the car. You are not *angry* when you do this. You are *calm* and *kind*.

Sit in the car, and, after a few moments, ask if he is ready to try again. (I realize your french fries are congealing on your plate, but this won't happen often once your child learns to trust that you will do what you say you will do.)

If the second try at sitting in the restaurant fizzles, it is time to ask that your meal be boxed for take-out and head out to the car to wait for the rest of the party to finish and join you. This whole thing might sound a bit grim, but children learn quickly.

Bon Appétit!

Prevent, prepare, and practice can change eating out for anyone attempting to include small children. Your child will become a far more delightful dining companion, even if the settings are not all that auspicious. Enjoy!

Age: Toddlers to Young Children

"It's Mine!" — How to Teach Sharing

Mark L. Brenner, MFCC
Author of *When No Gets You Nowhere*

Besides temper tantrums, most parents become acutely embarrassed when their children don't share. This reaction is usually followed by forcibly taking the object away or shaming the child into turning over the toy with expressions like, "It is not nice not to share," or "That is not the way to make friends." Parents who consistently intervene too quickly and grab objects away from their children in an attempt to teach sharing are doing little to encourage the behavior they desire to see.

Children, like adults, must come to their own insights for the right behavior to become permanent. A more helpful approach would be to say, "I see Kathy is not ready to give the ball to Bobby. Maybe later."

Here are some tips to encourage sharing. First, do not talk about the merits of sharing before age 2. Young toddlers think all possessions belong to them. If 20-month-old Bobby is not finished playing with a particular toy, just say, "Looks like Bobby is not finished playing with the ball." This kind of relaxed understanding will translate over time into making your child feel less nervous and afraid that objects might be taken for no reason. Second, we must be careful to limit expressions of ownership around the house: "This is Daddy's camera" or "This is Mommy's brush." It is more important where something belongs than who owns it: "The camera belongs in the bag," "The brush belongs in the drawer."

Let the child know you have confidence in him to make the right decision.

Parents who are also very restrictive in allowing their young child to explore freely in their own home send the message: "These areas are mine and I don't want to share them with you." This fuels the toddler's selfishness and the need to say, "It's mine!" longer. Parents must be prepared to think about such implications if they want to cultivate the values of sharing and generosity. If everything seems to always belong to someone else, a child will act more aggressively to prove his powers to control can match his parents' power.

More importantly, we must acknowledge children's feelings and reflect their behavior without making value judgments about their personality or character. Remember, what children hear they believe. If you cast them in a role ("you're a selfish person"), they will prove you right!

When a child won't share a toy, let him know you see he's not done playing with it. He will be expecting you to act as the heavy and force him to do what he is not ready for. So, surprise him! Casually tell him you see he is not ready to share the toy, or give him a time limit on how long he can play with it before giving it up.

Also, let the child know you have confidence in him to make the right decision: "Bobby, you play with the toy for another 5 minutes. I know at the end of 5 minutes you will make the right decision and let Alan play with it." Immediately, Bobby will feel as though he has an ally. Even if Bobby does not comply, at the end of 5 minutes he will rec-ognize and feel your respect.

In time, this will have a significant effect on his future behavior. If he does not give it up in 5 minutes, you tell him he has a choice: "Bobby, the 5 minutes are up and you can give Alan the toy or just leave it on the floor." If he still does not give it up, you can take the toy from him (show no anger or admonishment), remind him the 5 minutes are up, and he had a choice and chose not to act on it: "Bobby, you made the choice for me to take it. That was your decision." By doing so, the focus remains on the child's own behavior and diminishes the child's negative feelings for the parent as the target or enforcer.

The Best Discipline Is Strict Discipline

John Rosemond

Author of *John Rosemond's Six-Point Plan for Raising Happy, Healthy Children, Raising a Non-Violent Child,* and *Parent Power!*

The most essential element of successful discipline is good communication, not, as most people seem to think, correct selection of consequences for misbehavior. And as any public speakers will attest, the more relaxed you are (to a point), the better communicator you will be. Good disciplinary communication conserves on words. It's straightforward, to the point, and commanding (as opposed to demanding). I call it "alpha-speech," meaning that it is communication befitting a confident leader; in this case, a leader of children.

If, for example, a parent wants a child to pick up his toys, the parent should simply say, "It's time for you to pick up these toys." Then, in keeping with Grandma's wise observation that "a watched pot never boils," the parent should walk away, letting the child know that she is completely confident he will obey her instruction.

Alpha-speech prevents discipline problems. Not completely, mind you, but significantly. As dog trainers will confirm, the discipline of a dog is primarily a matter of how the dog's master gives commands. Again, the key is not punishment but communication. In a perfect world, disciplining dogs and children would be completely a matter of how dog trainers and parents speak to their charges. But, alas, the world is not perfect. Good communication will prevent up to 90 percent of behavior problems, but the remaining 10 percent requires that the dog, or the child, must experience consequences. That's where the need to be strict comes in.

Strict discipline is powerful but not harsh. Strict discipline is consistent but not necessarily predictable or repetitious. For these reasons, strict discipline puts a quick end to a problem—nips it in the proverbial bud. As such, it is in the best interest of both parent and child.

> *Strict discipline is consistent but not necessarily predictable or repetitious.*

Continuing the above example, let's say the child ignores the parent's command to pick up his toys. I'd advise the parent to calmly pick up the toys herself, and then inform the child that because of his neglect, he will go to bed immediately after the evening meal. The child protests, cries, pleads. The parent holds fast. Two weeks later, the child ignores another command. He is informed that he will not be allowed to play in that day's soccer game. He protests, cries, pleads. The parent holds fast. It's another 3 months before this child ignores a parental instruction. By being strict—in a relaxed, authoritative manner—the parent has made a disciplinary molehill out of a potential disciplinary mountain.

It's axiomatic that the fewer discipline problems a parent experiences with a child, the more relaxed the parent will be, and relaxed parents are the best disciplinarians. But one way to ensure that you will be a relaxed parent is to discipline well. In other words, effective discipline must come first. The relaxation is the payoff.

I'm aware that many parents don't really understand what truly strict discipline is all about. Instead of strict, their discipline is exhausting (to engage in, to be the recipient of, to witness), obsessive, and silly, but it isn't strict.

I've had occasion to watch some of these pretenders be "strict" with their children. Here's a composite example of how they corrupt the term:

"Rambo! Give me that!"

(Rambo, age 7, acts oblivious.)

"Rambo! Did you hear me?"

"Yes."

"Well?"

"I'm just playing with it."

"I don't care. Give it to me. It's not a toy."

"But Mom!"

"No! Give it to me."

"Just let me play with it for a while. Please."

"No! Now!" (Mom holds her hand out, expectantly.)

(Rambo jerks the "toy" back, away from Mom's hand.)

"Rambo! Give me that! Now!"

I think you get the picture. This game of Here We Go 'Round and 'Round and 'Round and . . . may go on for two or three minutes before Mom wins, Rambo succeeds at persuading her to let him play with "it" for a while longer, or Dad intervenes (upon which Rambo immediately hands it over). I don't mean to imply, by the way, that the so-called strict parent is always Mom. It might be Dad. It might be both Mom and Dad.

In a time not so long ago, parents of the above sort were known as nags. Other parents—truly strict ones—rolled their eyes at them. In those days, however, most parents were strict. Today, most parents are anything but strict. In addition to nags, today's parents are wimps, bullies, soul mates, playmates, bed mates, servants, absents, and codependents. There are very few true stricts.

To illustrate truly strict, I'll return to the above example, giving it a new outcome:

"Rambo, please hand that over to me. It isn't a toy."

(Rambo acts oblivious.)

(Mom, without any show or feeling of anger, takes Rambo by the hand, leads him to his bedroom, and says, "You're going to be in here for one hour, young man. Furthermore, I'm calling off your spend-the-night with Billy. Maybe some other time."

"Mom!"

"Rambo, you're a very smart fella. Smart enough, in fact, to figure out that when I talk to you, I mean business. I'm certainly not going to insult your intelligence by repeating myself. Now, I'll let you know when your hour is up." (Mom walks away.)

And that's that. I think you get the picture, but just in case: Strict is letting a child know that words are not simply exhalations of hot air. Rather, they mean something. Strict isn't mean (although children sometimes think it is), loud, threatening, or even punitive. In fact, my consistent personal and professional experience is that strict parents, because they convince their children that words mean something, punish less and enjoy their children more.

Learn to Give Praise and Positive Attention

James Windell, M.A.

Author of Discipline: A Sourcebook of 50 Failsafe Techniques for Parents, 8 Weeks
to a Well-Behaved Child, Children Who Say No When You Want Them to Say Yes,
and Six Steps to an Emotionally Intelligent Teenager

The great lessons that guide us in life are often very simple and direct. I believe this is true for being a parent and raising great children, too.

Raising children and teaching them self-discipline is not really that difficult. So, the greatest lesson I can give you is this: Learn to give praise and positive attention.

Of course, you already know this. And you, like every other parent, started out as a clever and conscientious parent offering your baby praise and loads of encouragement.

So why then are there so many discouraged, angry and unhappy children and adolescents?

Something typically goes wrong as babies become toddlers and active young children. And what goes wrong usually has to do with the stress of life and raising a child. For most of us, the stress and frustrations of life and bringing up a child get in the way of our intentions to stay positive and encouraging. Stresses and pressures in our job, in our interpersonal relationships, or in the raising of a challenging child may overwhelm us and derail us from our intention of being positive.

The result is that you gradually shift from being positive and encouraging to experiencing more anger and frustration, which leads to a creeping invasion of negativism and criticism. What comes out of your mouth instead of praise and positive attention? Angry comments, criticism, sarcasm, put-downs, nagging, and a hostile tone tell your child that he's not capable,

When parents relearn how to give praise and positive attention, amazing things happen with children.

worthy, or acceptable. His efforts and his motivation drop, and many times your child begins to strive to live "down" to what you're saying or implying about him.

Criticism and too much negative attention end up sapping your child's energy, robbing her of positive feelings about herself and her efforts. This negative attention is the biggest reason why children get discouraged, fail to try new challenges, or simply give up on themselves and become unwilling to work toward goals.

But the good news I've found over several decades of working with parents with discouraged, unhappy, and poorly motivated children and teen, is that a parent's negativism and criticism need not be a fatal disease for either parent or child.

When parents relearn how to give praise and positive attention, amazing things happen with children. Their attitude changes and their negative behaviors are reduced.

And good things happen to parents, too. They are less hostile. They are not as punitive, and they become able to ignore some misbehaviors they were giving too much negative attention to before.

These initial changes result in a new atmosphere in the family. There are more smiles, and communication between parents and kids takes place.

It's just like magic.

But it's not magic. All it takes is looking for good behaviors you'd like your kid to do more often. When you spot these behaviors, you say something positive about them, such as, "Hey, you hung your jacket in the closet. You're a big help to me. Thanks a lot!" Or, "I'm so proud of you for working so hard on your homework tonight. I'm really impressed!"

There's a simple four-step procedure for working this magic:

1. Find something in your child's behaviors or actions you like.
2. Describe what you like and want to see your child repeat in the future.
3. Add more positive and encouraging words.
4. Do it often and for various things.

To make sure you use praise and positive attention in the most effective ways, there are 10 important points to keep in mind:

1. *Give praise and positive attention during or immediately after a behavior or activity you would like to see your child repeat.* The younger the child, the more effective the praise if it's given immediately. In general, don't delay; give praise when it's deserved.

2. *Give praise only when your child is behaving—not when she's misbehaving.* Wait until a good behavior occurs and then praise it. But if you give praise after a behavior you don't want repeated, you might be reinforcing that behavior.

3. *Make all praise descriptive and specific.* Make sure you describe what it is you like. If you like your child speaking to you in a respectful tone, then say so: "I really like it when you speak to me politely and courteously. Keep it up!"

4. *Praise and honor efforts as well as accomplishments.* Accomplishments are important, but even more important are children's efforts. We want them to try new challenges and have a positive attitude about new experiences.

5. *Be genuine and sincere.* Don't just praise anything, but look for behaviors you really do appreciate and want to see repeated. In that way, you can't help but be sincere and genuine.

6. *Add physical affection to your praise and positive attention when possible and appropriate.* There's nothing like a hug, a kiss, and or a pat on the back to communicate to a child that she is loved and appreciated.

7. *Feel free to praise your child in writing.* Kids love to find a note praising them in their lunch at school, or an encouraging note on their pillow.

8. *Surprise your child—don't always be predictable in what you praise.* Children usually know what you like and don't like. But vary what you praise and the words you use. It helps to make sure your child is listening to you.

9. *Concentrate on giving praise in the area of your child's greatest weaknesses.* You want to increase behaviors that don't happen enough. If your child isn't making his bed every morning and you'd like to encourage this, praise it when it happens. You don't have to give praise to behaviors that are firmly established.

10. *Make sure there is no hint of criticism in your words of praise.* Don't spoil your efforts to praise and give positive attention by adding critical words or a hostile tone.

If you wish to be a great parent who uses effective discipline skills, just pay attention to good behavior every day. Remember the four simple steps for giving praise and positive attention and consistently follow the ten important points and you'll be a great parent—especially in your child's eyes.

~ *Lesson 32* ~
Age: Toddlers to Teens

The Wonderful World of Wits-End Parenting

(How to regain control
when things get really nuts)

Charles Fay, Ph.D.
Author of *Love and Magic for Early Childhood:*
Practical Parenting from Birth to Six Years

Wonderful kids can still bring us to our wit's end! When the kids haven't taken the trash out in days, they're fighting like hungry alley cats over the last mouse in town, their favorite response to anything you ask is a whiney, "But why?," and they're reaching Teachers'-lounge-legend status at their schools, it's easy to start feeling a bit . . . well . . . crazy!

A mother came into my office. Her face bore the same recognizable signs I'd seen painted on many others: bloodshot eyes resting on dark circles, a forehead creased with wrinkles, and prematurely gray hair standing on end. She struggled to find the strength to talk, but once she did, an almost endless flow of frustrations filled the air.

Mom: *Everything has to be a battle with Curtis. Everything I say, he has some sarcastic response to. And then his sister, Amy, gets in with how she thinks we let him get away with murder. Then they start arguing about who was supposed to feed the dog. And then Curtis just runs off and starts slamming the door.*

Me: *So let me see if I've got this right. He argues with you and . . .*

Mom: *And did I tell you about Amy's grades? She has so much potential, but all she wants to do is sit around and talk on the phone to her boyfriend. And the school's called three times this month about her brother, too. I mean, why does he constantly have to question everything his teacher says?*

Me: *You're unhappy about her grades.*

Mom: *Oh. That reminds me of mornings! Always forgetting their homework. They've made me late so many times I can't tell you.*

Me: *So it takes them a long time to get dressed and . . .*

Mom: *Yesterday she came out of the room wearing something . . . well, I just can't believe what kids wear these days . . .*

Those with kids affectionately termed strong-willed may find themselves feeling totally out of control more often than not.

There I sat with my Ph.D. in psychology with absolutely no idea of what to say! Panic started to settle in. Where was I supposed to start? Curtis? Amy? Grades? Arguing? Have you ever felt overwhelmed by the shenanigans your kids pull? Have you ever had brief fantasies about hiring kidnappers? You are not alone! All parents with kids worth keeping find themselves at their wit's end and in need of scream therapy. Those with kids affectionately termed strong-willed may find themselves feeling totally out of control more often than not.

How does a parent regain control when problems seem over-whelming? As I sat with this woman in my office, I stumbled upon a little exercise. I call it "Wishes versus Controls." People have told me that it's literally changed their lives.

Out of sheer desperation and sweat trickling down my forehead, I reached in my desk, grabbed a pencil and paper, and asked mom to help me make two lists. The first list I titled "Things I Wish I Could Control." The second list I titled, "Things I Really Can Control." I start-ed naming different things and asking Mom whether they belonged on the "Wishes" list or the "Controls" list. Our results looked something like this:

Wishes

1. The tone of their voices and what they say
2. Their attitudes
3. Whether they do their chores
4. Whether they want to learn and do their homework
5. The friends they choose
6. The color of their hair and the parts of their bodies they have pierced
7. Anything else that involves their muscles and brains instead of mine

Controls

1. The tone of my voice and my attitude
2. What I listen to and when I listen to it
3. Whether I cook what they want to eat
4. Whether I take them places they want to go
5. Whether I provide allowance
6. Which of their possessions I sell to pay for the chores they refuse to complete
7. When I leave in the morning

As we finished the lists, Mom's eye's lit up and she said, "I've been trying to control everything that I can't and nothing that I can! The *only* thing I can really control is myself . . . what *I* do!" Frankly, I'm glad she figured this out, because I was still lost. It's amazing what wonderful things other parents have taught me!

The only thing we can successfully control is our own behavior . . . not our kids' behavior!

Though I was a bit slow at the time, did Mom hit the nail on the head? You bet! The only thing we can successfully control is our own behavior . . . not our kids' behavior! Sadly, many kids unconsciously pull us into trying to control what we can't. I've known kids who were masters at getting their parents to fight with them over uncontrollable issues, such as their attitudes, nose rings, friends, and so on. A parent friend of mine calls this diversionary warfare. When parents fight battles over issues they can't really control, four very sad things happen:

1. Power struggles take place as the child reasons, "Mom and Dad can't tell me what to do. I'll show them!"
2. Ergs of parental energy drain away.
3. Parents have no energy or sanity left to control what they really can . . . their own behavior.
4. The child begins to worry down deep: "If it's so hard for my parents to set limits with me, I must be pretty bad."

How does all of this translate into day-to-day life with strong-willed kids? The answer? *Never tell your kids what to do.* Why? Because that's uncontrollable! If they decide to fight you, they will always win . . . and lose in the long run. Instead, focus on what you can control. *Tell them what you are going to do instead.* Stick to the "Controls" list!

Love and logic folks speak in what we call "enforceable statements." Simply put, when we use enforceable statements, we tell kids what we are going to do instead of what they should do. How does a parent turn things around when things get really nuts and out of control?

1. Make a list of "Wishes" and "Controls"
2. Say to yourself, "stick to the controllable, stick to the controllable, stick to the controllable."
3. Write an enforceable statement for each issue on the control list.
4. Experiment with one or two of these statements.

Our mom made a list of Controls and Enforceable Statements. A few are included below:

1. What I listen to: "I'll be happy to listen to you when your voice is as calm as mine."
2. Whether I cook what they want to eat: "I'll be happy to cook what you want to eat when I feel treated with respect."
3. Whether I take them places: "I'll take you the places you want to go when homework and chores are done."
4. Whether I provide allowance: "I'll give you your allowance when I feel treated with respect."
5. Which of their possessions I sell: "If you would rather not do these chores, I'll be happy to hire someone to do them, sell one of your things, and pay her with the money."
6. When I wash clothes: "I'll be happy to wash your clothes when I feel treated with respect."

Enforceable statements won't work if they are delivered with sarcasm or anger.

Remember! Love and logic teaches the importance of genuine compassion and empathy. Enforceable statements won't work if they are delivered with sarcasm or anger. Mom picked just two of these statements and experimented with them for a week. What happened?

Son: *Mom! When are you gonna wash my clothes? I don't have any-thing to wear!*

Mom: *(In the sweetest of voices) I'll be happy to wash your clothes when I feel treated with respect.*

Son: *Come on, mom! I need that stuff.*

Mom: *I'll be happy to wash them when I feel respected.*

Son: *This is stupid! Why are you being such a pain?*

Mom: *I'll be happy to listen when your voice is calm like mine.*

Son: *Fine! (ran to his room in a huff)*

The next day:

Son: *Mom! I need some clothes washed. What am I supposed to do?*

Mom: *I'll be happy to wash them when the yard is cleaned up.*

Son: *This is stupid!*

Mom: *I'll listen to you when your voice . . .*

Son: *(In a sarcastic tone) Oh. I know! You'll be happy to listen when my voice is calm like yours. Fine! (runs off in a huff)*

Three days later, Mom noticed her beloved Curtis out in the yard with a rake cleaning away. An hour later, he walked into the kitchen and said something very strange—so strange that it sent shivers up and down her spine. In a soft tone of voice, Curtis asked, "Mom, I finished the yard. Will you please wash my clothes?"

Warning! Focusing on the controllable and using enforceable statements may make your kids really mad in the short term.

The good news? Down deep, kids really need and want their parents to set loving limits.

The ultimate irony of parenthood? Sometimes we really have to make our kids mad in the short-term so that they'll have happier lives in the long run.

Raising Responsible Kids

Darrell J. Burnett, Ph.D.

Author of *Improving Parent-Adolescent Relationships, Raising Responsible Kids: 5 Steps for Parents, Parents, Kids, & Self Esteem: 15 Ways to Help Kids Like Themselves,* and *It's Just a Game! (Youth, Sports, & Self Esteem: A Guide for Parents)*

> "I didn't do it!"
> "Nobody saw me do it!"
> "You can't prove anything!"
> —*Bart Simpson*

Everywhere you turn lately, people are saying the same thing: "There's too much talk about being a *victim* and not enough talk about being *responsible* for your own actions. At what point do we stop making excuses for people's behavior and start to hold them accountable for their actions?"

It's almost stereotypic to expect a small child, like the cartoon character, Bart Simpson, to avoid taking responsibility for his or her actions. And yet, it seems as though over the past decade a large number of adults in our society have been equally irresponsible, crying "victim," spending their energy trying to get out of something, blaming everyone and everything (husband, wife, parents, economics, etc.) but themselves. What's going to stop this trend during our first decade of the twenty-first century? I think the best way to develop responsible adults is to develop responsible children who will develop to become responsible adults.

Responsible = Able to Handle Consequences

The dictionary defines responsible as "accountable, liable, able to accept consequences for one's behavior." If we're going to raise responsible kids, we have to start with consequences—teaching the three A's: be *aware* of consequences, *anticipate* them, and, most importantly, *accept* them.

Consequences:
The Key to Understanding Behaviors

Why are consequences so important? Because they help explain why a behavior happens. Behavior is a function of its consequence. Simply stated, if a child experiences a pleasant consequence after doing something, she is more likely to do it again. If a child experiences an unpleasant consequence, she is less likely to do it again.

If we want to raise responsible kids, our task as parents, in my opinion, is to teach them from their early years, that there is a *connection* between behaviors and consequences. We can do this by establishing a household where there are consistent

> *If a child experiences a pleasant consequence after doing something, she is more likely to do it again.*

pleasant consequences for positive behaviors and unpleasant consequences for negative behaviors. Then, children learn the meaning of the word *earn*, and learns to *think ahead* before acting. The more children are prepared for consequences, the better they can handle them.

Five-Step Game Plan for Parents

To give our kids a chance to become responsible adults, we need a game plan. I suggest using five practical steps within a system at home, teaching kids to associate behaviors with consequences and helping them to make choices based on anticipated consequences. The five steps for parents are:

1. Be consistent.
2. Say what you mean; and mean what you say.
3. Don't rescue.
4. Don't give in.
5. Look for the positives.

Be Consistent

To teach kids to handle consequences that result from their actions, parents need to be consistent in how they apply consequences.

Consistency means following through with promised rewards or negative consequences. For example, if you promise to rent a video game if homework is completed, do it consistently. Likewise, if homework is not completed, there is no rented game consistently. This is how kids learn to connect behaviors with consequences.

The other part of consistency is presenting a united front. Mom and Dad, as a team, should be consistent in presenting and discussing expected behaviors and consequences. Otherwise, kids will try to play Mom against Dad, always siding with the lenient parent. Consistency is extremely important but very difficult to pull off.

Say What You Mean and Mean What You Say

As parents, we need to say what we mean by spelling out our expectations ahead of time. This will help when your child tries to get off the hook on technicalities. For example, a little boy was told that if he didn't shower by 7:30 he couldn't watch TV. He did so, but didn't use soap, so his mom said, "No TV." The boy replied, "Mom, you just said to take a shower. You didn't say I had to use soap!" This is why it's important for us to say what we mean so that our kids know exactly what is expected, exactly what will be the consequence, and then they can make the choice as to whether they're going to perform the expected behavior.

To some kids, "no" often means "let's negotiate."

The other side of the coin is to mean what we say. To some kids, "no" often means "let's negotiate." If children know that their parents mean what they say, they will spend less time trying to get their parents to change their mind, and more time learning to accept the negative consequences for their actions.

Don't Rescue

As parents, it's natural to want to rescue our kids from danger. We don't want them to suffer any pain, but sometimes pain is inevitable and can often be a valuable teacher. If kids make mistakes, they can learn to see these as stepping stones for growth and genuine learning experiences. Some parents develop a pattern of rescuing their kids, letting them off the hook when they are caught in the act. Some become blinded to the truth, repeating those three words, "Not my kid!" unwilling to acknowledge that their kid could actually perform negative behaviors. Those parents run the risk that their kids will find it increasingly difficult to face negative consequences as they become adults. As an example: Mom catches her toddler scribbling on the living room wall with a crayon. As she is yelling at him, Grandma comes and picks him up and says it was "just an accident." The toddler, basking in the joy of being let off the hook, says to himself, "With grandmas, you're innocent even when proven guilty."

Don't Give In

As mentioned above, when a child is faced with a negative consequence, lots of energy goes into trying to get out of the consequence. In a cartoon, a psychologist is asking a small child if he goes along with the current thinking that kids can do as they please, regardless of their parents' wishes. The child replies, "No, sir. I believe in the good old traditional values: Scream your head off until they give in!" If a child learns that a screaming temper tantrum gets him out of eating broccoli, pretty soon the temper tantrum is used to get out of other things that he doesn't want to do.

As parents, once we have spelled out the expected behaviors and the consequences for behaviors, we have to make up our minds not to give in. It's tough. When kids are faced with a negative consequence, they will often play on our sympathy, or try to make us feel guilty. We have to realize that by giving in, we're perpetuating the behavior. When we give in and back off from administering a negative consequence for a negative behavior, our child's negative behavior will continue in the hopes that we will give in again.

Look for the Positives

If our goal is to get our kids to connect behaviors with consequences, there's no better way to develop this connection than through positive consequences for positive behaviors. Why? Because the earlier kids gets used to receiving and working toward positive consequences, the easier it is for them to handle negative consequences.

How, then, do you get kids to concentrate on getting positive attention? This can be done by keeping in mind four simple guidelines about positives:

1. Keep a 4-to-1 ratio of positives to negatives.
2. Praise with lots of animation.
3. Praise with specific actions.
4. Notice progress.

The reason for the 4-to-1 ratio is obvious. The more positives a child hears, in contrast to the negatives, the more likely it is that the child will remember the positives.

> *The more positives a child hears, in contrast to the negatives, the more likely it is that the child will remember the positives.*

The reason for animated praise is simple. Kids like action, emotion, and commotion. If you want to get their attention, be animated. If we don't make a big deal out of the positives, kids get bored and look for action through negative behaviors. A good rule of thumb: Be excited when you praise and calm when you correct.

The reason our praise needs to be specific is that kids can visualize specifics. They can remember and pay attention to specific compliments.

Finally, we have to notice progress in positive behaviors in terms of frequency (more often), duration (lasting longer), and intensity (done with more energy). The more we concentrate on positives, the more likely our kids will continue the pattern of positive behaviors for positive consequences.

Our Role as Parents
The Analogy of the Chinese Bamboo Tree

Raising our kids to become responsible adults is no easy task. It's something we work at from the time they're toddlers until they're out of their teens, realizing that we may not see the results until they're well into their 20s. The analogy of the Chinese bamboo tree is excellent when thinking of our role as parents.

If you purchase a certain species of Chinese bamboo tree, plant it as a sapling, water it, and fertilize it, for 4 years it will show no growth whatsoever. However, if you stay with it, in the fifth year, it is said to grow 75 feet in 6 weeks!

The analogy is clear. For years, as parents, our task is to tend to our children, offering them a consistent environment, with structure, warmth, love, and an opportunity to learn to be accountable, responsible adults. We may not see the results right away, but it will be well worth the effort. Giving kids every opportunity to develop into responsible adults is a gift that will last a lifetime. And, hopefully, it's something they'll pass on to their kids in turn, resulting in generations of responsible kids and responsible adults.

Practical Tools to Discipline Effectively

William P. Garvey, Ph.D.

Author of *Ain't Misbehavin': The Ten Discipline Issues
Every Parent Faces and How to Resolve Them*

There is no more challenging task for you as a parent than knowing how to discipline your children effectively. You need workable methods that not only enable you to train your children successfully but also prevent limit setting from resulting in ongoing battles and from turning into more serious problems between you and your children. This lesson will explain the basic principles that you need to discipline your children effectively.

Basically, there are two parts to discipline. First, you must have good discipline techniques at your disposal, for example, knowing how to make rules and administer consequences. The second concerns an aspect of discipline that is often overlooked but is crucial to a successful outcome. For discipline to go well, you and your child must interact and relate well during the process. Because this is so important and so often overlooked, I will discuss it first.

Discipline occurs in an interaction between you and your child, and how this interaction goes creates either a positive or a negative emotional tone between you. These emotional feelings have a huge impact on the results. For example, if you and your child habitually argue or yell, issues not only become much more difficult to resolve, but the hurt feelings that result adversely affect your child's willingness to cooperate and, at the very least, make it more difficult for you to be patient and understanding, especially when the same problems occur repeatedly. A good way to ensure that you and your children relate well is for you to have an effective parenting style and not allow your child to develop negative or oppositional styles in relating to you around discipline.

> *The best parenting style is one in which you are firm yet calm and gentle in your approach to your children.*

The best parenting style is one in which you are firm yet calm and gentle in your approach to your children. A style refers to the usual way that you interact. If you raise your voice on occasion, it is not something to worry about. You don't have to be perfect or saintly. If you regularly raise your voice, however, you need to make a change, because over time it will have a negative emotional impact on your children, making them feel angry and/or scared.

One of the characteristics of interpersonal styles is that, because they are so automatic, we tend not to pay attention to them. Many problems occur simply because parents are not aware of their style and how it affects their kids. To help you be more aware, here is a brief description of some common parental styles that interfere with discipline:

The Enforcer intimidates with words or actions. Kids become angry or scared or both.

The Threatener promises dire consequences but seldom follows through. Kids learn parents don't mean what they say.

The Pleaser doesn't want kids to suffer or feel pain and therefore doesn't create sufficient and consistent consequences for misbehavior. Kids often run the show in these families.

The Nag cajoles, because, like the pleaser, he or she doesn't want problems, but kids resent the nagging and soon learn to disregard what the parent is saying.

The Critic labels and/or blames the child with the result that the child's self, and therefore her self-worth, is called into question. Separate the deed from the person.

The Professor explains and explains and then gives a few more reasons why the child should behave, but seldom takes action. Kids soon learn that the parent is all wind and no teeth.

One way to learn more about your parenting style is to observe yourself while disciplining and watch its effects on your child. Another way is to ask others to give you feedback from what they observe. When you eliminate styles that don't work or are just plain ineffective, such as the pleaser, you will be able to set a positive emotional context within which you can discipline your child. Children will respond favorably and will be more motivated to cooperate.

Pay attention to your child's style. If your child has a negative style of interacting with you, setting limits can become formidable and stressful. The key to dealing with a child's lack of cooperation is to short-circuit the resistance by addressing the way your child interacts with you. The resistance is contained in the whining, nagging, complaining, demanding, yelling, bossing, arguing, talking back, being belligerent and defiant styles that children develop. Most kids, of course, will occasionally react in one of these ways. It becomes a problem if one or more of these styles is the usual way your child responds to discipline.

Nip negative styles in the bud. While you want to encourage your children to express themselves, how they do so is crucial. A whining style in a 6-year-old is not appropriate. Moreover, if unchecked, these styles often escalate into defiance and tantrums. Address the style specifically. Tell your child: "Use a better tone in your voice." Or, "It's not okay to argue with me."

On the other hand, if your child has developed one or more oppositional styles that interfere with discipline and therefore, he is becoming difficult to manage, correct that style before dealing with the particular problem in compliance or cooperation. Don't override or go around the style, and especially don't ignore it, because ignoring it subtly gives your child permission to talk to you in an unacceptable manner.

Kids who are discipline problems, who are uncooperative, and who misbehave all have resistive and oppositional styles of relating to their parents. The cardinal rule in dealing with these children is to deal with the oppositional style first. Do this without fail. By correcting their styles first, over time they will become less resistive and as a consequence more compliant.

Once you are sure that you and your child are relating well during discipline, you can turn your attention to the discipline techniques themselves. There are two aspects to setting limits and correcting your children. The first is that you have clear expectations for your children, particularly concerning rules and chores; the second is that you employ fair and appropriate consequences.

Here are three guidelines for communicating your expectations to your children. First, be clear. It is best to state things specifically. Rather than tell your child to be home by dinner, tell her to be home at a specific time, for example, 5:45. That way your child cannot say, "Gosh, Mom, I thought dinner was at 7."

Second, explain your rules. Child development experts tell us that explaining is helpful in eliciting cooperation because it involves them in the process. "I want you to come at 5:45 because your Dad gets home then, and he likes to eat right away."

Third, mean what you say. Don't make a rule that you don't really care about or create a chore that you are not going to follow through on. For instance, you tell your child that he must finish his homework before he can go out to play. Then, when a friend comes over, you let him go out without checking to see whether the homework is done. Your child will think that you don't really mean what you say because you haven't followed through.

The next part of discipline involves the use of consequences. How to best employ consequences is often unclear to parents. What do you do when your children misbehave? Obviously, you can talk to them, and it is certainly good to do so, but many discipline problems arise because parents only use words (as noted in the information on parental styles). Words have little impact unless they are linked to specific consequences.

Your child will think that you don't really mean what you say because you haven't followed through.

This is not about being mean or punitive. It is about teaching your children responsibility and preparing them for life.

Don't simply use generic consequences, such as sending kids to their room or taking away TV or allowances. Some kids like to be in their room, and some kids don't care much about TV. Tailor consequences to your child by choosing consequences that are meaningful to her without being unfair or harsh. One way to accomplish this is to watch how your children spend their time. If a child spends a lot of time playing with matchbox cars, removing them would probably be an effective consequence.

Another strategy is to make the consequence fit the situation as closely as possible. If your child has developed a habit of coming home late, then time is important and can be used as a consequence. One strategy is to subtract the amount of late time from the next day's playtime. So, if she is 15 minutes late, then she loses 15 minutes from her playtime the next day. It won't take her long to figure out that being late doesn't work.

Whenever you can, use natural consequences. Suppose your child has developed a careless attitude toward possessions. Subsequently, he leaves his bike outside overnight, and it is stolen. The loss of the bike is a natural consequence. There is no need to harangue or punish him. Discuss his behavior with him, of course, so that he can learn from the situation and become more responsible with his possessions. After a few days without the bike, he will be unhappy enough and will be well on his way to learning his lesson.

Finally, don't forget the positive side of consequences. Acknowledge your children when they behave well. Let them know that you appreciate their cooperation. On occasion you might provide a special little treat of some kind, which they understand is a reward for their cooperation. It could be a trip to their favorite ice-cream shop, or in the case of lateness, additional playtime as a reward for being on time.

Managing and disciplining children can be a trying experience at times, and your buttons will get pushed. The tools discussed in this lesson will help considerably. Above all, in all your endeavors with your children, remember to come from your heart.

Waist-High Fences:

An Approach to Discipline

Marilyn E. Gootman
Author of *The Loving Parents' Guide to Discipline*

A s a parent of three children, I have found that one of the greatest challenges for me has been setting limits and rules, knowing when I am being fair and when I'm either too lax or too strict. Over the past 25 years, as I have worked with parents and teachers, I have found that they too share my concern. That's why I chose this excerpt from my book, *The Loving Parents' Guide to Discipline*, to include as a *Parent School* lesson. The following analogy provides us with a framework for discussing rules and limits:

> The hikers trudged through the woods to reach a magnificent waterfall. The path up was steep and their hunger and exhaustion growing, yet they forged ahead, propelled by the exciting prospect of seeing the waterfall. Their anticipation was building as they neared their destination. Up one hill,

160

then another, over a few rocks and slippery spots, and then they were there. They finally arrived only to find a huge barricade blocking most of the view. On it was posted DANGER, DO NOT PASS BEYOND THIS FENCE.

Fuming, they ranted and raved about the park rangers—how could they be so insensitive? Didn't they realize how important the view was to the hikers? One hiker vowed to get back at them and wrote obscene messages all over the barricade.

Another, blinded by his fury, decided to scale the eight-foot fence—he was going to see the waterfall regardless. He may have seen the waterfall but does not recall anything about the moments before his twenty-foot plunge.

A second group of hikers trudged through the woods to another waterfall. Up one hill, then another, over a few rocks and slippery spots, and then they were there—ah, what a view! Straight before them, in all its raw beauty, was a raging waterfall. A fine mist of refreshingly cool water sprayed their faces. But one hiker became panicky. "What if I slip? What if I get too close and fall down the slope?" He cowered near the path, unable to relax until they descended.

The waterfall, however, fascinated one of his friends. He edged closer and closer to get the best possible view, until . . . A third group of hikers trudged through the woods to yet another waterfall. They all ran up to the waist-high fence, held the rail, and gazed with awe at this majestic scene. A gentle cool mist sprayed their faces as they relaxed, soaking up the beauty that lay before them.

So, too, as they hike through childhood, do our children need waist-high fences to keep them safely on the path to adulthood. They need waist-high limits—limits that will provide them with safety and security as well as the freedom to enjoy life. When rules are unreasonable, children may react with stubbornness, sneakiness, or resentment. When no rules exist, children may react with fear, impulsivity, risk-taking behavior, and rejection.

Many parents assume that when disciplining their children, they have before them two options—to be permissive and build no fences for protection of their children, or to be strict and build huge barricades. Just as with the hikers, neither of these approaches works.

Life and learning are our children's waterfall. Our rules are the fences that keep them on the path to enjoying life and learning, providing our children with safety and security as well as with the freedom to enjoy and benefit from their experiences. As parents, we have the choice whether to build barricades, no fences at all, or waist-high fences.

Expressing rules in terms of the behaviors we expect, rather than in terms of those we do not want to see, sends children a clear message about how to act.

In choosing our rules, they C.A.N. be successful if they are *clear*, *appropriate*, and *necessary*.

Clear

We need to spell out clearly for our children just what it is that we expect of them. "Don't be home late" will not work with children. What is late to us may be early to them. It's always safest to specify the time by which we want them to be home. Whenever possible, our rules should be stated in the affirmative: *do* rather than *don't*. Expressing rules in terms of the behaviors we expect (e.g., "Use the crayons on paper") rather than in terms of those we do not want to see (e.g. , "Don't use crayons on the wall") sends children a clear message about how to act. Often when we tell children "do not," they seem to have selective hearing. They hear the "do" but not the "not," or they may hear only the end of the sentence and not the beginning.

What do you think the first thing a young child who is told "Don't put beans in your nose" will do?

Appropriate

It's helpful to examine our rules as our children grow. The limits we set for our children will change as our needs and our children's needs change. When our children are younger, we may have to restrict them to playing in the yard. The older they get, the farther they can venture from home. A 6-year-old should not use the food processor, but a 16-year-old might.

Ideally, as our children get older, they can assume more responsibility for themselves and need fewer limits. For example, bedtimes get later as children get older. By the time they are in high school, they can set their own bedtimes. Ironically, as our children get older, we often give them harsher rules than when they were younger. Relaxing and changing our rules as our children mature presents a difficult challenge to many parents. It's hard to let go.

Necessary

It is helpful to ask ourselves, "How important is this rule to me? Do I have a really good reason for sticking with it?" Be sure that your limits really matter to you and that they are truly worth upholding. The fewer rules the better. The more you have, the harder it will be for your children to remember them. If you spend too much time trying to enforce low-priority rules, you may be winning a lot of little battles and losing the war. Often, we do not realize the need for a rule until we are faced with a problem.

One day my 7-year-old daughter went straight from school to her friend's house. It never occurred to her that she should tell me first, since she often went to this friend's house to play after she came home and had her snack. After spending many anxious minutes tracking her down, I realized that I had never told her to check with me first.

Yes, it is a challenge, but we C.A.N. set limits for our children, and, in fact, we must. In so doing, we give them safety and security as well as the freedom to enjoy life.

Who's in Charge at Your House?

Managing Kids' Testing and Manipulation

Thomas W. Phelan, Ph.D.

Author of *1-2-3 Magic: Effective Discipline for Children 2–12*,
*All About Attention Deficit Disorder, Surviving Your Adolescents, Self-Esteem
Revolutions in Children, Adults with Attention Deficit Disorder,*
and *Medication for Attention Deficit Disorder*

Parent School is filled with useful ideas regarding the art of managing children. However, while it's one thing to suggest strategies for parents to use with their kids, it's quite another thing to figure out how to manage the children's reactions to what Mom and Dad are trying to do.

One of the most important things parents need to remember is this: Kids will not thank you for your efforts to discipline them effectively and make your house a happier place in which to live. In fact, many children will test you immediately when you attempt something new.

That's the bad news. The good news is that we have discovered the six kinds of testing and manipulation (T&M)! These are the efforts children use to weasel their way out of something unpleasant, avoid discipline, or otherwise sidetrack their parents.

The purpose of children's testing and manipulation, obviously, is to get their way rather than have you impose your will on them.

Testing occurs when a child is frustrated. You are not giving him what he wants; you are counting him; you are making him do homework or go to bed. He doesn't like this and looks for a way out.

Testing, therefore, is purposeful behavior. The purpose of children's testing and manipulation, obviously, is to get their way rather than have you impose your will on them. In fact, T&M can have two purposes, which often occur in sequence.

The first purpose of testing and manipulation is for the child to get what he wants. The second purpose of T&M kicks in if the first fails. If the child cannot get his way, he may try to get something else—revenge.

When using T&M, children have a choice of six possible tactics. All six can serve the first purpose (getting their way); five of the six can serve the second purpose (revenge). When your kids use manipulative tactics for these purposes, it does not mean they are sick, mentally ill, or are destined to become professional criminals someday. It's perfectly natural; it's just kids being kids.

All parents and teachers recognize T&M tactics because they have seen them many times. These adults also will usually know which strategies are used by which children. In addition, parents, teachers, and other caretakers may recognize some of their own favorites, because adults simply use different versions of the same basic T&M methods that kids use.

Here are the six tactics that frustrated children use on adults:

1. *Badgering.* Badgering is the "Please, please, please" or "Why, why, why?" business. The child just keeps after you and after you and after you, trying to wear you down with repetition. "Just give me what I want and I'll shut up!" is the underlying message. "Mom! Mom! Mom! Mom! Mom!" Some kids sound like machine guns and can be amazingly persistent.

   If a parent attempts to verbally respond to everything a child says every time she says it, Mom or Dad is in for a very long and frustrating time. Many parents continue on a wild-goose chase looking for the right words or reasons to make the youngster be quiet.

2. *Intimidation.* Intimidation is an aggressive attack that often involves temper tantrums. The aggravated child may yell at you or otherwise storm around the house. Younger children throw themselves on the floor, bang their heads, and kick around ferociously. Older kids sometimes swear or produce arguments accusing you of being unjust, illogical, or simply a bad parent in general.

3. *Threat.* "I'll never speak to you again!"
   "I'm going to kill myself!"
   "I'm not eating dinner and I won?t do my homework!"
   "I'm going to kill the parakeet!"
   "I'm running away from home!"
   These are all examples of threats. The message is that something bad is going to happen to you unless you cease and desist from your ridiculous parental requests, restrictions, or discipline at once.

4. *Martyrdom.* As opposed to threats, actually not talking, not eating dinner, or sitting in the closet for two hours may be examples of martyrdom.
   "No one around here loves me anymore. Might as well look for another family to live with."
   Crying, pouting, and looking sad or teary can also be effective. The goal, obviously, is to make the parent feel guilty, and martyrdom is surprisingly effective. Many moms and dads have a guilt button the size of the state of Wyoming! All the kids have to do is push the

button and then they run the house.

The first four tactics—badgering, intimidation, threat and martyrdom—share a common, underlying dynamic. The child, without quite knowing what he's doing, is saying to the parent, "Look, you're making me uncomfortable by not giving me what I want. But now I'm also making you uncomfortable with my pestering, temper, ominous statements, and feeling sorry for myself. Now that we're both uncomfortable, I'll make you a deal: You call off your dogs and I'll call off mine."

Sound good? If you do give in and give the children what they want, you are almost guaranteed that the testing and manipulation will stop immediately. The problem, though, is who's in charge at your house then? It certainly isn't you; it's the kids. All they have to do in a difficult situation is get out their big guns and they've got you.

I hope each of us who cares for children will inspire others with a real passion for parenting.

5. *Buttering up.* The fifth tactic takes a different approach. Instead of making you feel uncomfortable, the child tries to make you feel good.

"Gee, Mom, you've got the prettiest eyes of anybody on the block." Or, "I think I'll go clean my room. It's been looking kind of messy for the last three weeks. And after that, maybe I'll take a look at the garage."

As opposed to the other kinds of testing, now the child is going to do something nice. Sometimes children use buttering up in anticipation of a potentially frustrating event. Have you ever heard a parent say, "The only time he's ever good is when he wants something?" That's probably buttering up, or what is also called "sweetness and light." This type of manipulation is sometimes tricky, because it's hard to tell it apart from genuine affection.

6. *Physical tactics.* This is perhaps the worst strategy. The frustrated child either physically attacks you, breaks things, or runs away. Children don't usually start acting this way all of a sudden. Many of them have a long history of this kind of behavior, and the bigger they get, the scarier their physical testing gets.

Once we took a survey of parents and teachers, asking which testing tactics they thought children used the most. Interestingly, both groups mentioned the same three: badgering, intimidation, and—the overwhelming favorite—Martyrdom.

The $64,000 Question

Now comes the big question. Think of your kids, one at a time, and ask yourself, "Does this child have one—or perhaps two—tactics that he or she uses frequently or all the time?" If your answer is yes, that is bad. Why? Because the tactic most likely is working for the child. People repeat things that work for them.

What does "work for them" mean?

Remember the two purposes of testing and manipulation? First of all, the child may be successfully getting her way by using the tactic. How do you know if a child is getting her way by testing? It's obvious—you just give in to her! You turn the TV back on, stop counting, or don't make her do her homework or go to bed.

"Work for them" can also refer to the second purpose of T&M: revenge. How do you know if a child is effectively getting revenge? Think back to the no-talking, no-emotion rules that are critical to good discipline. If this child can get you all upset, or get you talking too much, she knows she's got you. It's obvious to her that you are uncomfortable. You are "paying for your sins."

Let's say, for example, you want homework done, but your child pulls a number two on you (Intimidation). He yells, screams, and bangs things around. Your response, however, is a "counter" temper tantrum. You get more upset than your son did! Final score: Child 5, Parent 2. He got you: The smaller youngster got the "big splash" from the larger, "more powerful" adult.

Or let's say when asked to go to bed your child does a number 4 (martyrdom): "Well, it's obvious that nobody around here loves me anymore. I might as well hitch the next freight to Iowa and find a family more compatible with my basic needs" (touch of number 3, threat). You feel frightened and guilty. You are certain that unloved children grow up to be homeless people or serial killers.

Your response is to sit the youngster down on your lap and for a half hour you tell him how much you love him, how much Dad and the dog love him, and so on. You have just been had by tactic number 4, Martyrdom. Unless you are a grossly neglectful or abusive parent, your kids know that you love them, and by all means tell them that you love them. But never tell them that you love them when they're pulling a number 4 on you.

Doing It Right

Now, let's say you're beginning to understand testing and manipulation and you're toughening up a bit. Your 10-year-old child wants to go to a friend's house at 9 P.M. on a school night. You say no, and the following scene occurs:

"Why not? Come on, just this once!" (Badgering)
"Can't do it."
"You never let me do anything!" (Martyrdom)
"I don't think you're too underprivileged."
"I promise I'll clean my room later." (Buttering up)
"Your room looks okay."
"This stinks. I hate your guts!" (Intimidation)
"Sorry."
The child tries to hit you on the arm. (Physical)
"Watch your step, pal."
"Oh, please, please, oh, come on, it's not so late." (Badgering)
"No way."
"If you don't let me go, I'm gonna split for good." (Threat)

Although this is aggravating, this scene is also encouraging! Why? Because something constructive is happening. The child is switching tactics—fishing around and probing for your weak spot. But he can't find it. You are sticking to your guns, and not only that—you are remaining fairly calm in spite of the aggravation.

There is one thing wrong with this example, however. It has to do with how you handle testing and manipulation. You would not let the child switch tactics that many times. Why? Because if you look at the original six T&M tactics, five of them are obnoxious behaviors (except for number 5, Buttering up). So if the child is going to push you this much, you are going to make the revolutionary switch from talking to counting.

Here's an example. It's 5:45 in the evening and you are making dinner. You are going to eat in 15 minutes. Your 8-year-old daughter enters the kitchen.

"Can I have a Twinkie?"
"No, dear."
"Why not?"
"Because we're eating at six o'clock."
"Yeah, but I want one." (Badgering)
"That's 1."
"You never give me anything!" (Martyrdom)
"That's 2."
"This is so stupid! I'm going to kill myself and then run away from home!" (a 2–3 pattern: intimidation plus threat)
"That's 3. Take 5."

A brief rest period or time-out follows. Remember: With the exception of buttering up, testing and manipulation should be counted.

Counting and Testing

When you start the 1–2–3 (counting obnoxious behavior), the kids will fall into two categories: immediate cooperators and immediate testers. The immediate cooperators you can simply enjoy.

The immediate testers, however, will get worse at first. When you try to take away the power of their favorite T&M method, they will initially respond in one of two ways. They may up the ante with a particular tactic, making it much worse. The volume or length of a tantrum, for example, may double. The kids' other response can be to switch tactics, perhaps trying new ones or returning to some behavior they haven't used for years. Tactic escalating and tactic switching are aggravating, but remember that these changes are almost always a sign that you are doing well at remaining firm and holding your ground.

So, when confronted with testing, keep your mouth shut except to count when necessary. Eventually tactic escalation and tactic switching will diminish, and the result will be that the youngster will begin to accept your discipline without having a cow every time he is frustrated. You then have won the battle. You are the parent, they are the children, and your home is a more peaceful place. You will have what all parents want: kids who listen and children you can enjoy.

You Can't Make Me—
But I Can Be Persuaded!

Cynthia Ulrich Tobias, M.A.
Author of *The Way They Learn*

"You're not the boss of me!"

"I don't have to!"

"You can't make me!"

If you are struggling right now with a strong-willed child (SWC), it may be hard to recognize what a compliment God has paid you by giving you this boy or girl who can literally change the world. You're probably frustrated and exhausted. You may even feel guilty that you look forward to the times when you don't have to be in the same room with your own offspring. You are not alone. Your feelings are familiar to many parents all over the world. Don't despair—there is so much hope!

Almost two years ago, I sat across the table from Dr. James Dobson, well-known psychologist and best-selling author of *The Strong-Willed Child*. I looked at him and said, "Dr. Dobson, I *am* that strong-willed child you defined and wrote about. I *have* one of those children, and I've talked to hundreds of others, of all ages. I want to write a book that will let the rest of the world know how we think, why we do the things we do, and how to get us to do the right thing without so many power struggles and emotional arguments."

Since that day, when he gave his nod of approval, I worked very hard to bring a book into existence that would not only be my experience but would share insights from the hearts and lives of strong-willed individuals of all ages. *You Can't Make Me (But I Can Be Persuaded)* is designed to give a rare behind-the-scenes look at the nature of the strong-willed child. Although we have been led to believe that strong will always denotes defiance, rebellion, and difficulty, that steely determination does *not* have to be a negative trait! When you know how to bring out the best in that fiercely independent gift from God, you'll find incredible strength and possibilities without sacrificing bottom-line accountability.

Let me give you a small sample of the facts and feelings I found to be very consistent among my strong-willed friends and acquaintances. Keep an open mind. I think you'll find these truths very helpful!

1. We don't have trouble with authority— we have trouble with how you communicate your authority.

Even some of my most outrageous SWC cohorts agree that we want our parents to maintain authority. We know we shouldn't get by with bad behavior or be excused from the consequences. Believe it or not, when we push, we *want* to have a point where you push firmly back. It's not the authority we argue with—it's the manner in which you *use* that authority. We don't want you to just be the boss, telling us what to do and not to do. We don't respond well when you simply issue orders to be obeyed. We want to be treated with respect, and yet some parents think it will signal weakness if they speak politely to a child instead of laying down the law. The fact is, you may be amazed at how much easier it is to get us to cooperate when instead of saying: "Get downstairs right now and get in that car!" you say: "The car leaves in two minutes—everybody on board!'"

I personally have a problem with a national television advertisement that tries to sell an expensive carpet-cleaning machine. At the end of the commercial, the announcer quips, "Life is messy—clean it up." It makes me frown. *You* clean it up! You've got the machine; *you* clean it up. They could change my entire attitude toward them with just one word: "Life is messy—*let's* clean it up." Okay—no problem. I'm not that hard to get along with. Just stop being so bossy!

2. We don't need to control you—
we just can't let you take all control away from us.

We know there is nothing we really *have* to do—except die—which we are willing to do. If we are willing to die and you're not, we win. Okay, we're dead, but we win. We know we always have a choice. That means we have ultimate control over what we will and will not do. If you find yourself saying, "You will . . . " or "You're going to . . . " or "This is how it's going to be . . . " we may interpret that as an attempt to take all control away from us, and we can't let you do that. We need to keep at least *some* control over our own lives, so we end up exercising the only option we have left—even if it is unpleasant or harmful. I do always have a choice—I can choose the consequences if I want to. That may be difficult to accept as a parent, but even at 18 months old, I know you can't *make* me swallow those peas or keep that piece of clothing on if I don't want to.

> *You can and should enforce the rules, but the reality is that you cannot force me to comply with them.*

My mom tells me that when I was just 3, she warned me: "If you stand on that table, I'm going to spank you." In my toddler head, I thought about it. How hard could it be? How long could it last? Okay—it's worth it. To my exasperated mother, I must have seemed defiant and difficult just to frustrate her. But I was already figuring out that I always had choices. My parents may have been able to control the circumstances and dictate the consequences, but in the end it was in my control whether to obey or pay the price.

You can and should enforce the rules, but the reality is that you cannot force me to comply with them. God is the only one who can force anyone to do anything against his or her will. He has never done it—and He has said He never will. Be careful about backing yourself into a corner by telling me what I will and will not do—what if I decide to prove you wrong?

3. **The quality of the relationship you have with us determines the effectiveness of your parenting strategies.**

Although establishing and maintaining a good relationship is important to do with each of your children, it is absolutely critical with the strong-willed child. We are not likely to accept what you say solely on the basis of your being older or bigger, or to do something just because you said so. In the beginning, at least, we are not going out of our way to show you disrespect; we are simply trying to figure out why we *should* respect you or do what you say. If you have cultivated a relationship with us that we want to preserve, we will try much harder to cooperate and keep you happy. On the other hand, if you don't seem to like us much anyway, why even bother? If your time spent with us seems to mostly consist of you ordering us around or yelling at us for doing or not doing things, why would we want to hang onto that relationship?

My father was the unquestioned authority in our household while I was growing up. Although I was and still am strong-willed, I never brought shame to my dad or did anything that would hurt or embarrass him. I knew he loved me and valued me, and even as an adult, I wouldn't dream of disappointing him or jeopardizing the strength of our relationship.

But I'm the Parent!

Some parents get a little defensive about seeking the cooperation of their children. After all, isn't it mandated that children simply obey their parents?

I am living proof that when a parent (even a parent who is just as strong-willed as the child) respects and values a child's individual gifts or bents, that child will be more motivated to follow the parent's desires and live according to his or her values. You do not have to surrender your parental authority in order to live in peace and harmony with a strong-willed child. You may, however, need to learn to back off of certain issues and to modulate your voice and adjust the *manner* in which you require your child to obey.

It sounds a little overwhelming at first, but there are two very simple questions you can ask yourself repeatedly that will help you keep things in perspective:

Some parents get a little defensive about seeking the cooperation of their children. After all, isn't it mandated that children simply obey their parents?

What's the Point?
• What do I need to accomplish?
• Is there another way to reach the goal?
• What's the bottom line?

Is It Worth It?
• Is this battle worth fighting?
• Will this improve the relationship?
• Is this a negotiable issue?

Your strong-willed child will keep you forever challenged. You won't have to worry about becoming bored or getting into a rut. There's something to be said for that! Life is too short to constantly battle with those you love. If you can begin to understand the inner workings of a strong-willed child's mind, you may hold the key to his or her heart. It sure beats knocking down the door!

Remember,

You can't make me . . .

So don't
- Back me into a corner and leave me no choice
- Tell me what I will or will not do
- Insist that something can't be done
- Demand I obey without question

But I can be persuaded!

So do
- Value my ability to see the world from a unique perspective
- Find ways to inspire me to change the world
- Ask for my input
- Recognize my uniqueness even if it bothers you

This is excerpted from *You Can't Make Me (But I Can Be Persuaded)*:

The Strong-Willed Child (SWC)...
❑ Almost never accepts words like *impossible* or phrases like "it can't be done"
❑ Can move with lightning speed from being a warm, loving presence to being a cold, immovable force
❑ May argue the point into the ground, sometimes just to see how far into the ground the point will go
❑ When bored, has been known to create a crisis rather than have a day go by without incident

❏ Considers rules to be more like guidelines (as long as I'm abiding by the spirit of the law, why are you being so picky?)
❏ Shows great creativity and resourcefulness—seems to always find a way to accomplish a goal
❏ Can turn what seems to be the smallest issue into a grand crusade or a raging controversy
❏ Doesn't do things just because you're supposed to—it needs to matter personally
❏ Refuses to obey unconditionally—seems to always have a few terms of negotiation before complying
❏ Is not afraid to try the unknown, to conquer the unfamiliar (although each SWC chooses his or her own risk)
❏ Can take what was meant to be the simplest request and interpret it as an offensive ultimatum
❏ May not actually apologize, but almost always makes things right

What's Your SWC Quotient?
How many items apply to you?

0–3   You've got it, but you don't use it much.
4–7   You use it when you need to, but not on a daily basis.
8–10 You've got a healthy dose of it, but you can back off when you want to.
11–12 You don't leave home without it, and it's almost impossible not to use it.

Face Reality

Valerie Wiener, M.A., M.A.

Author of *Gang Free: Friendship Choices for Today's Youth* and *Winning the War Against Youth Gangs: A Guide for Teens, Families, and Communities*

Of all the hard lessons parents can teach their children, one of the hardest is a direct one: Face reality. Children must learn to accept responsibility for their own behaviors . . . for the choices they make.

Parents need to understand the difference between behavior and identity. What the child *does* is not the same as who the child *is*. Therefore, when a child does not meet certain parental expectations, that child's parents must address the specific behavior, not attack the character of the child. The real identity of the child is the *who* of that person, not the *what* performed by the child.

> *Children must learn to accept responsibility for their own behaviors . . . for the choices they make.*

When teaching children about choices, parents should teach them that life is filled with actions and reactions. They should stress that each of us has total control over how we react to what happens to us. This awareness helps children make real choices. Knowing this and taking advantage of this reality gives children genuine power over their own lives. This power translates into their ability to assert themselves in positive, productive ways.

Turning Conflict into Cooperation:

The Power of Loving Guidance

Becky A. Bailey, Ph.D.

Author of *There's Gotta Be a Better Way: Discipline That Works!*
and *Easy to Love, Difficult to Discipline: The 7 Basic Skills For
Turning Conflict Into Cooperation.*

Recently, I was staying in a hotel in Chicago on the 27th floor. A woman riding on the elevator became irate because the elevator was stopping on a number of floors letting people on and off. I thought to myself, "Relax, Honey, this is what elevators do. It's their job." She would look at her watch, accentuate the exhaling of her breath, and mumble comments such as, "This is ridiculous." "We can't be stopping again." "I'm going to be late." This woman seemed convinced that if she complained and huffed and puffed enough, the elevator would get to the lobby more quickly.

How often are we all convinced that if we become irate ("You stupid driver") or show our irritation ("The grocery sign clearly says ten items or less. Can't people read?"), life will somehow go our way? We have come to believe that our upset will change others. It is as if we are saying, "If I get upset enough at my husband/wife/children/co-workers/bad drivers, etc., point out their faults and wrongdoings enough, they will see the error of their ways and this will lead to change." Of course, what ends up happening is they become angry with us, either attacking us with blame, or withdrawing into silence. Days become filled with power struggle after power struggle.

When we approach life with the notion that our upset will change others, we end up teaching our children that if they want life to go their way, they too must get upset, have fits, or become irritated. We then create children who are easy to love but difficult to discipline.

As I thought about what is the most important lesson I have learned that might be helpful to parents, my mind immediately went to the word *acceptance.* When we learn to accept what life has to offer (instead of fighting events we think *should* happen differently), we are able to more effectively respond to the problems we encounter. This is true for life and especially helpful in regard to parenting. Most of us do well when life runs smoothly. We are able to live and model our highest values for children. We are respectful of others, kind to one another, and grateful for what we have.

> *If we rely on discipline based on fear, then our children will use those exact skills on others.*

What happens, though, when life does not go our way? The elevator is too slow and we are late. The children are not dressed and it is 7:45. Your spouse is not coming home until late, *again.* How, then, do we behave?

Discipline is about what we do when life does not go our way. This is when we must dig deep and rely on the power of love to help guide us. Love is about accepting *what is* in order to make changes. Fear is about resisting *what is* in order to create conflict.

Discipline based on love is about (1) accepting what is, and (2) solving the problem together.

Discipline based on fear is about (1) negating what is happening ("Itshouldn't be like this"), and (2) blaming others for our upset. In our blaming of others, we then attempt to get them to feel bad in order to behave better.

If we rely on discipline based on fear and upset when our children are little, then they will use those exact skills on others and us when they are older.

How, then, do we shift from reliance on fear to reliance on love in order to discipline our children? For *Parent School*, here are four guiding principles to help you on your journey from fear to love:

Guiding Principle #1
The only person you can change is yourself

As simple as this sounds, it is difficult to implement in everyday life. How often have we attempted to make a smoker quit smoking, a miserable person become happy, or our 8 month-old eat her peas? The more we attempt to force or coerce others to change, the more out of control we become. Attempting to make our children behave is a guarantee they will be difficult to discipline. Then you, as a parent, will rely on every fear, force, and coercive or manipulative strategy in your arsenal. As you rely on these ineffective strategies, you teach your children to use these same skills in their attempts to get the world to go their way. You will not be able to make your child sleep in his own bed, stop bickering with siblings, or complete his homework. It is impossible. Attempting to do so turns you into a person you dislike. More importantly, it also models for children the exact same skills you are trying to eliminate. I wish I had a nickel for every time I heard myself screaming at children to be quiet.

> *By changing yourself first, you can help change your child's behavior.*

To discipline your children based on love instead of fear, change your thought processes. By changing yourself first, you can help change your child's behavior. For example, instead of attempting to make your children stop fighting, take a deep breath and ask yourself, "How can I help my children be more likely to choose to cooperate with each other?" Changing your original intent from force to choice is the first step to loving guidance. Focus on helping your children be successful, not on making them mind.

Change your original question from "How can I get my children to _____?" to "How can I help my children be more likely to choose to _____?" If you ask yourself, "How can I get my child to do his homework?" you might say, "If you do your homework before dinner, you can watch TV. No homework, no TV." If you ask yourself, "How can I help my child be more likely to choose to do his homework?" you might elicit cooperation by saying, "What would help you finish your homework before dinner?" Or, you might offer some positive choices by saying, "You could work in your room or at the kitchen table. Which would be better for you?"

Guiding Principle #2
Conflict is an opportunity to teach

Most of us do not have a healthy relationship with conflict. Growing up, conflict signaled something bad was happening or was going to happen. Either our parents argued and our hearts sank, or we were in trouble and our defenses mounted. Conflict was seen as a disruption to life, an aggravation that need not be, or disrespect for one's authority. A messy room was seen as a result of a child who refused to listen, instead of one who got distracted by toys and friends.

If you think conflict is bad, when it arises you set out to nail the "bad guy" ("Who started this?"). You seek a culprit so that you can decide who must be made to feel bad for causing your upset. By changing our perception of conflict, we can then change our response to it.

When you and your child have a conflict, think of it as a call for help. Children are either doing one of two things. They are extending love (being nice, polite, and doing what they are told) or they are calling for help (being rude, obnoxious, giving the silent treatment, and other forms of resistance). By seeing misbehavior as a call for help, we put ourselves in a positive mindset. This allows us to teach our children what to do instead of reacting to their errors.

In order to use conflict as a teaching moment, we need to learn the skill of *positive intent*. Positive intent is what we can offer those in our world who do not act as we think they should. Instead of

> When you and your child have a conflict, think of it as a "call for help."

screaming at a reckless driver, we could stay calm and wish him well in hopes he gets where he is going safely. This calmness allows us to access the highest part of our brains. It allows us to be firm, fair, compassionate, and strong at the same time. It also provides a sense of safety for our children as it teaches them how to respond to life when it does not go their way. It allows their brains to function optimally and ultimately enhances their ability to take responsibility for their actions. Positive intent allows you to diffuse an intense moment and turn conflict into cooperation right before your eyes. Offering negative intent creates more conflict.

Attributing positive intent to a child's poor choices allows you the opportunity to teach the child another way of interaction with others. The following examples outline the whole process:

Situation	Negative Intent	Positive Intent
Child hits	Was that nice? Why did you hit her?	You wanted the remote control.
Child pushes	We don't act like that. That is bad.	You wanted her to move.
Child name-calls	Name-calling is ugly. Stop it this minute.	You wanted your brother's attention.

As one child pushes another, you might say, "You wanted your brother to move, so you pushed him. You may not push. Pushing hurts. When you want your brother to move, say, 'Move please.' Say it now for practice so that I can help him listen to you." As your child is willing to practice a new way, show him how effective his new strategy was. You might say, "Your brother was willing to move when you asked nicely instead of hitting him." Encourage your children each step of the way.

Guiding Principle #3
The motivation to behave comes from
being in a relationship with one another

Children who are chronically saying, "You can't make me" or "I don't care" are really saying they don't feel cared for. Slow down and spend time with your children. Let go of the clutter in your mind. All too often our bodies are present, but our minds are somewhere else. Bring your mind to where your body is and be present with your children instead of buying them presents for your shortcomings and absences.

Bring alive your family rituals. Rituals are sacred times you spend with each other for no other reason than to connect. For young children, add the following to your bedtime ritual:

> *Take your child's hand and give it a deep hand massage, while saying, "A wonderful woman who lived in a shoe . . . " Then, as you say the next line, touch each of the fingers on your child's hand. "She had so many children, she knew exactly what to do." Fold the child's fingers into a ball and cover them with your hand securely and say, "She held them." Rock them gently side to side and say, "She rocked them." Tuck the child's hand up under her chin and say, "She tucked them into bed." End the verse by saying, "I love you. I love you is what she said."*

For older children, clear your calendar, clear the "to do" chatter in your head, snuggle up on the couch and read together, talk, or engage in some activity you both enjoy.

Guiding Principle #4
Treat yourself as you would have others treat you

How you treat yourself is how you will treat your children and how you will teach them to treat others, including you. Think of the last time that you made a mistake. Did you immediately say to yourself, "Oh, another opportunity to learn"? Or did you start with berating self-bashing talk like, "I am so stupid. I can't believe what I have done," or blaming and listing the faults of others? If you immediately start by saying, "I can't believe how stupid I am," this will be the same reaction your children will have when they make a mistake or misbehave. If you are going to discipline your children with love and use conflict as an opportunity to teach, you must start with yourself. If guilt, feeling rotten, and beating oneself up were effective tools in promoting behavioral change, we would all be saints by now.

The next time life does not go your way, take a deep breath, relax, and say to yourself, "This moment is as it is." . . . Your job at this point is acceptance.

Loving guidance is an inside-out job. The next time life does not go your way, take a deep breath, relax, and say to yourself, "This moment is as it is." Your children are not dressed, not fed, and you are going to be late. That is what is—whether it should be that way or not is irrelevant. Your job at this point is acceptance.

Work on disciplining yourself with love first, then it will be natural to do the same for your children. Instead of saying, "I forgot the bread. I can't believe how stupid I am," say, "I wanted to take care of so many things that I forgot the bread. All is well. I can go now or I can pick it up tomorrow."

Loving guidance is a process of shifting from fear to love to discipline ourselves and our children. It requires self-control. This comes from understanding the only person you can make change is yourself. It requires teaching your children what to do instead of condemning them for what they didn't do. This can be accomplished by attributing positive intent and using conflict moments as opportunities to teach. Conflict will never be resolved without willingness. This willingness comes from feeling connected to one another. Changing from fear to love is an inside job. As we learn to treat ourselves with respect, we then will naturally teach our children to respect us and others.

Keeping Your Teen from Remaining a Tribe Apart

Patricia Hersch

Author of *A Tribe Apart: A Journey into the Heart of American Adolescence*

The 6 years I spent tracking the lives of eight "regular" kids, seventh through twelfth grades, in my book *A Tribe Apart: A Journey into the Heart of American Adolescence,* chronicled growing up in today's world from the inside out. I wanted to learn from the experience of the adolescents themselves how it felt to *be* them as opposed to my analysis of how they seemed to me. My conclusions, reflected in my title, are that today's teens are a tribe apart not because they have separated themselves from us but because adults have abandoned them.

The most stunning change for adolescents today is their aloneness. Today's kids are more isolated and more unsupervised than previous generations. Not just parents are gone; all the grown-ups are some-where else. Over time, the hours roll into days, the days into years, so by graduation from high school, a teen may have spent years without meaningful, consistent adult contact. As one 16-year-old explains it, "You basically have a life of your own."

This freedom changes everything. Mostly we focus on how it changes access to a bed, a liquor cabinet, or a stash of pot. But the effects go beyond issues of rules and discipline to the connections between generations that used to occur naturally. This contact provid-ed role models. How many of us were never going to be like Mom or Dad, yet greatly admired a friend of theirs or a relative? The fact that other adults were role models for us presupposes their presence in our lives. Generational contact creates idea exchanges, conversation, and guidance, and assures the passing down of traditions. It's a way of learning values and negotiating life.

Teaching about life cannot be just another thing heaped on the schools. I have discovered that the informal lessons of growing up absorbed from the previous generation, or chosen in reaction to the previous generation, are lost. Kids today need to experience loving relationships to learn how to have them themselves; they need to acquire methods of conflict resolution, ways of connecting and of expressing themselves.

How can kids imitate and learn from adults if they rarely talk to them? How can they form the connections to trust adult wisdom if there is inadequate contact? The mere presence of adults nearby has always been a time-honored way for kids to avoid a troublesome situa-tion; "I can't—my folks will be home any minute," is fairly useless when every kid knows no adults will be around for hours. The generational threads that used to weave their way into the fabric of growing up are missing, leaving the life stage threadbare and easily torn. We don't have to look very far to see the results of this weakness making teens vulner-able to responding in unhealthy ways to life's normal pressures, let alone the extraordinary ones they often face. It is so easy to blame kids for their failings, but it is tough to grow up in a vacuum.

Believe it or not, today's adolescents yearn to be known through more adult interaction. They do not need a mom or dad in the kitchen

When I talk to adolescents, their message is clear: Don't give us so much space. Pay attention to us.

baking cookies as much as parents who make it clear that they are available, interested, and involved. Besides, kids will never accept guidance from adults who are unaware of their reality. "Let us finish what we are trying to say," implore kids from all across this country. "When you have to buy groceries or take us somewhere," they counsel, "don't always choose shopping over us." When I talk to adolescents, their message is clear: *Don't give us so much space. Pay attention to us. Reach out even though it sometimes seems we are backing away.*

Adolescence is a journey that requires guides. Only the years from birth through age 2 are comparable in terms of the breadth of social, intellectual, and physical development. Think of the adult time spent studying, planning, buying toys, and interacting with the little ones. Why would we abandon kids at this hugely important developmental stage? We instinctively get on our knees to talk to a toddler, yet how many of us actually look our adolescents in the eye? We smile and applaud each developmental leap of small children, yet we tend to leave adolescents alone. A seventh-grader observed this about adults: "You pay attention to grades but not our needs; you always tell us what we do wrong but never praise us for what we do right."

My many years of speaking to adolescents across the country, as well as raising three sons of my own, has taught me that the best advice for parents is the simplest and most straightforward:

1. *Be available.* Most kids think their parents are available to them during the workday for life-threatening emergencies only. Many dilemmas of adolescence are less dramatic by adult standards, but vitally important to a teen. Kids won't know they can call you unless you make it explicit. Just knowing that you are there for them makes a big difference.

2. *Be involved.* Trust me here. No matter what they say, kids like it when their parents show interest in what they are doing.

> • Attend your child's activities. Sounds self-evident, but I have been amazed at the lack of parent participation at sporting events, concerts, plays, and even back-to-school nights. Volunteer to do concessions at games or to chaperone trips. Start early so that they get used to your being around. If your child has a job, arrange a visit to see what she does. We visited the restaurant where one of our sons worked for dinner over his objections, and he waited on us with a secret grin.

> • Make a date with your child. Let him lead the way. Let the kids choose the family activities. In my home, they range from National Symphony concerts to wrestling matches; fossil-hunting expeditions to hockey games. Go to a rock concert (but offer to sit somewhere else in the audience). Your children can open new worlds to you.

> • Volunteer to drive the carpool. That's "found" time you can spend with your child. It shows you care and often leads to wonderful conversation. If there is a group of kids in the car, they often forget you are there and you will hear things that you never would have known.

> • Visit them in their space. If their bedroom door is closed, knock and ask to pay a visit. There is something positive about going to them because you want their company.

3. *Be the adult you are.* Neither be intimidated nor gullible. You can set boundaries and they will be secretly appreciated. Enforce curfews, which means staying awake until the kids come home. If there is a party, call the house and see if the parents will be there. Don't buy the time-honored cover of a late-night decision to sleep over at a friend's house; it is most likely an excuse to party all night or who knows what. Sleepovers need to be arranged before 10 P.M. This is

not a perfect system, but when carried through consistently, it gets across that life is not a free-for-all.

4. *Get to know each other.* Communication is a two-way street. Share information about your day, your youth, and your feelings. It will broaden kids' perspectives and connect them more closely with the adults in their lives. This is not to suggest parents bring their children in as their confidants, but rather that they share their humanity.

5. *Network with other parents.* Since adolescents are always on the go, the best safeguard of healthy fun for your child is knowing and communicating with the parents of their friends. You might find that some have wildly different values than you do, but at least you will know. I ran into families that served alcohol to minors, smoked pot with the kids, and allowed sex in their homes. But these parents are still the exception.

6. *Create wholesome options.* Ultimately, adolescents want mostly to be with each other. If adults in the community are persistent in setting boundaries and diligent in orchestrating healthy, fun opportunities for kids to socialize, eventually new options can become popular. But involve kids in planning and be patient; it will take a while for something different to catch on.

7. *Hug them.* If you've always had a warm connection to your child, don't change because he suddenly seems so big and grown up. Don't embarrass children by giving them a huge smacker in front of their buddies, but a warm hug or an affectionate touch is a reminder of how some things remain the same even when everything else is changing.

My experience with my own three children and with all the other kids I got to know working on my book convinced me without a doubt that adolescents need us and want us. Furthermore, knowing them enriches our lives—not that they won't drive you crazy at times, or be exasperating and totally annoying. That's how it is with human connections. But one of the great untold stories of adolescence is how much we miss by not knowing them.

Adolescents cannot grow up on their own. They need their rightful place among the generations to be drawn into something beyond them that has meaning and makes them feel connected to a larger world. Otherwise, they will remain a tribe apart.

⤳ *Lesson 41* ⤵
Age: All

Better to Prepare or to Punish?

Paula Statman, M.S.W.
Author of *The Good Son, The Wonder of Boys* and *A Fine Young Man*

Recently my 14-year-old daughter and her friend were harassed by a group of boys on the street. The girls tried to avoid them by ducking in and out of stores, but to no avail. The boys followed them wherever they went. Finally, my daughter called me to come get them.

As we drove home, I asked if it any point they had turned to the boys and said, "Leave us alone!" They told me they had not. When I asked why, they said they hadn't thought of telling the boys to stop following them.

This incident reminds me of how important it is to continually prepare our children with "What would you do if ...?" conversations before granting more independence and new privileges. Asking "What if ...?" questions will reveal areas of confusion or gaps in our children's judgment and help us gauge how much freedom to grant at that particular point in time. If we miss that opportunity and something distressing happens, we must focus afterward on how to better prepare our children instead of reacting with fear or anger or imposing a punishment.

In this case, the solution my husband and I chose was to enroll our daughter in a course that teaches teenage girls how to set verbal and physical boundaries (a course that I had previewed and a friend's daughter had liked). In addition, we will resume our regular "What if ..." conversations, so that regular checkpoints are built into our decision making.

Helping our children make a safe passage to adulthood is a continual process that takes vigilance and courage. Whether we're parents or professionals, we all make mistakes. I try to accept mine with humor, humility, and forgiveness because it helps me do better the next time. I hope you will do the same, treating yourself and your children with compassion and fairness as you learn and grow together.

Excerpts from
Rebel Without a Car

Fred Mednick, Ed.D.
Author of *Rebel Without a Car: Surviving Your Child's Teen Years*

"Could you get your sister to pass the
salt?"
—*A 46-year-old father of a
teenager and a 9-year-old*

Here are a few lessons for effectively parenting your teenager:

1. *Be still.* Kids freak out at the most unpredictable moments, not necessarily connected to anything real. They feel a sense of impotent
   rage from time to time. The fact is they really are powerless in our
   society. Because they can't vote or place a newspaper ad or make any
   real and significant decisions in their lives, they often feel claustro-
   phobic and trapped. My advice: Keep still and listen to your child.

Your anxiety is not going to make your children's anxiety any better. Much of the time, they just want to vent. They don't want you to blow the hot air back in their face. They just need a listening post. Don't fix anything—yet.

Think back to this commonplace scene: Your child is 2½ years old and you are sitting on a bench in the park watching him play. He is climbing all over the jungle gym and digging holes in the sand and running around the perimeter of the play area. Once in a while, he calls your name to watch him or he comes up to you and pats you on the knee and then goes off again. Johnny just wants to know that you acknowledge him; he wants to know you're there. You're that steady presence, there on the bench; that's all he needs, and if he bumps his knee, he needs more emotional than medical attention. In the same way, that's what your teenager needs, too. Some parts of this syndrome simply heal themselves. Don't pick at the scabs.

Allow your kids to feel pain, suffer the consequences, and deal with setbacks.

Certainly, an adolescent crisis is more likely consequential than a skinned knee at the park. Teens are able to articulate their fears and disappointments or simply express their frustration, and fury, vulnerability. Sometimes kids feel that they have no skin; everything that touches them hurts. You may not be able to stand your child's pain, but if you end up overinvested in what you hear, going nuts as they go nuts, you do no one any benefit. I observed a sophomore wailing into the pay phone that the teacher just failed her on a test. "Mom, she, like, failed the whole class. She's out of control. She's the teacher from hell." Trust me. She did not fail the class. It was just a hard test.

2. *Allow your kids to feel pain, suffer the consequences, and deal with setbacks.* This is a notion foreign to most modern parents. In our desire

to protect our children from the harsh realities of life, we shield them from an essential coping mechanism, the ability to come to terms with failure. Bailing our kids out may rob them of the opportunity to recoup their losses. These parents may spend an inordinate amount of time worrying about all the bad influences in the world. They see life as one big minefield and will do anything to prevent their child from feeling sad. Some may even view the school—as an institution—as some kind of invidious adversary; they'll be damned if their child will experience any form of suffering or injustice. Some parents will march into school to fix the situation; the teacher gets six "While You Were Out" messages, the principal gets a few calls, and then the situation escalates. In essence, parents end up colluding with their kids to transfer all that pain someplace else, in this case onto the school or an individual teacher.

However, there is a price, because these same children, though appreciative that their parents are fighting their battles for them, develop little self-reliance. They are incapable of handling suffering. Some educators have commented that—rich or poor—this kind of response is a form of "affluenza" and may cause complications for the adolescent syndrome. There is a qualitative difference between working in a child's service and working in a child's best interest. The former may help for a while, but only builds dependence. The latter may hurt for a while, but ends up building independence. It may be in a child's best service to solve the problem now, to demand that the teacher explain the grade, for example. Yet such an approach may not be in that child's best interest, namely the necessity that a child learn the life skills of coping—talking with the teacher alone, for instance, or working on the means by which he or she can improve the grade the next time.

Just as the Chinese word for crisis is opportunity, so must we view the failed test, the abandoned relationship, and the hurtful glare as an opportunity for growth and for conversation. Kids are bound to suffer—it's the effect of the syndrome—but we can help them with tools to solve their own problems.

3. *If you're a couple, stand united.* The barracuda syndrome comes into

play here. Adolescents are sophisticated enough to run to Mom when they don't get what they want from Dad; they'll also take it a step further and turn inconsistencies into a chasm. Parents end up feeling that the entire problem is theirs. Be careful. When and wherever possible, go for the united front. Let's say that you disagree with your spouse on whether to allow your son to drive 40 miles in the rain to a club named the Grunge Room. When clarity and resolution cannot immediately happen (and it inevitably won't), stay in the room during such conflicts and try, despite your cynicism, to work things out with your spouse so that you come to some form of agreement in front of the kids. Kids need to see adults confront problems and work to resolve them. Many children experience the tension and the anger, but they're often shut out during the time when parents reconcile behind closed doors.

Kids need to see adults confront problems and work to resolve them.

In earlier generations, parents protected their kids from everything—politics, scandal, and inner turmoil. Nevertheless, the kids detected all the permutations and combinations. They felt the arctic draft in the room. Although there is something to be said for staying together for the sake of the kids, all cannot be presented as peaches and cream. It's too suspicious. In recent generations, however, the opposite is equally destructive. Kids have been privy to everything, even the sexual and emotional parts of parents' relationships. I cringe when I hear kids talk about their family's intimate secrets. The problems you may experience in the natural course of your own relationship may not be resolvable in ways that you want your child to emulate. Kids cannot possibly resolve these conflicts; they cannot act as therapist or intermediary, for they can easily end up feeling a significant measure of panic, helplessness, and anger. If there are deep-seated problems—sexual, emotional, relational—parents need to get some assistance.

The adolescent is a master at nothing, yet he or she wants to be the master at everything. No wonder it feels like World War III at home. (And, by the way, it can at school, too.) You say up; they say down; you say black; they say white; you say jump, and they ask why.

A parent told me about her child. "I don't know where she's at from day to day. It's as if I'm living in a nightmarish marathon of Mutual of Omaha's Wild Kingdom."

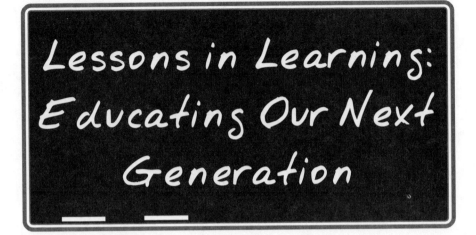

Lessons in Learning: Educating Our Next Generation

"Our society simply can't afford to fix any more broken adults. It's so much easier and cost-effective to build a healthy child."

—Steven W. Vannoy, from The 10 Greatest Gifts I Give My Children: Parenting from the Heart

"My interest does not lie in raising parrots that just rehash 'their master's voice,' but rather in passing the torch to independent and inventive, innovative and creative spirits."

—Viktor E. Frankl, from Man's Search for Meaning

Learning Really Is Fun!

Naomi E. Singer and Matthew J. Miller
Authors of *A+ Activities for First Grade* and *A+ Activities for Second Grade*

Innumerable times in our experience as teachers, we have been asked by parents, "What can we do at home to support our child's learning?" Our books are our best effort to answer this question.

We teach in an inclusive school system that celebrates diversity. The parents, teachers, and administrators of our school communities have developed core values that emphasize a love of learning, respect for self and others, academic excellence, and commitment to school and community. Each of these values has been a driving force in the work we do each day with our students. Just as we embrace these values in our classrooms, so do parents embrace them at home.

We truly believe that parents working in partnership with teachers make a huge and positive difference in the education of young children. Our goal is to extend classroom learning to the world around you. As you use these activities, build on your children's strengths to enhance their self-confidence and positive self-image. Have fun and enjoy learning! By taking an active and participatory part in your children's learning, you not only support their developing skills but also demonstrate the value that you place on learning.

Ask questions, explore, and observe together. Celebrate your children's learning by praising, encouraging, and valuing all efforts. In doing so, you create a safe environment for learning and share the joyful experience of discovery.

Below you will find some samples taken from our book, *A+ Activities for First Grade*.

Drizzle and Griddle

Recognize numbers and eat them, too! Have a pancake breakfast that is sure to be a hit with every member of the family. Prepare your usual pancake recipe. Pour the batter from a mixing bowl to a spouted measuring cup or pitcher. Then supervise the fun as you drizzle the batter onto the griddle in the shape of numbers. Griddle the number of people in the family. Griddle a lucky number. Note the way numbers reverse when you flip the pancakes. Then flip them again to demonstrate correct directionality on the plate. Serve with butter, maple syrup, and a whole lot of fun!

Verb Charades

Verbs are action words that can tell you how people, animals, or things move. Play Verb Charades to build your children's awareness of the action words. To get ideas going, brainstorm a list of physical action words. Tell your children that you will act out an action word without using words. Then hop, skip, or jump to see if your children can guess the verb. Each player gets a point for a correct guess. Alternate turns and set a timer to one minute for fast-paced fun!

Family Read-In

Cuddle up in front of a cozy fire or stretch out on a blanket under a shady tree! Whatever the season, wherever you are, a Family Read-In is a wonderful way to show your child that reading is special for everyone. Choose a time on a snowy weekend afternoon or a summer blue-sky day. Designate the time as a Family Read-In. All family members gather, each with a chosen book, magazine, or newspaper. Have hot chocolate and cookies or lemonade and munchies as everyone gets comfy and reads.

Imagine That . . .

We learn about a character in a book from what the character says and does and from what others say about the character. Illustrations and descriptions also show how the character looks and acts. Sometimes a character is described and we are left to imagine how that character appears. For example, in Kevin Henkes's *Owen*, we read about the Blanket Fairy but never see the Blanket Fairy. The reader is left to wonder how the Blanket Fairy looks and acts.

Imagine That . . . with any book you read. Imagine that there really are blanket fairies, wild things, whatzits, two-headed giants, and trolls. Talk about the characters in the books you read, and how they look and act! Then draw them!

Drinking-Straw Skeletons

Make drinking-straw skeletons to help your first grader become familiar with the location of bones in the human skeleton. Cut drinking straws to use as bones. For the upper body, cut twenty-four 1-inch sections for the vertebrae of the spine, twenty-four 3-inch sections for twelve pairs of ribs, two 3-inch sections for collarbones, two six-inch sections for upper arm bones, and four six-inch sections for forearm bones. For the lower body, use six 7-inch straws for calf bones, shin bones, and thigh bones. Cut two 4-inch sections for hip bones and twenty 3-inch sections for fingers and toes. Cut a skull from a sheet of paper, and draw a nose, eye sockets, and a mouth with visible teeth.

Construct your skeleton using a picture or model as a guide. Hold a 12-by-18-inch sheet of construction paper vertically. Glue the paper skull 1 inch from the top. Build the skeleton by gluing straw sections in appropriate locations. Upon completion, identify and label the bones.

Family Crest

You don't have to have lived in the Middle Ages to have had a coat of arms! Create a family crest to show what makes your family unique.

Explain that a family crest is an emblem designed to show what makes you special. Talk about characteristics unique to you. Record any and all ideas. On a large sheet of construction paper, draw a shield into quarters. Based on the recorded ideas, designate and label each quarter with a theme. Select from themes such as family members, traditions, celebrations, hobbies, occupations, and goals.

Invite family members to contribute to each section of the family crest with drawings, paintings, or words. When your family crest is complete, cut it out, mount it on cardboard or poster board, and display it with pride for all to see! As an option, you may want to visit the library to examine books on heraldry and view samples of a coat of arms or family crest.

Celebrate The People

Celebrate our diversity by making a collage of people of the world. Talk about how exciting it is to know, meet, and live and work with people of different cultures and backgrounds. Then spend time looking through recyclable magazines for faces that represent the people of the world community. Cut out and collect pictures of children and adults—

black, white, yellow, and red; people at work, people at play. When you have a wide and representative sample, make a Celebrate the People collage on a large piece of poster board or construction paper. Arrange the pictures to cover the entire paper, leaving space across the top for the heading. Glue the pictures to the paper and Celebrate the People.

Cloudscapes

Look up and let your imagination soar with the cloudscapes. Take a thermos of lemonade and a bag of cookies outside on a day when the sun is out, the sky is blue, and puffy clouds are flying. While looking up, ask your child what he or she knows or believes to be true about clouds. What is a cloud? Come to an understanding that a cloud is made from tiny drops of water or ice that float in the air.

Lie back on the grass and watch. What do you see in the clouds—a lion leaping, a dragon dancing, a giant jumping, a snake slithering, or a crocodile crawling? Find animals, objects, or shapes and point them out to each other. To extend your child's knowledge and appreciation of clouds, visit your local library or bookstore on a rainy day and read books such as *Little Cloud* by Eric Carle, *Cloudland* by John Burningham, *It looked Like Spilt Milk* by Charles Shaw, or *Now I Know Clouds* by Roy Wandelmaier.

Dissect a Seed

Every seed has potential! Soak a lima bean, kidney bean, or any large bean in water overnight. The next day, remove the bean from the water. As your child watches, gently cut it to examine the inside. If available, provide your child with a magnifying glass to heighten observation. Ask your child to draw a cross-section diagram of the open bean. Then, working together, use your fingertips or the tip of a toothpick to remove the baby plant from the bean. Place the tiny plant on your work surface and examine it. Again, ask your child to draw a diagram, this time of the baby plant. Talk about all observations. Predict what will happen to a bean when it is planted in soil.

Coin Sort

Do you ever wonder how much money you have in that big jar of change sitting on a shelf or in a corner? Let your first-grader help you find out.

Use four paper cups as sorting bins. Tape a penny to the outside of the first cup, a nickel to the outside of the second cup, a dime to the third, and a quarter to the fourth. Supply your child with a handful of loose change including pennies, nickels, dimes, and quarters. Ask your child to sort the coins by putting pennies in the penny cup, nickels in the nickel cup, dimes in the dime cup, and quarters in the quarter cup.

Variation: For an extra challenge, label the cups with the coin value. Ask your child to sort the coins, find the value of the coins in each cup, and find the total value of all the coins.

Bedtime Rhyme:

Enjoy a few minutes together before lights out and build your child's sense of rhyme at the same time! Be ready at bedtime with a rhyming book that you've chosen from either your local library or your child's personal library. Some favorites are *Sheep in a Jeep* by Nancy Shaw, *Is Your Mama a Llama?* by Deborah Guarino, *The Lady with the Alligator Purse* or *Skip to My Lou* by Nadine Westcott, or *Noisy Nora* by Rosemary Wells. Read the book once, enjoying the rhythm, rhyme, story, and illustrations. Read the book a second time, omitting rhyming words at the end of the lines so that your child can fill in the missing words. From *Noisy Nora*, for example you read,

> Jack had dinner early,
> Father played with Kate,
> Jack needed burping,
> So Nora had to _____.

Your child chimes in, "Wait." Praise whatever suggestion your child makes. Sleep tight!

What Is Smart?

Understanding and Nurturing the Multiple Intelligences in Your Child

Laurel Schmidt

Author of *Seven Times Smarter: 50 Activities, Games and Projects to Develop the Seven Intelligences in Your Child*

Have you ever caught a glimpse of your kid as you peeked in his bedroom and wondered *What's he doing? He looks so weird!* Air dancing to a commercial jingle and talking to three people who aren't in the room. Did you think . . .

    a. What the hell?
    b. We need to see a shrink.
    c. This kid is so smart!
    d. All of the above.

The best answer is c. That's right. Many of the puzzling things that kids do are actually signs of intelligent life.

Smart kids:

- Repeat lyrics, poems, jokes, and stories word-for-word
- Tap fingers, sticks, or toys rhythmically on a surface
- Draw on the bathroom mirror in the steam
- Take toys apart or put together collections
- Create and entertain imaginary friends
- Build with blocks or other objects and knock them down
- Ask why and how things work
- Want to hear the same story over and over

You probably have dozens of these "smart" pictures of your kids, but you might be thinking, *Who knew? I just thought he was being a pain!* Researchers are discovering that many of those curious behaviors are clues to the special ways that kids are smart. If you learn to recognize the clues, you can help them get even smarter.

Researchers are discovering that many of those curious behaviors are clues to the special ways that kids are smart.

What Are the Seven Intelligences?

Most people still think of school and smart in the same context. But history books are full of famous people who never made the honor roll. Isaac Newton, Leo Tolstoy, and Winston Churchill all failed at some point in school. Thomas Edison was dismissed by his teachers as too addled to learn anything. And Albert Einstein didn't read until he was 7—you'd have found him in the low group for sure. All of these people went on to make major contributions in science, politics, and literature despite their poor performances in class.

So it shouldn't surprise us that there might be a whole bunch of intelligences that people use to succeed. That's exactly what Howard Gardner proposed in his theory of multiple intelligences. According to Gardner, intelligence isn't a single IQ number but a mosaic of abilities located in many different parts of the brain—at least seven distinct intelligences or ways of knowing: verbal/linguistic, visual/spatial, musical, kinesthetic, logical/mathematical, interpersonal, and intrapersonal. Simply put, we're word smart, picture smart, music smart, body smart, logic smart, people smart, and self smart. Gardner recently suggested an eighth intelligence—naturalist. The best news is that these intelligences aren't fixed at birth. They're like muscles. Use them and they grow, which means that in the right environment, kids get smarter.

The Seven Intelligences Go to School

With all these ways of being smart, why do so many kids feel dumb? One big reason is school, which can be a crushing experience for kids, unless they have strong linguistic and mathematical intelligence. Many schools are so focused on producing good readers and "math-ers" that they routinely dismiss the other five intelligences, even though research shows that all seven intelligences contribute to success in school. Studying music helps kids improve in math. Visual intelligence can unlock the mysteries of reading or geometry. Ignoring these areas is like asking kids to navigate through school blindfolded.

I believe all kids are smart, but many are smart in secret ways.

Another problem is that far too many schools ask kids to sit still, keep quiet, and perform repetitive tasks in rooms devoid of art, music, and human comfort. In effect, to learn with their brains tied behind their backs. Or worse, in suspended animation. When kids don't respond well, the explanation usually involves some deficiency in the child, the parents, or both. You'll hear: "He's not trying." "There's no support at home." "She can't focus."

"Maybe there's a learning disability." But just for a moment, imagine yourself in that environment, 30 hours a week. How well would you perform?

I believe all kids are smart, but many are smart in secret ways. So parents and teachers need to get better at recognizing the many different signs of intelligent life. Otherwise, kids may never get a chance to feel and act as smart as they are.

A Word on How Kids Learn

You may be thinking at this point, *Of course, I want smart kids, but I don't know the first thing about teaching. Should I hire a Seven Intelligences tutor?* Happily, it's much easier than that. Learning is a natural human activity, especially for children. And this is what research tells us about how children learn best:

• Children learn through play. It's the work of childhood.
• Children learn through hands-on experiences. Seeing, touching, tasting, and smelling are the strongest modes for early learning.
• Children master communication by having conversations.
• Children learn by trying to solve real problems.
• Children find exploration and investigation intrinsically rewarding. The driving force is "What if . . ." and "I wonder . . ."

So you can be your kids' best teacher simply by turning them loose in your basement, backyard, or garage. On their own they'll discover hundreds of ways to get smarter, with little prompting and no money changing hands. Using simple things like muffin tins, scrap wood, recyclable cans, and old shoes, they can launch a learning festival that will run for years.

At first, the sight of a kid pawing through your kitchen drawer to snatch up rubber bands and toothpicks for an "invention" may not strike you as brainwork. But it is. If kids paint their faces, don old hats, and serenade you standing on kitchen chairs, applaud. That's smart stuff. When they dismantle a radio, make a bug collection, or build a miniature golf course in the living room, they're doing mental aerobics. And the more they do, the smarter they get.

Once your kids get hooked on collecting, composing, or building, they may not want you around. Don't feel bad. Enjoy the break, because it won't be long before they drag you outside to witness their latest miracle. There are rules for responding to miracles. Follow them:

1. *Be a good listener.* When your kids talk about their projects or inventions, behave as you would with an adult friend. Don't repeat what they say (echo). Don't turn their statements into questions: "You built a house?" Just respond with genuine curiosity. And smile. Kids watch like hawks for signs of approval. Give until it hurts.

2. *Ask good questions.* What made you think that? How does it work? What else could you do? How did you figure that out? What would happen if . . . ? What part do you like best?

3. *Avoid criticism.* Encourage kids to judge their own work. Reinforce their conclusions rather than giving your own critique.

4. *Be patient.* Leonardo da Vinci used to sit motionless and stare at his paintings for hours. He'd paint furiously one day, without eating or drinking, then days would pass without a single stroke of work. It may take weeks or months for kids to complete a project. It may evolve, languish or be destroyed. But habits of mind are continually developing, sometimes with little physical evidence.

5. *Don't do anything for kids that they can do for themselves.* Don't finish their models, solve their engineering problems, or tell them how their poems should end—even if you have to sit on your hands and bite your tongue.

When kids really tap into their intelligence, you'll see the signs. They're excited. Their ideas grow and take up more space. They work longer and return to the activity over and over. Step back and enjoy the view.

You're probably a lot like my mom and dad—already doing lots of the right things. And I'll bet there are a lot more that you've forgotten, including some wonderful pastimes from your own childhood. Like making your own scooters or organizing your pets into a circus. You probably thought you were just having fun, but chances are you were also getting smarter. Now your kids can, too.

Remember, there's no reset button on childhood. That kid you adore could be missing out on an amazing life because he's too busy watching reruns of *Gilligan's Island*. But it doesn't have to be that way. Be a smart parent. Have a smart kid.

～ *Lesson 45* ～
Age: All

Children and Books

Trish Kuffner

Author of *The Toddler's Busy Book, The Preschooler's Busy Book,*
The Children's Busy Book and *Picture Book Activities*

"The man who doesn't read good
books has no advantage over the man
who can't read them."
—*Mark Twain*

Reading good books is one of the greatest pleasures in my life, and
it has been as far back as I can remember. Long before I became a
mother, I looked forward to the day when I would share my favorite
picture books with a sweet-smelling, pajama-clad child or two cuddled
on my lap. When my husband and I were finally blessed with a baby, a
bookshelf was an essential part of the nursery furniture. It was soon
filled with many children's classics just waiting to be shared. My best
memories of my daughter's early years were the hours we spent snug-
gled together reading Ludwig Bemelmans's Madeline, PD Eastman's
Are You My Mother? and Robert McCloskey's *Blueberries for Sal.*

I don't know when I discovered the joy of reading. I do clearly remember the day I learned to read: I rushed home from first grade and proudly followed my finger along the first page of my *Dick and Jane* reader as I read aloud to my mother. Learning to read was exciting.

But discovering the joy of reading—feeling the sheer pleasure of holding a good book in my hand and anticipating the world to which it would take me—I don't know when that happened. I don't even know who to thank for it: My parents? A teacher? A librarian? Maybe good books were just something I happened upon. Until I became a parent, I never thought much about the joy of reading. But as a brand-new mother I read in Gladys *Hunt's Honey for a Child's Heart* (Zondervan, 1989) that, "children don't stumble onto good books by themselves; they must be introduced to the wonder of words put together in such a way that they spin out pure joy and magic." I learned that in most cases, children learn to love books when significant adults in their lives take the time to share their own enjoyment of books and reading. Reading to my children and passing on my own love of books became one of my priorities as a parent.

• Why is reading good books to children so important? For starters:
• Reading aloud to a preschooler prepares him to succeed as a reader.
• A child may learn new ideas from books that are read to her.
• Reading helps instill a family's or society's values in a child.
• Reading is a good way to spend time with a child.
• Reading may calm a child and be a vital part of a bedtime routine.

These are all great reasons to read to your child, but none is as important as this: Reading good books to your child helps him discover the pleasure they can give and thereby helps him develop a love of books.

Helping Your Child Develop the Reading Habit

As parents, we can and should actively help our children take those first steps toward the habit of reading. There's no sure-fire formula that guarantees your child will learn to love reading, but you can provide

> *Parents willing to invest time in reading to their children must also invest effort in finding good books.*

two very effective tools.

The first tool is time: Parents must be willing to invest the time it takes to read to the children in their lives. A busy schedule is the enemy of reading, so parents must be willing to turn off the TV, slow down the hectic pace of activities and outings, and read to their children every day.

Parents willing to invest time in reading to their children must also invest effort in finding good books. Just as a steady diet of junk food hampers a body's ability to thrive, poor-quality books hamper the development of a love of reading. Children can discover the pleasure of reading and learn to recognize quality in books only by exposure to good books.

Choosing Books for Children

The biblical wise man Solomon said, "There is no end to the writing of books" (Eccl. 12:12). Solomon wrote that about 3,000 years ago, but he could have been talking about children's books in the twenty-first century! With about 40,000 children's books in print and roughly 4,000 new books published each year, choosing books to read to your child may seem like an overwhelming task. Don't despair; it's not as difficult as it may seem.

- The best way to determine which books your child will enjoy is to read children's books—lots of them.
- Choose books *you* enjoy, and trust your judgment.
- Avoid books that are too cute, too boring, too preachy, or too condescending or those with explicit themes. Implicit themes are more effective and more memorable. In *Choosing Books for Children* (Delacorte, 1990), Betsy Hearne writes, "In general, the less a moral

shows through, the better."

- Read many different kinds of books, and don't expect your child to enjoy every book you choose. Just as an adult book is not good for all people, neither is any one book good for all children.

- Read old classics as well as new treasures. Books give young children a picture of their world, so as Alice Dalgleish says in *First Experiences with Literature* (Charles Scribner's Sons, 1932), "We need to keep the best of the old, and add to it the best of the new, for literature must reflect life and to reflect it truly it must keep pace with our ever-changing world."

- Hundreds of books receive special recognition each year. Award-winning books usually hold to a high standard of literary and artistic excellence, but don't limit the books you choose to award winners. Many excellent books for children are runners-up or receive no special mention at all.

- Read books about children's books. For in-depth study, read Zena Sutherland's *Children and Books*(Addison-Welsley Publishing Company, 9th Edition, 1996), the leading textbook on the subject. Other favorites include *The Read-Aloud Handbook* by Jim Trelease (Penguin Books, 1995) and *Honey for A Child's Heart* by Gladys Hunt (Zondervan Publishing House, 1989).

- Make the children's room of your library your second home. Get to know the librarians and ask for recommendations. Popular books are usually checked out as soon as they are returned, so reserve if you can. If you have Internet access, you may be able to reserve books from home—a lifesaver if you have an infant or toddler! Alternatively, you could schedule an afternoon or evening to visit the library without children in tow to spend some time familiarizing yourself with the best in old and new children's books.

- Visit your local bookstore and browse the shelves of the children's section. Be cautious when asking for recommendations. Many clerks aren't experts on children's books and may simply recommend what everyone else is buying. That's not necessarily a bad thing, but bear in mind that today's buying trends tend to be based more on advertising and popular culture than on quality.

Trish Kuffner

Evaluating Picture Books for Children

A true picture book has little or no text and contains only picture of objects a child may recognize and point to. A picture book is also understood more broadly as one that tells a story, but in which the picture is the dominant feature on each page. Children should be able to "read" a picture book simply by looking at the illustrations.

Good picture books maintain high literary and artistic standards. When evaluating picture books for your child, keep in mind the traits that distinguish a truly good picture book:

• A good picture book has brief text written in a simple and direct style.
• A good picture book retains a child's interest after many readings.
• A good picture book has solid characters.
• A good picture book combines action, wordplay, humor, and poetry.
• A good picture book includes few concepts and only those a child will comprehend.
• A good picture book contains high-quality art that perfectly complements the text in mood and subject matter. A picture book's illustrations are very important because young children usually pay more attention to its pictures than to its words.
• A good picture book will stand the test of time, remaining in print many years after it was first published.

Ultimately, a good picture book is one that children will read and enjoy. Knowing how to evaluate and choose picture books for your child will help her learn to love books and develop a lifelong habit of reading for knowledge and pleasure.

One Last Thought

While listening to a radio discussion about raising better readers, I heard an "expert" advise parents to stop reading aloud to their children once the children could read on their own. He reasoned that children would then be forced to read for themselves.

I was horrified! Some of the best times I share with my older children are when we are immersed in a reading adventure together. Although my children are excellent readers and love to read on their own, they still enjoy and benefit from hearing good books read aloud. I believe that reading aloud is a priceless, irreplaceable family activity that's often overlooked and

> *I believe that reading aloud is a priceless, irreplaceable family activity . . .*

undervalued in our hurried world, and I encourage you to keep doing it as long as you like.

I also urge you to hold to high standards when choosing books for your children and to continue doing so long after they're reading independently. Too often I hear parents say, "I don't care what they read, as long as they're reading." Don't forget that although we can't remember everything we read, what we read changes us. It feeds our minds and nourishes our souls. Good books help us grow and add to our inner stature. I pose to you the challenge Gladys Hunt so eloquently makes in *Honey for a Child's Heart:* "A young child, a fresh uncluttered mind, a world before him—to what treasures will you lead him? With what will you furnish his spirit?"

A Father's Place Is in the School

Aaron Kipnis, Ph.D.

Author of *Knights Without Armor,* and *Angry Young Men: How Parents, Teachers, and Counselors Can Help "Bad Boys" Become Good Men*

Extreme acts of school violence have become a disturbing and persistent feature of the cultural landscape in twenty-first century America. Once largely thought of as an urban street gang–related problem, one in five, adolescent boys now owns a gun; even more have been threatened with one according to the Justice Department. Many suburban boys today have something in common with inner-city gang boys—a profound feeling of alienation and a perceived lack of protection from others who corrode their emotional self-esteem or threaten their safety.

Contrary to the widespread image of American boys as tough, independent, and relatively advantaged, they actually suffer the highest rates of violent trauma for an industrialized nation. In 1999, males were the majority of abused, neglected, and abandoned children. They were three out of four assault victims, homeless youth, and drug addicts, and four out of every five suicide and homicide victims. We also have more young men incarcerated in juvenile halls, jails, psychiatric hospitals, youth corrections, and adult prisons than any other nation. Homicide is now the second leading cause of death for American youth; ten times the youth homicide rate of Canada, fifteen times Australia's, and twenty-eight times Germany's. Handguns kill thirteen children a day in the United States. and thirteen people a year in Sweden. But guns alone are not the problem. Drugs, the media, video games, and rap can't carry all the blame. Tougher laws and more prisons won't solve the crisis nor will ten commandments posted in "zero tolerance" schools expelling record numbers of boys today. As Jesse Jackson puts it, the problem isn't that we have failed to make young men afraid enough. "The real problem is that our young people are not hopeful enough."

Expulsions and suspensions for boys have skyrocketed to over two million per year.

Today, most school safety guidelines list behaviors that are typical for at least a third of adolescent boys as predictive of students most at risk for violent outbreaks. Expulsions and suspensions for boys have skyrocketed to over two million per year. Because "bad boys" are generally referred to programs in which the staff usually has the lowest level of training, the poorest tools, and the most dilapidated facilities, our highest-risk students tend to become the least well cared for. Few teachers are trained or equipped to deal with boys who act out. Boys sense this. Teachers legitimately fear both personal injury and lawsuits for using excessive force. Yet the small incidents that lead to most fights, such as pushing, scuffles, name calling, and "mad dogging" (stare-downs), tend to settle down when a serious and capable adult male shows up in the immediate vicinity.

Recent research in social psychology increasingly confirms that one thing the majority of boys at risk have in common is an absent or abusive father. In the late 1980s, at Arlington High in Indianapolis, students were so out of control that the school could no longer hold large events like dances. For years, this school, where one-third of the students came from fatherless homes, was a troubled, dangerous place. Things began to change, however, when a new principal, Jacqueline Greenwood, simply asked for help. She told the fathers, "Come to the school anytime that you can and be with your kids. We need you to get involved."

In response to this call, one student's mother, Mrs. Linda Wallace, said to her husband, "Those are big kids and no mother can yell at them and make them behave. But maybe a father could." She printed a T-shirt emblazoned with "Security Dad." Her husband, Anthony, saw looks of surprise the first night he showed up at a football jamboree wearing the shirt. Students smiled and waved: "Hi Mr. Wallace— how're you doing?" Whenever students started to get unruly and he moved in their direction, other students would say, "Hey, that's Lena's dad. Be quiet. Sit down." When he asked them to move out of the aisles, they did so without a fuss.

His wife recalls, "He talked to them with respect and they listened. He treated them like they were his own kids. It was fantastic." After more fathers joined the "Security Dads," the school was able to reinstitute events previously canceled out of fear of violence. Also, about two dozen fathers got together to patrol the school during classes to increase security for all students.

> *The power of a father's presence to lift his children's academic performance transcends class, race, ethnicity, and his level of education.*

"What works is that father image," said Ron Cheney, another father who joined the group. "So we don't need to say very much. Just being there is what counts. With a [police] officer they think, 'Hey, I must be in trouble.' With us, they smile and say, 'Hey, what's up?' And we love it."

One student said, "It's much happier to have fathers around, rather than guards. Our dads are like real people. They don't intimidate us. Where parents are involved, our lives are a lot easier. It's like a family."

In 1997, the U.S. Department of Education found that better grades and behavior both result when men are more involved in school activities. The power of a father's presence to lift his children's academic performance transcends class, race, ethnicity, and his level of education. The rate of suspension, expulsion, and repeating grade levels is also lower for father-involved students than those for whom only the mother is involved. The success rate declines much further when neither parent is involved.

Over the years, through many consultations with couples and families, I have noted that fathering often complements mothering with slightly different attributes. Frequently, mothers seem more concerned with the emotional life, safety, and health of their children. Fathers often appear more focused on encouraging achievement, discipline, motor skills, and independence. Neither approach is better or worse. Together, they are a balanced parenting "meal" that better nurtures children. Of course, not all couples fit these tendencies, and sometimes when these differences are present, they create conflict between women and men vying for the preeminent approach to parenting. But for single parents of either gender, it's often tougher to balance a boy's needs for consistent discipline and fierce direction with tenderness, nurturing, and protection.

Children from fatherless homes account for: 63 percent of youth suicides, 70 percent of juveniles in state-operated institutions, 71 percent of all pregnant teenagers and high school dropouts, 85 percent of all youths in prisons, and 90 percent of all homeless and runaway children. Children who live with both biological parents have the lowest reported rates of maltreatment (3 percent). Divorced fathers with custody show slightly higher rates, and children living with single mothers, particularly those with a nonbiological male in their home, suffer the highest abuse rates (19 percent). Why do single fathers show lower rates of abuse and neglect of boys than single mothers? The generally better economic welfare of single fathers may partially account for this, since child poverty is also highly correlated with abuse. Children from families with annual incomes of less than $15,000 report maltreatment almost seven times more frequently than children from higher-income families. Single mothers with young children living below the poverty line, together with alcoholic and drug-addicted parents of both sexes, have the greatest statistical risk of abusing or neglecting boys.

Even though research continues to document the essential importance of father involvement in children's academic achievement and emotional well-being, approximately 50 percent of mothers see no value in the father's continued contact with his children after a divorce. One study of 500 women showed that only 11 percent of mothers value their husband's input when it comes to handling problems with their kids. By comparison, on the same survey, 45 percent of teachers and doctors rated the input of fathers as important and 16 percent of close friends and relatives agreed. In the same way that women want men to open doors to arenas where women have historically been excluded, men need women to assist them in moving into women's traditionally held domains. For example, in the past, because most fathers felt unwelcome in the delivery rooms of maternity hospitals, they were seldom present at the birth of their children. The prevalent myth of past eras was that they just didn't care. But when obstetricians' attitudes toward fathers started to change in the 1980s and fathers were actively welcomed, they showed up in droves. Now more than 80 percent of married fathers are present at the birth of their children.

In the same way, when fathers feel welcome and invited into the schools, they fill a personal need to play a role in their children's lives from which they have historically felt excluded. In the wake of more schools' recognizing the value of father involvement, their numbers are increasing. In California, the Dads Club and Dads in Action are getting rave reviews from school officials. Nationally, Mad Dads and other such groups have similar positive impacts. Some schools provide a parents' lounge and other supports to encourage sustained school involvement from fathers. The fathers in these programs often report that their school involvement also improves relationships with their own children. Even the busiest executives somehow find a few hours a week to do their stint at school, and many do more.

Secrets to
Self-Esteem

"Never tell a young person that something cannot be done. God may have been waiting for centuries for somebody ignorant enough of the impossibility to do that thing."
—*Dr. J. A. Holmes*

"Teaseproof" Your Kids

Jim Fay

Author of *Parenting with Love and Logic*
and *Parenting Teens with Love and Logic*

"Mom, I don't want to go to school. It's not fair. Mrs. Taylor tells the kids not to tease me, but they still do it when she's not watching 'em. I try to ignore 'em just like you said, but they just do it all the more."

Loving parents who are confused with this type of situation feel like a piece of their hearts is being ripped out. What a hopeless feeling we have when our kids are being rejected or teased by other kids. It is not uncommon at these times to have feelings that include both heartache and rage.

We think to ourselves, *Why can't the school people protect my child? Don't they realize that we put our kids in their hands and therefore our trust?*

The sad truth is that the more a teacher protects the child who is teased, the more resentful and aggressive the other children become. A teacher who tells kids to be nice to a specific child actually "marks" that youngster and sets him or her up for more intense rejection and ridicule.

When it comes to teasing, the only person who can protect your child is *himself*. Kids have some sort of built-in sonar that causes them to zero in on certain kids, and they can be unmerciful in the torment.

Watching this happen can be a gut-wrenching experience for any adult. But the good news is that we can actually help kids, become "teaseproof."

Have you ever noticed that some kids never get teased whereas others are constantly subjected to teasing? There is a pattern to this.

Kids who are never teased never worry about being teased. They have an aura around them that says, "I can handle myself!"

Kids who are never teased never worry about being teased. They can't imagine that it would ever happen to them. They have an aura around them that says, "I can handle myself!"

Kids who do get teased constantly worry about being ridiculed and send out non-verbal messages that indicate lack of confidence and fear of teasing. Children are especially in tune with nonverbal signals of weakness. Without realizing what they are doing, they zero in on these kids. Two subconscious goals come into play. The first is, "I can show others that I am superior to that kids" and the other is, "That kid's weak and I better show him that he needs to toughen up."

Remember that none of this happens at the conscious level. It just happens and appears to be human nature.

The trick to teaseproofing a youngster is giving her skills to be able to handle teasing. Once the child realizes she can actually handle the problem, you will see a change in the nonverbal attitude. The other kids will recognize this and start looking for different targets.

Mr. Mendez, a wonderful second-grade teacher, teaseproofed his whole class. He said to the class, "Kids, the reason kids tease other kids is that it makes them feel superior. Now you can let them get away with this or you can use an adult one-liner. But first of all, we all have to practice the 'cool look.'"

This teacher had the kids practice standing with their hands in their pockets, rocking back on their heels, and putting a cool grin on their face.

He practiced this over and over. Every now and then, he would yell out, "Let's see your 'cool look.'" The kids would all jump out of their seats and put on the "look."

Once they had all mastered the cool look, he said, "When kids start to tease you, put on your cool look. Keep the look going while they tease. As soon as they get through putting you down, use your one-liner."

The one-liner he taught them is one of the famous Love and Logic One-Liners: "Thanks for sharing that with me." Mr. Mendez had the kids practice this, making sure that they kept the cool look on while they said the words.

Every now and then, when the kids would least expect it, he would yell out, "Let me hear your one-liner!" And the kids would practice saying the words, making sure to grin while they said them.

Once the teacher felt that the class had mastered saying, "Thanks for sharing that with me," in the appropriate way, he started having them practice jumping out of their seats, putting on the cool look, and saying their one-liner.

The next step was for the kids to learn to turn around on the last word and walk away fast without looking back at the teasing child. Needless to say, they all practiced until the skill was mastered. They even spent some of their recess time practicing this on the playground.

Now that the skill was learned, practiced, and mastered, Mr. Mendez could implement his part of the operation. When the children came to him to tattle about others teasing them he consistently asked, "Did you let him get by with it or did you use your cool skill?"

In the event that the child admitted that he had not used his skill, the teacher said, "How sad that you let him get by with it. Do you suppose you are going to continue to let him get by with it or are you going to use your skill? It's your choice, but tattling to me is no longer a choice."

Mr. Mendez tells us that the amount of tattling and complaining has been reduced by over 90 percent. He also proudly tells about one of his students who asked if the one-liner he taught him had to be used, or if the children could they make up their own one-liners.

This second-grader wanted to demonstrate to the class the one-liner that he used so successfully on the playground.

All the kids clapped for this skillful second-grader and the teacher beamed with pride as he thought to himself, "Now that kid is really 'tease proofed' for sure."

He stood before the class and said, "This other kid on the playground was dissin' me. He said I had the skinniest arms in the whole school. I put on my cool look, I grinned, and said, 'Bummer, I thought I was cool, man.' I walked away before he could figure out what to say. Man, I blew his mind!"

All the kids clapped for this skillful second-grader and the teacher beamed with pride as he thought to himself, *Now that kid is really teaseproofed for sure.*

You don't have to wait for the teacher to teaseproof your kids. You can do it in your home the same way Mr. Mendez did in the classroom. What a gift you can give your child, and come to think of it, what a gift it is to parents to know that we can send teaseproofed kids into the world.

Since the development of the cool look skill, many different kids have found sanctuary in its use. One of the most creative applications was seen at a local school where the kids seem to take great pleasure in claiming to do research on the behavior of other kids' mothers and attacking each other with this information when they are mad.

One kid yelled out to the other, "Yo momma's a ho!" The youngster being attacked put on his cool look and retorted, "I tell her to be nice, but she gets mad when I tell her what to do." With this he turned and walked away.

The teacher who witnessed this reported that the attacker's mouth fell open and all he could say under his breath was, "Man, that guy's weird."

Now the kid who pulled this one off is absolutely teaseproofed. Even if kids try to tease him, the attacks will bounce like Ping-Pong balls off a stone wall.

Helping Your Child Develop Meaningful Self-Esteem

Maureen Stout, Ph.D.

Author of *The Feel-Good Curriculum: The Dumbing-Down
of America's Kids in the Name of Self-Esteem*

While parents may differ on many issues regarding how to raise their children, there is one issue on which virtually all parents agree: that kids need to have confidence in themselves—what we refer to today as self-esteem. There have been many books written on the topic, and courses are even offered in schools aimed at helping children feel good about who they are. But what is self-esteem and how do we get it? I believe we need meaningful, healthy, enduring self-esteem: the self-confidence that naturally develops from effort and achievement and is based on a sense of personal and social responsibility. Kids need

233

to feel secure in who they are for the long term, but they also need to have a realistic and balanced perspective on life.

What does this perspective mean in practice? It involves two main lessons: first, teaching your child how to interact with the outside world, and second, teaching him to develop confidence in himself. Children need to learn as early as possible that they are very important people in the world, but so is everyone else. They need to know that they are unique and valuable individuals, but other people are also unique and have qualities that need to be respected. Young children are naturally egocentric—that is, they tend to be concerned only with their own physical and emotional needs. Part of the parent's responsibility, of course, is to attend to those needs, but it is also the parent's job to begin to socialize the child, to teach him that he is part of a family and a larger community. Parents can do this in very simple ways, by getting their children involved in the community, going with them to do volunteer work, and giving them responsibilities in the family. This will begin to instill a sense of empathy in children that provides a healthy balance to the second task: developing self-confidence or self-esteem.

The best way to promote meaningful self-esteem is to relate it to effort and achievement. This does not mean that only those children who are A students or excellent athletes deserve to feel good about themselves. Kids need to know that they have unique gifts and that part of our responsibility as individuals is to develop and nurture those gifts to the utmost. So if a child is not very academically inclined but has a talent for working with her hands or paints well, parents should encourage the child to develop those talents. But the child should also be encouraged to work on those skills that need more attention, as we may have talents of which we are not aware until we apply ourselves to a task that requires them.

Sometimes, of course, this means applying ourselves to something that isn't necessarily the most fun thing at the time. How many of us remember the hated piano lessons of our childhood but found we were grateful for them as adults? Of course, some of us decide as adults that we are not grateful for them, and it is probably not productive to make a child work at something he really hates or for which he has no interest or little talent. But there is no question that dedication to any task, and the feeling of confidence that comes from accomplishing it, is central to developing self-esteem.

The key to remember here, and the core of true self-esteem, is that none of us really knows what the potential of any child is, so the most important lesson is encouraging children to achieve the utmost in every area of their lives. One thing on which virtually everyone agrees is that if you set high expectations for children and encourage them to set high expectations for themselves, they will rise to meet them. If you don't, they won't. This is what is known as the self-fulfilling prophecy. Once again, this does not mean pushing children into anything, but nurturing the best of who they are intellectually, emotionally, and spiritually, helping them be the best Jennifer, Juan, or Matthew they can be.

If you set high expectations for children and encourage them to set high expectations for themselves, they will rise to meet them.

But the road to self-esteem can hit two potential roadblocks that we need to be aware of and understand: comparisons with others and the possibility of failure. Children, like adults, compare themselves to each other all the time in terms of looks, athletic abilities, popularity, and so forth. It is natural and inevitable, and, indeed, a healthy dose of competition never hurt anyone. Here parents must help their kids try to strike a balance between healthy self-respect and respect for others, and learn the difference between relevant and helpful comparisons from which they can gain something and irrelevant and destructive comparisons that make them feel bad.

For example, let's say 12-year-old Jose compares himself to his friend, David, who is several inches taller and feels like he doesn't (literally!) measure up. Jose's parents should try to explain to him that his worthiness as a person does not in any way depend upon his height. Now that might not totally assuage Jose's insecurities, but it will certainly help. Then let's say David has been taking homework home for

Janice, who is sick, and Jose thinks perhaps he should have thought of doing that for her. Such a scenario provides a golden opportunity for Jose's parents to discuss the importance of thinking of others, to see David's actions as something Jose can learn from and let Jose know that he has shown himself to be a good person by thinking about this whole issue.

Jose doesn't need to feel bad about himself because David thought of doing a good deed before he did. However, by recognizing David's thoughtfulness, Jose can both respect him and reflect on his own actions and perhaps think more about the welfare of others in the future. Children can learn about their own worth not only by achieving something but by learning about the worth of others. Self-esteem without humility is narcissism, and part of growing up is growing out of narcissism to a healthy interaction with others.

Comparison is part of competition, and, like it or not, competition is built in to society and into schools. Children are acutely aware of who does well and who does poorly in school and in sports, and if they believe their worthiness is dependent upon doing better than others, then to them failure could mean they are not worth anything. This is where we need to rethink our definition of failure and success, however. As I have noted, we all have talents, and one of the more important roles of parents is to identify and help develop those gifts in their children. But part of growing up is also acknowledging the fact that some people will always be better at some things than we are, while recognizing that this does not make us less important as individuals.

One way to promote this mindset is to take the stigma out of failing. That is, if we fail at something, it should be seen as an opportunity to learn what we need to improve upon and to devise strategies to do better. That does not mean that in schools A's should be given out for effort, but that effort should be recognized and encouraged, and failure should not be made shameful. After all, we have all failed at something somewhere along the line, and the important thing is to learn from the experience. As a matter of fact, many of the most important lessons in life are acquired from failure, for it is only when we are truly tested that we truly learn.

And perhaps that is what is core here: Becoming the responsible, mature, happy, successful adults that we all want our children to be is part of a lifelong learning process. Meaningful self-esteem involves developing a realistic view of one's strengths and weaknesses, a respect for hard work, a recognition of others' talents, and an acknowledgment of both one's importance and the importance of others. But most important it involves knowing what is possible and achieving it; letting kids know they can make a difference in their own lives and in the lives of others, and that if they believe in themselves, nothing can really stand in their way.

Lesson 49

Age: Young Children to Teens

Help Children Learn to Believe in Themselves

Michele Borba, Ed.D.

Author of *Building Moral Intelligence: The Seven Essential
Virtues that Teach Kids to do the Right Thing* and *Parents Do Make
a Difference: How to Raise Kids with Solid Character,
Strong Minds, and Caring Hearts*

Regardless of what state or country I'm in, the question parents at my workshops ask me most frequently is, "What's the most important thing I can do to help my child succeed?"

I have been asked the question so often, I decided to pose the same question to teachers attending my seminars. After all, they deal with hundreds of children and certainly know what helps students succeed. For the next 5 years, I surveyed more than 10,000 teachers from coast to coast, and their number one response everywhere was, "Help children learn to believe in themselves." Scores of child development experts have reached the same conclusion. Simply stated: For our children to succeed, they must first believe they can succeed.

Without feeling "I can do it," a child is gravely handicapped from succeeding in every arena: at school, at home, with others, at work, on athletic fields, and in life. With little faith in himself, the child will approach experiences with a "Why bother, I can't do it anyway" attitude, greatly minimizing his chances for happiness and personal fulfillment. The cumulative impact that an "I can't" attitude has on his self-esteem is tragically predictable: How can he possibly feel good about himself with so few positive experiences to affirm that he is worthwhile and competent?

Parents who expect their children to succeed and communicate the belief, "I know you can," produce children who do.

"I can do it" attitudes don't develop automatically; our children learn them, and the first place they learn them is from us. Clear-cut evidence shows that parents who expect their children to succeed and communicate the belief, "I know you can," produce children who do. And nurturing this belief is one of the greatest gifts you can give your child, because it is the foundation for healthy self-esteem and successful living.

Sometimes, though, parents and teachers unintentionally send messages that diminish children's self-beliefs. One of the deadliest habits that chips away at children's self-confidence is any form of stereotyping.

Nicknames like Shorty, Clumsy, Crybaby, Slowpoke, Klutz, or Nerd can become daily reminders of incompetence. They can also become self-fulfilling prophecies. Regardless of whether the labels are true, when children hear them they begin to believe them. And the label very often sticks and becomes difficult to erase.

For my *Parent School* lesson, I'd like to share four ideas (from my book, *Parents Do Make a Difference*) that you can do to help prevent your child from forming negative self-images:

1. *Avoid using negative labels about your child*, whether you are in front of him or with others. Labeling children with such terms as shy, stubborn, hyper, or clumsy can diminish self-esteem.

2. *Never let anyone else label your child.* Labeling is deadly, but you can immediately turn any negative label into a positive one. Negative label: "Your son is so shy!" Positive new label, "Not at all. He is just a great observer."

3. *Avoid making comparisons.* Never compare your child to anyone—especially siblings! "Why can't you be more like your sister? She's always so neat, and you're such a slob!" Making comparisons can strain a child's individuality and undermine her sense of self-worth.

4. *Refrain from using genetic labels.* Labels can limit your child's view of himself. "You're as lazy as your uncle." "You're going to be poor in math like I was." "You take after your Aunt Sue; you're shy just like her."

What follows shows how you can turn negative, demeaning labels into more affirming terms that help children develop more positive self-images. One good rule to remember about labeling is, *If the nickname does not boost your child's feelings of adequacy, it's best not to use it.*

Creating a Positive New Label

Think of your own child and identify any current label that could be destructive to her self-esteem: lazy, selfish, dumb, slow, irresponsible, sloppy, unreliable, uncoordinated, inconsiderate, stubborn, rebellious.

Now develop a new, more positive term you could use to replace the negative label, and write it down. Use the new term with your child as well as around others to help her see herself more positively. Here are a few to get you started:

Old Negative Label	*New Positive Label*
Hyperactive	Energetic
Shy	Cautious
Unpredictable	Flexible
Daydreamer	Creative
Aggressive	Assertive

There's much we can do to enrich our children's lives, to help them become their best. And that's really what raising kids is all about. Good parenting and great teaching are not about how to turn out little prodigies, but rather how to help our children live their lives to the best of their abilities. That, in itself, is an immensely powerful role.

Teaching Self-Reliance

Excerpt from Being the Parent
Your Child Deserves

Rae Turnbull
Author of *Being The Parent Your Child Deserves*

The most important thing you can teach your child is self-reliance. At the beginning of my intensive ten-session seminar, "The Parent Forum: The Parent as a Teacher," I ask parents to make this pledge:

> *I will be the teacher my children deserve.*
> *I will prepare them for their eventual independence*
> *by teaching them how to become*
> *self-reliant, self-confident adults,*
> *able to love themselves and others,*
> *willing to lead decent useful lives,*
> *and capable of pursuing their own happiness.*

You will note that the pledge states self-reliance first. That's because the rest of the pledge cannot be fully realized without it.

What is so important about self-reliance?

Self-reliance is the foundation for self-respect. When we encourage our children to rely on themselves, we are proving to them that we believe them to be capable individuals. What is one of the first things that brings pride into a small child's eyes? When that child is able to complete a task and say, "Look, I did it all by myself!"

In that moment, the child feels the freedom of being able to do something, independent of anyone else. Self-respect has begun to be a reality for that child. All sorts of examples come to my mind, but I will use only one, because it so clearly demonstrates the link between self-reliance and self-respect. It also illustrates how early this need for self-respect begins.

Daniel, my youngest grandson, is not yet 3 years old. One recent Saturday, I was spending the afternoon with him and his older brother, Jacob, who is 5 years old. The three of us just returned from a long walk, and the boys raced for the house to get a drink. Jacob, playing the big brother role, reached for two cups on the sink drain board, and handed one to Daniel. *How nice*, I thought, *he's going to get a drink for his little brother.*

But as I watched, Jacob reached into the refrigerator, pulled out a fairly heavy plastic container of water, poured some into his cup, then put the container back on a low shelf in the refrigerator, without pouring any water into his brother's cup. Daniel just watched patiently, with none of the whining I expected to hear because of what I perceived to be his brother's neglect.

"Jacob," I said rather sharply, "Why didn't you get some water for Daniel?" Jacob's answer was quick and to the point: "Because he likes to get it for himself."

As he spoke, I watched Daniel struggle with the water container, needing both small hands to heft it off the shelf, then lugging it over to the table and heaving it onto the tabletop. Beaming proudly, he turned

243

to me and said, "Me do it!" Jacob smiled knowingly and filled his brother's cup for him. Apparently, the two little boys had already learned, probably through trial and error, that the container was too heavy for Daniel to be able to pour the water. Daniel was perfectly willing to accept his big brother's help when it was really needed. But he didn't want to be insulted by having his brother do the part that he knew he could do for himself. Jacob, by honoring his little brother's need to be self-reliant, allowed Daniel to add another small layer to his gradually building self-respect.

How had Jacob learned to encourage his little brother's self-reliance? The lesson was learned from his parents' example. From the time Jacob was Daniel's age, he remembered that he was encouraged to do things for himself whenever possible. His parents were ready to help when help was needed, but they were also willing to wait while the child took the extra time to try to do things on his own. This big brother was doing for his little brother what had been done for him. I'm sure it would have been much easier, in many instances, for his parents to simply do the task themselves, thus providing Daniel with the result, instead of teaching the child how to get the result for himself. Easier for them and for Daniel in the short term, but much more difficult for all of them in the long term.

Clinging to the role of provider may be a way to avoid making the necessary changes that you need to make in yourself, in order to be an effective teacher.

Unfortunately, many parents prefer the role of provider over the role of teacher. They want to provide everything for their children. If you are one of those parents, remember that one of the things you learned in the beginning of this journey was the importance of honesty, especially honesty with yourself. If you are being honest, you will see that clinging to the role of provider may be a way to avoid making the necessary changes that you need to make in yourself, in order to be an effective teacher.

As a teacher to your children, you need to develop patience and consistency, and constantly keep your ultimate goal in mind. As a provider, you have no such constraints on your own behavior. Providing everything you think your child needs, or you want him to have, can be very personally satisfying as a short-term goal. It makes you feel important, necessary, in control. Best of all, it requires no real effort on your part, in terms of self-improvement. Without changing yourself at all, you can purchase, make, or do everything for your child. In this way, you believe that you ensure your child's happiness. I urge you to understand that not only is that a selfish goal, but it is an impossible one. Here are some of the reasons why:

As a classroom teacher, I meet many parents who want to be able to say, "I gave my children everything they ever wanted." But if they do, they are keeping from their children the one thing those children want and need most: the opportunity to respect themselves and their own abilities.

It's useful for us to remember that it is not our responsibility, as parents, to provide our children's happiness. Each of us must make ourselves happy.

The self-reliant individual will be able to find his or her own happiness. Remember that's what your goal must be, for no matter how hard you try, as a parent, you cannot provide your child's happiness. That role is rightfully reserved for each individual.

Happiness is not an external thing. It must come from within the self. It cannot be given to someone. It must be gained by each individual for his or her own self. What better way to do that than to pursue our own interests, struggle toward our own goals, and claim our victories as our own? We must struggle. It is the struggle to reach them that gives true value to our goals. Without struggle, we may get the desired results, but there is no real achievement when that happens.

Self-respect is not enhanced when luck takes on greater importance than struggle. No one gains self-respect from accidental victories. We all like to feel that we are in control of our lives. When we stop the struggle and rely on luck to get what we need in life, we lose that control. In order for us to feel truly successful in our lives, we need to know that our success comes from our own effort, not from the handouts or gifts. Both are fine, in the right time and place, but as a way of life, they are self-defeating and demoralizing. We do not want our children to be the victims of our own selfish need to make them happy.

Another reason for avoiding the pitfalls of the provider role is the fact that it's not the things we have that give us true satisfaction. It's the journey toward obtaining those things, the effort it took, which marks their real value. On that journey to acquire what we think we desire, we learn much about ourselves.

One of the lessons we learn is that sometimes the things we think we need or want are not really that important to us after all. The thing itself is only the symbol of the journey and the goal reached—tangible evidence of the effort it took to acquire it. When too much is provided for us, it makes us lose confidence in our ability to provide for our-selves. Remember the Parent Pledge as you guide your child toward self-reliance.

❧ Lesson 51 ❧
Age: Young Children to Teens

"My Child is Being Teased! How Can I Get This to Stop?"

From: Good Friends Are Hard to Find

Fred Frankel, Ph.D.
Author of *Good Friends Are Hard to Find.*

Children tease because it's fun for them to see someone become upset when his buttons are pushed. How children tease changes with age. Children up to second grade tease by name-calling. Older children who tease use more elaborate statements. They attack the dignity of family members (especially moms, because it hurts more). Anything that will get someone upset, or get laughs at another's expense, will do as a tease.

My experience shows that the most effective technique you can teach your child is to make fun of the teasing. Your child makes fun of the teaser's inability to tease well. This is different from teasing back:

Your child does not sink to the level of the teaser, but shows through humor that the teasing does not push his buttons (even if it does). Children who learn this tell me they have success the first time they use it. They get sympathy from onlookers and take away the fun of teasing.

The most effective technique . . . is to make fun of the teasing.

Mothers are better than fathers at getting their child to practice responses to teasing. If the teasing is about mom (for instance, "Your Mom's fat") and the person being teased doesn't seem to care about the content ("So what?"), then it takes a lot of the hurt out of the teasing. Your child no longer feels he has to defend the family honor, so he has less reason to be upset when he's teased.

Step 1:
Get as much information as you can about the teasing.

Talk about the teasing in a calm, matter-of-fact way. This will help neutralize your child's hurt feelings. Find out who is doing the teasing and as much information about what they are saying as your child will comfortably tell you. Don't get angry or laugh at the teasing. Don't give advice at this point. Only gather information. Making suggestions too early will end the conversation before you get what you need.

The best way to neutralize the hurt of teasing is to remain neutral yourself. Be patient and let your child tell you about it as slowly as he wants. Example:

Mom: *How did things go in school today?*
Timothy: *[Visibly upset] Okay.*
Mom: *Did something happen today that you would like to tell me about?*
Timothy: *No.*

Mom: *Okay.*

Timothy: *[After 10 minutes of silence] The other kids were teasing me again today.*

Mom: *[In a serious tone] Oh, I see. It happened today?*

Timothy: *Yes.*

Mom: *Who teased you today?*

Timothy: *A whole bunch of kids.*

Mom: *What did they say?*

Timothy: *Sam called our family the "fat butts," and the other kids laughed.*

Mom: *[Serious but neutral tone of voice] Was Sam the only one calling us the fat butts, or was someone else doing it also?*

Mom should watch Timothy's reaction when she says "fat butts." If Timothy doesn't react, Mom continues. If Timothy becomes upset, Mom should refer to it as "the teasing" after this point.

Timothy: *Just Sam, but the rest of the kids laughed.*

Mom: *Does anyone else tease you, besides Sam?*

Timothy: *No, just Sam, and the other kids laugh.*

Timothy had said all the kids tease him, but he now realizes it is only Sam.

Mom: *Is this the only thing Sam says to you when he teases you?*

Timothy: *No. He says I come from the fat family.*

Mom: *You know, I don't care if Sam calls me fat, so you don't have to worry about me.*

Mom makes this last statement (regardless of how accurate it is) after she gathers the facts. It helps Timothy stay calm the next time he is teased. This will not be enough to take care of teasing. Sam thinks he can push Timothy's buttons. He won't give up unless Timothy makes fun of the teasing.

Step 2:
Rehearse making Fun of the Teasing with your child.

You need to teach your child what to say in these situations to take the fun out of teasing but not tease back. Your child will answer every tease with a reply. Read aloud the following list of replies to see if your child likes any of them:

"So what?"
"What?"
"Can't you think of anything else to say?"
"That's so old it has dust on it."
"That's so old it's from the Stone Age."
"I fell off my dinosaur when I first heard that."
"Tell me when you get to the funny part."
"And your point is . . . "

This is not a complete list. You and your child can probably think of more.

1. Have your child pick ways to make fun of the teasing from the list above or similar statements.

2. Practice a few replies to teases several times.

3. Laugh with your child after each reply he tries.

Making fun of the teasing shows the teaser that your child:

• Is not going to cry or get angry
• Thinks teasing back is beneath him
• Has an answer for any teasing

With a younger child (below third grade), you have to tell him exactly what to say (and keep it simple). With an older child, try getting him to use replies from the list of examples or have him come up with his own. Here's how it's done:

Mom: *[Reads the above list to Timothy] Want to try any of these? What might you say the next time Sam calls us the fat butts? Remember, don't sink to his level and tease him back. You have to show him that teasing is not going to get you angry anymore.*

Timothy: *[Reads from list without any intonation] I've heard that one before.*

Mom: *[Laughing] Yeah, that's a good one. [Repeats in a confident, mildly disparaging tone of voice], I've heard that one before. So what do you say when Sam calls you fatty again?*

Timothy: *[This time with a little more confidence] I heard that one before.*

Mom: *[Laughs] Yeah, that's a good one. Let's try some more. What other one do you like?*

Timothy: *That's so old I fell off my dinosaur when I heard it.*

Mom: *[Laughs] That's great. So what do you say after Sam says you're one of the fat butts? . . .*

I find that one session is all the practice most children need.

Step 3:
Ask if your child used the technique and whether it worked.

I always like to find out how my advice turned out. The next day, Mom has this conversation with Timothy:

Mom: *Did you get a chance to try making fun of Sam's teasing?*

Timothy: *Yeah, he teased me and I said, "So what!" He didn't say anything. He just walked away.*

Mom: *That's great!*

The first time Timothy makes fun of his teasing, Sam will not know what to say next. He will either stop teasing, or when he tries again, he will stop after Timothy comes up with one or two differently replies. That's why it is better to rehearse several different replies: is Your child will not run out of replies before the teaser runs out of teases.

You've helped your child deal with teasing without you getting into the thick of it. I remember being teased when I was about 9 years old. I remember repeating back a phrase I heard someone else use: "Sticks and stones will break my bones, but names will never hurt me." I felt awkward saying it and the boy teasing me teased me about saying it, but I said nothing. He never teased me again. I felt much better when I realized this.

Family Values

"In an ever-changing world, we must have some absolutes—some values. I've learned that children feel more secure, more grounded, when there are things to hold on to, like believing in God, respect for ourselves, compassion for others and sharing. Traditions can change, but values are eternal."

—*Brenda Nixon, MRE, Parenting Speaker, Parent Educator, Adjunct University Instructor, "Parenting Power!" columnist (www.parentpwr.com)*

～ *Lesson 52* ～
Age: All

What Really Matters

Alvin Rosenfeld, M.D., and Nicole Wise
Authors of *The Over-Scheduled Child: Avoiding the Hyper-Parenting Trap*

What really matters in life? What do I really believe in? Who am I, really?

When, exactly, are we busy parents supposed to find time to ponder deep philosophical questions like these—between kindergarten drop-off and a grocery store run? Most of us cannot imagine ourselves—or anyone else who is both a parent and a homeowner, not to mention a professional, son or daughter, coach, friend, or any of those other roles we work so hard to juggle in our lives—making time to wrestle with questions like these. The meaning of life? Most of us would rather have the mortgage paid off, thank you very much.

Nowadays, it seems possible, even reasonable, to live a full life without ever facing an existential question bigger than "What's really better, buying or leasing a Ford Explorer?" When confronted with life's big questions, many of us are inclined to give a reflexive, *Cliff's Notes* kind of answer: "I'm on this earth to make a good life for myself and my family." But this rote reply fails to specify what, exactly, that "good life" means to us, let alone what ingredients go into creating the particular one that will best suit the unique needs of our own family. As our media culture endlessly dribbles out values, priorities, and standards, we—like some sort of superabsorbent paper towels—just soak them up. It is easier to pick up what is lying around than to take the time to figure out what it is *we* consider worth caring about.

Whether we intend it or not, the things we do and say, as well as those we choose not to do or say, make clear what we value and what we do not.

But life's big questions aren't big because some celebrated philosopher wrote a book and a publishing company hired a publicist to get the buzz going. They are important because, even without conscious thought on our part, the answers to them help define what our lives are about, and direct the decisions we make every single day. Whether we have consciously thought them through or not, our answers to these questions—in the form of how we live them in our lives—broadcast our core values to the world, and more importantly, to our children.

Whether we intend it or not, the things we do and say, as well as those we choose not to do or say, make clear what we value and what we do not. Do we believe pleasure has a place in our lives? Is love a risk worth taking, even if being open and vulnerable means you might get hurt? Do we believe in charity, even if it requires sacrificing something important—like free time? Do we believe every person is created equal—or do we see those of higher status, lighter skin, greater wealth or talent, or of a particular religion as somehow more better than others?

We parents simply cannot be neutral about values. By acting in a certain way, by saying we approve of this, applaud that, find this idea weird and that one reprehensible, by saying yes to this play date or activity and no to that one, we pass on our values, beliefs, and culture to our children. Not a child alive really listens to what his parents *say;* children watch what we do and come to their own conclusions, accepting or rejecting them based on how well, from the child's perspective, that way of life seems to be working. So the question "What do I believe in?" is not hypothetical; it is the foundation for how we raise our children and what we teach them about life.

Values are everyday matters. Do you give back the dollar of extra change the waitress mistakenly gave you, even if no one has noticed? Do you apologize for yelling at your child? Do you let Daniel have that sleepover, even though he just called his brother a sphincter-hole? Do you remonstrate your own dad for yelling at your daughter, or do you ask *her* to forgive and forget, because right or wrong, we must respect our elders? Actions always speak louder than words.

That's not to suggest that life is a deadly serious business, that both adults and children must be ever on the watch, never able to cut loose and have fun. We adults can no more live our lives as saints than we can ask our children to be angels! Who wants a conscience so severe there is no room for fun?

Our children benefit enormously from seeing a real picture of what a good life looks like—and joy and pleasure are key components. One woman we know, who had a grim upbringing, needed a professional to teach her that life wasn't supposed to be an endless turn on the treadmill, that her whole family would benefit if she started taking time for herself. Aware of the irony in having to learn to have fun, she reports that her life has been transformed by this revelation, and her children are happier, too. Not that they exactly cheer when she heads out the door without them, but they definitely like the more relaxed mom who knows how to laugh and doesn't care so much about the mess.

One New York–area mother structures her life around auditions and rehearsals for her talented 10-year-old son, whose modeling and acting career is ever on the edge of that big break. He has appeared in two national TV commercials and has come close to getting a movie role—but the child is losing interest in his "career" and his mom complains endlessly about the insanity of it all. Still, she urges his agent to keep looking and her son to keep trying, just one more time. "It'll be worth it," she promises him, and herself. Maybe it will. But more likely, it won't.

If all we do is work and act as though life is a serious business indeed, our children will never believe that we see family as a priority. They may not realize that we consider joy integral to a good life. If our most intense efforts go toward manicuring reality so that the world sees only the deceptive, highly polished surface of our lives, our children won't grow up believing that we think truth and honesty are important. If we push them to be better than everyone else, they won't absorb cooperation and caring as values. If we aim always for achievement and act as though acing the upcoming diving competition is the most important goal in sight, they will certainly not consider balance an important human trait.

> As we parents race our families from activity to activity, we should ask ourselves whether we are really doing what is best for our children and ourselves.

As we parents race our families from activity to activity, we should ask ourselves whether we are really doing what is best for our children and ourselves. By doing all these things, are we really providing our children with the sort of childhood we want them to have? Do our actions teach them what we want them to know? What are they learning as they watch us run so fast? We grown-ups don't really have to do all the things we have jotted down in our calendars; it may be that we are running so that we won't have to look hard at our lives. We may fear reflection, shrink from recognizing that our adult lives have become so empty that we are look to our children to give meaning to our existence.

Our achievement-oriented, consumerist culture does not fill our deeper needs. Material goods are like a sugar high—a quick boost with no sustenance at all. As one man, a thrice-divorced member of a phenomenally wealthy family put it, "Without the right relationships, all money does is enable you to be miserable in nicer surroundings."

Most of us try to be decent, kind, and do what is right. We sacrifice a great deal for our families, and are willing to do even more if that is what it takes to make life better for our children. However, despite our best intentions and great sacrifices, sometimes what we do in the short run is not what we, and our children, need in the long run. As parents it is our job to find an ethical road map that our children can follow— a path that eventually will guide them when they come to a fork in the road, when it is unclear which is the right path to take. Relationships, not possessions, make life good. We need stronger connections, more time with our families, not more activities that distract us from what is really important in our lives.

To become independent and successful parents, to give our children the real tools they need to go through life well, to teach them to think *for themselves*, we have to think for ourselves, to decide what life means *for us*. It is not an easy task. Nor is it one that everyone *consciously* chooses to take on. But like it or not, we take on that task every day in the choices we make and the actions we take.

As parents we have to ask what is the right way for us and for our families. What values do we want to impart? How firmly do we want our children to have faith in something they can believe in and value? What are we doing to make the right choices more likely to happen? The goal is not heaven or endless activities to avoid a long stay in pur-gatory. The goal is to be living a life we are involved in passionately, one in which we feel active and alive. It is to be fully involved with our lives so that we make the deep connections with our children that they, and we, need. And out of that, if we are lucky, happiness may emerge.

It may be easier to try and avoid this issue entirely, to bury ourselves in our work, the children's academic life, Little League, piano lessons, and the American Heart Association. Then we can feel we have covered all the bases, including charity. But if we have not ourselves faced the question of what gives our adult lives meaning, we will not be equip-ping our children to face it, either. And they do need a guidebook to help with the hard questions of life, which start out as "What do I do when one of my friends is mean to the other?" and end up far more serious than that.

It isn't difficult, really, to tune in to what we are all hungriest for. But usually it is not what we are working so hard to serve up. Only rarely do epiphanies occur on moonlit mountaintops at midnight—in fact, when they involve how we are living our daily lives, they are as likely to hit us over the head in the kitchen, as the kids are bickering, the phone is beeping, and the casserole bubbling in the microwave has just exploded, and you are already running late for basketball practice, the PTA meeting, or homework. Yes, a major personal crisis—like diagnosis of a serious illness, dissolution of a marriage, or loss of a loved one—can give you cause to reevaluate how you are living. But so, too, can the realization that happiness has eroded, bit by bit, while you have been so busy chasing the American dream.

Let's face it. Most of us who can afford the lifestyle that allows us to hyperparent and overschedule are living lives that are truly charmed. We have everything we really need, and much of what we want. Our children may not be perfect, but most are doing just fine in their lives—performing well enough in school, involved in activities they enjoy, have friends, and have plenty to be happy about. On a given day we may have our complaints, but we already have more than enough of what it takes to live a good

> *In putting a stop to our overscheduling and hyperparenting . . . the resentment that so often characterizes family life today will dissipate.*

life. If you can awaken in a warm, comfortable bed, with a healthy child (or several) asleep a few rooms away, if you have people who love you and a life that sustains it all, aren't you blessed?

In our quest to polish and perfect it all, we lose sight of that essential truth.

Our lives are rich and full. Overfull, in fact. Not satisfied with having 95 percent of what it takes to be happy, too many of us are pushing to get to 110 percent. And it is often that last bit that pushes us over the edge.

If we really learn to know ourselves, we will know when it is time to slow down and where we can safely cut back. We will know what we need and what our children need. If our relationships are sound and solid, we will also know when the scales are well balanced, or tipping too far in one direction. We adults will know how much space we need in our own lives, how much our children need in theirs—and how much space we can afford before the mortgage becomes too large to leave time for the things that matter more.

In knowing ourselves, we will also come to know our children as the people they really are. There is no greater gift or any better parenting advice. In putting a stop to our overscheduling and hyperparenting, in measuring what we value, in making sure that everyone gets enough of what we all need, the resentment that so often characterizes family life today will dissipate. And what a good life that will be—not only for our very lucky, much loved children, but also for us!

∾ *Lesson 53* ∾
Age: All

Ten Ways to Show Gratitude Within the Family

Mimi Doe, M.Ed.
Author of *Busy But Balanced, 10 Principles for Spiritual Parenting—
Nurturing Your Child's Soul* and co-author of *Drawing Angels Near:
Children Tell of Angels in Words and Pictures*

1. Thank your partner for everyday thoughtfulness—in front of your kids.

2. Create a *thanksgiving sheet* to hang on your fridge—a place for the family to jot down their gratitude, from passing a spelling test to sharing life with a warm purring kitty.

3. Begin family dinners by thanking someone at the table for a special kindness he or she has shown you.

4. Start your children on the wonderful habit of looking the person who they are thanking right in the eye.

5. Frequently remind your kids how grateful you are they were born.

6. Thank-you notes never go out of style. Even the youngest child can draw a picture or dictate a note. Remember, thank-you notes don't have to be just for gifts.

7. Begin the magical tradition of a thank-you fairy who leaves little goodies and notes for jobs well done.

8. Go the extra mile to thank the people in your life—from the dry cleaning lady to the guy who bags your groceries. Your kids are watching.

9. Be thankful for your friends and let them know how you feel. Ask your kids to take some time to appreciate their friends.

10. Thank God, or whatever your family calls the source of your being, right out loud when you are moved to do so. "Thank you, God, for this glorious morning."

Excerpt From:

How to Talk to Your Kids About Really Important Things

Charles E. Schaefer, Ph.D., and Theresa Foy DiGeronimo, M.Ed.

Authors of *How to Talk to Your Kids About Really Important Things*
and *How to Talk to Teens About Really Important Things.*

What your children don't know *can* hurt them. They want to know about birth, death, and everything in between—and, eventually, they will find the answers to all their questions—but who will tell them? If you want to be your children's primary source of information, let them know that right from the start by talking to them openly, matter-of-factly, and honestly about the many issues that are important in their lives.

Starting today, strive to be an "askable" parent—that is, someone your children feel will not judge, tease, or punish them for asking questions. As an askable parent, you will respond to your children's often unending list of questions with words and actions that say, "I'm so glad you asked." This attitude will let your children know that you are open to talking about the things that are important to them, even sensitive or embarrassing subjects. Children

Be forthright about what you know and honest about what you don't know.

are very intuitive about this. If you avoid talking about emotionally sensitive topics—like death, adoption, or an alcoholic parent—they learn to keep their concerns to themselves. If you ignore "embarrassing" issues—like pornography, homosexuality, and masturbation—your children will get their information (or misinformation) from someone else. If you slight the importance of such life experiences as moving to a new home, starting school, or staying at the hospital, your children will assume you just don't understand their fears. Every one of these life experiences and issues offers you opportunities for talking to your children.

In fact, open communication is the most valuable parenting tool you have during this time when your children are developing the foundation for basic beliefs, values, and attitudes, so use it wisely. Remember: The *way* you talk to your kids is just as important as what you say. Keep the following communication tips in mind the next time you sit down to talk to your child:

1. *Know what you're talking about.* To be effective in giving advice or counsel, you have to establish yourself in the eyes of your child as an expert on the subject. So before offering advice on a topic such as sex or alcoholism, you should read up on these topics. Your opinion will be more credible if you offer supporting evidence instead of just stating your view.

2. *Be trustworthy.* Be forthright about what you know and honest about what you don't know. Avoid exaggerating the truth to make an impression or distorting the truth to spare your child or yourself discomfort. Let your children learn that they can trust what you tell them.

3. *Be brief.* Don't beat around the bush; get right to the point. You will keep your child's attention and respect if you can avoid the tendency to give a lecture or a lengthy, involved argument.

4. *Be clear.* Use simple, concrete language geared to your child's level of development.

5. *Respect your child's view.* Ask your children what they think about issues rather than just telling them what to do or think. Remember to listen to and respect children's opinions so that you talk with them rather than at them. Respect also involves giving children reasons for behaving in a certain way. Reasons help develop a child's thinking powers and independence of judgment.

There's no doubt that talking to kids can sometimes be difficult, awkward, and even frustrating, but the end result is well worth the effort. If you can talk to your kids often and openly about any subject in the world, they'll quickly learn that they can trust you with their secrets and fears. As your children grow, this trust will enrich your relationship and encourage them to look to you, not the streets, for the information they need to stay safe and healthy.

Encourage Your Loved Ones

Judy Ford, M.S.W.

Author of *Wonderful Ways to Love a Child*, *Wonderful Ways to Love a Teen: Even When It Seems Impossible*, *Wonderful Ways to Be a Family*, *Wonderful Ways to Be a Stepparent*, and *Wonderful Ways to Love a Grandchild*

We all need encouragement—you do, and so do your husband and your children. In some ways, we're all helpless people trying to cope in a complex world. The rules change practically every day and it's hard to keep up. In this nine-to-five society full of daily frustrations, we need all the support and encouragement we can get.

As a family therapist, I frequently see husbands and wives, mothers and fathers who do the opposite—they discourage each other. They blame and find fault—sometimes in small and subtle ways. Here are two examples:

> *Clara signed up for a cake-decorating class and told her husband, Eric, that she hoped to open a small bakery some-day. Eric put a damper on her enthusiasm saying, "You don't know anything about business."*
>
> *Ten-year-old Nick told his mom, "I want to be an astro-naut." She warned him, "There aren't that many jobs for astronauts."*

Unfortunately, these small and subtle ways of discouraging each other add up and are ultimately lethal to thriving relationships and families.

Regardless of our age, we all have aspirations, wishes, hopes, secret longings, and ambitions. When you're beloved shares an innermost desire or a wish with you, he or she is revealing a vulnerable, private, personal side. By trusting each other with these precious aspirations, you're creating togetherness. It's through self-revelation that you grow closer.

If your spouse or your child has a dream, tell them it's a wonderful dream.

If your loved one—be it your spouse or your child—has a dream, tell them it's a wonderful dream. Whatever they try to do, stand behind them. Let them know you believe they can accomplish their goal by saying, "I think you can do it." Don't knock down their aspirations by pointing out all the roadblocks. Whatever they want to do, encourage them to go for it. Acknowledge their accomplishments, however small.

We all have more talents than we're using, so try to see what talents your children have and tell them about their talents. Don't push them, though, and be honest. Everyone is gifted in some way. When you acknowledge how special your children are, you help them see their gifts and they feel loved by you. Their inadequacies are relatively unim-portant. What is most important to your relationship is how special they are to you.

∽ *Lesson 56* ∽
Age: All

"What Do You Say?"

Sandra E. Lamb
Author of *How to Write It: A Complete Guide to Everything You'll Ever Write*

Raising thankful children has, perhaps, never been so difficult. Or so important. And how key is teaching thankfulness to helping children develop an appreciation for others, and their contributions? It's essential, and it's pivotal.

Welcome to the new—and old—civility!

You may even be able to hear the echo of your mother's voice playing that refrain in the back of your brain: "What do you say?" Or, maybe your grandmother. And you'll probably also remember that it didn't always number among your "Top Ten" desired tunes.

But you may also remember how your mother and/or your grandmother carried out their social duties in acts of graciousness such as

268

RSVPing and writing thank-you notes. Acts that kept them connected; acts that strengthened social bonds; acts that even made the world a little better place and the hearts of others just a little happier.

Yes, that's right, writing thank-you notes. It is a way of telling others that you value their efforts, you desire their company, and you number them among your friends.

It's often been said that George Bush, the first Bush president, paved his way to the White House by his attention and care to the business of writing personal notes. Ronald Reagan, too, often recorded his appreciation of people and deeds. And some of those personal Reagan essays are now causing former Reagan detractors to even reevaluate the "Reagan mind" and Reagan's contribution to history.

But, of course, the best way to teach (here's your grandmother's voice again) is by example. When last did your child see you sit down and write a thank-you note for a gift given to you, or for an act of kindness? How about a note for no particular reason at all, other than the fact that you appreciated a job well done and the person who did it? If you're like most parents today, your child may never have seen you do this. But it offers the best opportunity to talk positively about what our values are concerning the character and acts of others, and it allows us to teach by example how we should and can express our appreciation.

Here are some simple and easy ways to ensure that this task becomes an integral part of your life, and therefore what you teach your child:

- Be prepared. Keep your own supply of personal notes ready.
- Do it immediately. And engage your children when you do it, and tell them when and how they can.
- When your child, for example, is invited to a birthday party, you can increase the value of the festivities and the anticipation. Have your child select a note card and address an envelope before leaving home.
- Write the thank-you note immediately upon returning. This can be coupled with talking about the party and sharing the experience together.
- When your child has received a gift, use the same approach. Allow

him to decide how the thank-you will be written. For the very young child, he may dictate and you can write. Maybe a finger-painted picture or a photo of him using the gift can be used to create a thank-you card to Grandma and Grandpa.

If your child is stuck, do the following:

• Ask, "What do you like about this gift?" (There's something, even if it's the color. This will get the process started. You may have to ask the second question of "How can you use the gift?")
• Help your child connect himself to the gift in his note.
• Connect the gift and appreciation back to the giver.

Here's a simple thank-you that Jack sent to his grandmother for a pair of mittens:

> *Dear Gram:*
>
> *Thank you for the red mittens. I like red, and they go great with my blue-and-red ski jacket. Here's a picture of me skiing with them on. I wore them today because we went to Keystone for my birthday. They kept my fingers nice and warm, even when my feet got cold.*
>
> *It looks like you didn't make any mistakes in knitting.*
>
> *I love you and Grandpa,*
Jack

Being thankful—from the smallest acts to the really important acts—will ensure a grateful child and will also enforce the concept of how good it feels to be a giving person.

∽ *Lesson 57* ∼
Age: Toddlers to Teens

Little Things Long Remembered

or Filling Your Child's Memory Bank

Susan Newman, Ph.D.

Author of *Parenting An Only Child: The Joys & Challenges of Raising Your One & Only*; *Never Say Yes to a Stranger: What Your Child Must Know to Stay Safe*; a gift book series: *Little Things Long Remembered: Making Your Children Feel Special Every Day*; and *Little Things Mean a Lot: Creating Happy Memories with Your Grandchildren*

The time and know-how to create positive memories can easily escape today's harried parents whether or not they work. No matter how little time you have left after carpooling, running errands, or attending your child's events, you can fill it with realistic, simple, and fun gestures and activities that strengthen family ties and fill your child's memory bank.

By grabbing pockets of time, if only a few minutes with your child each day, you can build tradition and your child's strong feelings of being cared for and loved. What is second nature to some parents never occurs to others—and we all need reminders now and again.

As my *Parent School* lesson, I would like to share fifteen doable ways for overextended parents to connect with their children quickly and effectively—and to stay connected:

- Ask caring questions each day: How was your spelling test? The book fair? The game?

- Tell your child you love him a minimum of once a day.

- Wear whatever "jewels" your child makes or buys for you. Display her artwork; use her clay vases and bowls.

- Get excited when your child tells you about his day or latest accomplishment. Nodding your head is not enough.

- Request a "kid fix" (a hefty hug and kiss) whenever you feel the need, and let your child know it makes you feel better.

- If you're out for the evening, call in a good-night kiss and promise an in-person one as soon as you return.

- Sing while she plays; play while she sings or dances. Duets are very supportive, often memorable, and usually hilarious.

- Use the mail to surprise your child with a comic book, a sports player's card, or a fancy pencil. Send an e-mail card if he has his own e-mail address.

- Ask your child what was the best and worst part of her day—every day.

- Put a note in her lunch box that says, "I love you."

- Keep a chair next to your desk so that your child can visit or chat.

• Ask about your child's friends regularly.

• Prepare the grocery list together; ask your child for dinner suggestions.

• Compliment your child and let her overhear you complimenting her to someone else—for example, a relative or friend.

• Do something ridiculous: Chase your child through the house or start a pillow fight.

You never know what silliness or gesture will become a little thing long remembered—embedded warmly and happily in a child's mind forever. Simple acts, more than expensive gifts, have a way of becoming treasured remembrances of growing up—and of you. Little things do mean a lot, especially to children.

Raising a Giving Child

Jackie Waldman

Co-author of *The Courage to Give, Teachers with the Courage to Give, Teens with the Courage to Give, and Amierca, September 11th: The Courage to Give*

The courage to give is the courage to first give to ourselves so that we can know who we are, what we want in life, and what we have to offer to the world.

Below are four descriptions of giving styles. See if you can find one that best fits you and one that best fits your child:

1. *I'm easygoing and make things fun.* Instead of planning, I act on a moment's notice. I may not like routine. I love action. Instead of long explanations, I like to make things happen. I love to make an impact and do the unpredictable. I live for this moment. I am great at finding a way to do things. I am best at jumping right in and solving a problem, without needing a long thought process. I want variety in my life, because I get bored easily.

2. *I'm practical, orderly, and dependable.* I am responsible, work hard,

and stay organized. I like to follow rules. I love family and tradition. I like a structured environment. I am loyal and trustworthy. Others know they can count on me to help out wherever I can. I want to feel needed and I want to be appreciated.

3. *I enjoy theories and ideas.* I love to research to find answers. I'm independent and curious. I'm philosophical. I see the big picture. I love a challenge. I have very strong interests. I love to discuss ideas rather than engage in small talk. I want to use my intelligence to analyze a situation and consider new possibilities.

4. *I want to help create peace and harmony.* I'm always trying to do something nice for someone else. I'm encouraging, motivating, and empathetic. I am always working for a greater good for our world. People and relationships are the most important part of my life.

Once parents and children know which giving style applies to them, a family can use those styles to grow and learn together by giving back to their community.

Parents teach best by example. A parent can set good examples for their children by going together to a shelter to volunteer. Each member of the family can help out at the shelter by doing what he or she does best. If one child likes to organize, you can suggest that he look around to see what may need organizing. Or even find some books for him to alphabetize. If another child likes other children, you can get a group of kids together to play games. This will help increase your children's self worth and, at the same time, allow them to feel good about themselves because they are giving to the community.

It's important to recognize your children's ability and giving style and match it with things they can do. They will learn generosity while enjoying their task.

In this example, not only will the family impact the shelter and the people needing their help, but they will impact themselves. Giving together outside of the home creates small miracles—improved communication, a new perception of each other, gratitude, improved relationships, and a new respect for each other's uniqueness.

When siblings observe each other being kind and sharing their unique qualities, they will come away from the experience with a greater appreciation for each other.

For our children to learn how to give from their hearts—no matter what—is every parent's hope. When a family finds their courage to give—their courage to step out of their comfort zone or their danger zone—and step into the lives of each other and strangers in the community, doing what each enjoys and sharing it, love radiates.

⤳ *Lesson 59* ⤳
Age: Toddlers to Young Children

Building Empathy in the Preschool Years

Myrna B. Shure, Ph.D.

Author and co-author of *I Can Problem Solve, Raising a Thinking Child, Raising a Thinking Child Workbook,* and *Raising a Thinking Preteen*

I recently read in the newspaper about a seventh-grader who exclaimed, "I won't steal anymore 'cause I don't want to get caught." Her parents were ecstatic. So was her teacher. I was not.

Why not? The girl won't steal anymore. Isn't that what we want? Only partly. I believe that the girl's parents and teacher were focusing on the wrong half of the sentence. If this girl could figure out a way to not get caught, would she still refrain from stealing?

What this girl and others like her really need is a sense of empathy—a genuine desire to not want to hurt other people not out of fear of punishment but out of an inner feeling of another's pain.

How early can a child feel empathy? Research has shown that this is possible as early as age 2—perhaps even younger. And my own research over the past 30 years has shown that children can also think (or learn to think) of different ways to meet their needs and to resolve conflicts that come up with others as early as age 4.

How can parents help their children beginning in the preschool years to develop empathy and to make good decisions in light of what might happen when they do what they do? To a 4-year-old, a very important problem is wanting a toy another child has. We can help children this young think about what might happen next if they grab the toy or hit the child.

Before children can genuinely care about others, they have to first care about themselves.

We can also help them think about how what they do affects their own and others' feelings, such as, "He'll be mad if I hit him," or, "I'll feel bad if he cries."

Children can think of other ways to solve the problem, such as, "I can let him play with my toy," "I can let him play for a little while," or, "I can tell him I'll be his friend."

Before children can genuinely care about others, they have to first care about themselves. I once talked with Gary, a 4-year-old boy who hit his younger brother to get his truck. When I asked him what happened when he did that, he told me, "He hit me back, but I don't care. I got the truck." If Gary truly didn't care or could endure his own pain (however temporary), how could he care about or feel the pain of others—now, or later in life?

For my *Parent School* lesson, I have likened the way we talk to our kids when they do things we don't want them to do to the rungs of a ladder, with the goal being to climb to the top—to the problem-solving rung. Using our example of one child wanting a toy another child has, we can contrast each style of talk and how each style might affect children's ability to think about the problem and how they solve it.

The Ladder

Rung 1: Power Assertion

Power assertion includes negative punishments such as frequent spanking, commands, demands, and threats: "If you two can't share the toy, I'll put it away and neither of you can will it!" or "How many times do I have to tell you to share your toys!"

I have also placed a time-out on Rung 1 of my ladder. Time-out? When used as a cooling-down period, time-outs can be helpful. But as is often the case, children are sent to the time-out chair in front of their brothers and sisters, making them feel humiliated. They build up more anger, and if they are thinking at all, it may be about how to get revenge with the sibling who got them into trouble in the first place! The children fighting over the toy are separated from the toy and from each other. What are they learning? What are they thinking? What will they do the next time they want to play with the same toy at the same time?

Here are some possibilities:

- They might stop hitting their brother or sister to avoid being spanked, yelled at, or sent to a time-out.
- They might feel anger and frustration and take it out on a peer at school.
- They might, like Gary, become altogether immune to their own pain and use aggressive means to end up with what they want.

Rung 2: Positive Alternatives

This approach focuses on telling children what *to do* instead of what not to do. If, for example, one child starts hitting his brother or grabs the toy, a parent might say, "Ask for what you want." Although this approach is more positive than the power approach, it is still doing the thinking for the child. Here are some possibilities for the impact of this approach:

- The child may not know what to do the next time the same problem comes up if the solution given to him by his parents does not work.

• The child may become dependent upon others to get her out of situations that may become overwhelming for her.

Rung 3: Reasoning and Explaining

Behind this approach is the belief that if children understand why they shouldn't be doing what they do, such as "You will hurt your brother if you hit him," "The toy might break if you grab it," "Your brother doesn't like to be hit," or even the popular "I" message, "I feel angry when you hit your brother," they will feel guilt and will inhibit these kinds of behaviors. I have learned that these kinds of explanations and reasons are important for children 2 to 3 years old. But by the time they are 4, most children have heard these explanations a thousand times, and the thousandth and first time likely won't make any more difference. In fact, here is what could really happen:

• The child may tune out because you're telling him what he already knows.
• You become exasperated and angrier because you're thinking *My child never listens to me.*

Rung 4: Problem Solving

This approach turns statements, including suggestions and explanations, into questions that involve children in the process of thinking about what they're doing. This includes the impact of their own and others' feelings, potential consequences, and, if needed, alternative solutions. Now when your child grabs a toy from his brother, you can ask:

• What happened? What's the problem?
  (Child tells you his view of the problem)
• How did your brother feel when you hit him?
  (Guides child to think of his brother's feelings)
• What happened next?
  (Guides child to think of consequences of his actions)

- How did you feel about that?
  (Child thinks about his own feelings)
- Can you think of a different way to solve this problem so that you both won't feel that way and that won't happen?
  (Child thinks of alternative solution to the problem)

One problem-solving mom talked with her 4-year-old son, who grabbed his toy from his friend, this way:

Mom: *Peter, what happened? What's the problem?*
Peter: *He's got my truck. He won't give it back.*
Mom: *Why do you have to have it back now?*
Peter: *'Cause he's had a long turn.*

Had this mom demanded, or suggested, he share his truck, she could not have learned that, from her son's point of view, he had *already* shared his toy. Now the problem shifted from Peter's grabbing to how he could get his toy back.

She asked him how he and his friend felt, and what happened next. Based on what he said, she then asked, "Can you think of a different way to get your truck back so that you both won't be mad and you won't fight?"

Peter thought for a moment, and said, "I could let him play with my new video game."

Instead of feeling angry and frustrated, Peter felt proud. He was able, and free, to think for himself. If Peter's parents continue to talk to him the problem-solving way, in the future it won't be fear of getting caught that will keep him from stealing or otherwise upsetting others. He will grow up as a thinking and feeling human being who won't want to hurt other people. It will come from within.

Always Make the Highest Choice

Judy Ford, LCSW

Author of *Wonderful Ways to Love a Child*, *Wonderful Ways to Love a Teen: Even When It Seems Impossible*, *Wonderful Ways to Be a Family*, *Wonderful Ways to Be a Stepparent*, and *Wonderful Ways to Love a Grandchild*

> "A harmonious family is possible. It should be your goal, because it provides the best opportunity for everyone to grow."
>
> —*Judy Ford*

If you're an adult, you have a sacred covenant to the wonderful family of human beings—the family to which we all belong—to make the highest choice and to ceaselessly do the right thing. It's a sacred obligation that comes with being human.

In order to make the highest choice and do the right thing, it's imperative that you understand the dynamic of ambivalence.

Ambivalence is defined as the coexistence of opposing attitudes or feelings, such as love and hate, toward a person, an object, or an idea.

Ambivalence is part of our inner makeup—meaning we all can feel contrasting feelings at the same time. For example, you can like your mother one minute and hate her the next. You can adore your husband yet get so mad at him that you wonder why you married him in the first place. You can cherish your baby with all your heart yet in a moment of frustration come very close to shaking her.

By recognizing ambivalent feelings, instead of building a case against them, you're better prepared to make the highest choice and do the right thing.

Ambivalence is a fact of life. It resides in you and in your children. You can feel two ways about the people you love. You can love them and dislike them. You can feel admiration for your sister's success and jealous that you haven't made it yet. You can be devoted to your friend and secretly hold hostility.

If you aren't aware of these double sets of feelings, you're likely to be mixed up, messed up, confused, and not sure what to do when you and your mom, or you and your husband, don't see eye to eye. By recognizing ambivalent feelings, instead of building a case against them, you're better prepared to make the highest choice and do the right thing. You have free will to act.

People who aren't comfortable with their own ambivalent feelings get intrigued by them. It's like this: If I were to point and tell you, "Don't look over there," you'd be really tempted—in fact, you might become obsessed. Likewise, if I say, "Don't be mad," you might not be able to get over it. But if I said it's okay to look, it's okay to feel, you are free to choose how long to look and what action to take.

In confusing situations, becoming aware of your ambivalence helps you choose the right thing. Jason was thinking about quitting the team.

His dad said, "You feel two ways about your coach—you like him and you dislike him. You want to quit the team because you don't like the way the coach yells, but you want to stay on the team because you like your teammates and the coach lets you pitch." After Jason said all that he had to say, his dad asked, "What do you think is the right thing to do?" Jason said, "Stay on the team," and that's exactly what he did.

When you're confused and not sure what to do, ask yourself, *What is my highest choice?* Get in the habit of asking, *In this situation what is the right thing to do?* Your immediate family, your extended family, your innocent children and pets are counting on you to make the highest choice and do the right thing.

Parenting Kids with Labels

"The labels A.D.D. and A.D.H.D., especially the latter hyperactive variety, are considered by many pediatricians and child development specialists to be a diagnostic wastebasket."

–*Eli H. Newberger, M.D.*
from The Men They Will Become:
The Nature and Nurture of Male Character

"Children can recover from many problems of motor, cognitive, or emotional development. The earlier these are identified, and appropriate ways to support and compensate are found, the better the outcome. It is therefore very important to seek help when you are worried."

—*T. Berry Brazelton, M.D.*
from Touchpoints

"A wise person knows that to label a person is to disable him. This applies especially in the case of young children, whose minds are like wet cement. The diagnosis may become the disease. A child may often live up to his parent or teacher's negative prediction."

—*Azriel Winnett*
Author of the popular ezine Effective
Communication *(azriel.hodu.com)*

Great Expectations: The Only Child

Susan Newman, Ph.D.

Author of *Parenting An Only Child: The Joys & Challenges of Raising Your One &
Only*; *Never Say Yes to a Stranger: What Your Child Must Know to Stay Safe*; a gift
book series: *Little Things Long Remembered: Making Your Children Feel Special
Every Day*; and *Little Things Mean a Lot: Creating Happy Memories with Your
Grandchildren*

Families are getting smaller, giving parents more time to devote to
each child. As a result, parents today all seem to be pushing for
"star" children. Children would benefit if parents could temper their
dreams. In parents of only children, the tendency to want their children to excel can be so focused that it becomes counterproductive.
This information adapted from *Parenting an Only Child: The Joys &
Challenges of Raising Your One & Only* also offers helpful suggestions
for parents of more than one.

Parents have fantasies about babies before they are born. While the fetus moves about in the womb, parents make predictions: "This will be a very active baby; this one's going to be an athlete." As years pass, the fantasies change form. With an only child there is almost always a level of expectation that is too high. No matter how much you restrain it, it's there. If you're honest with yourself, you'll recognize it, as will your child at a very young age.

Chances are your only child will do well in one or more areas because of the special opportunities and attention that "onliness" affords. Only children show up with more frequency among leaders; they are intellectually advantaged and socially well adjusted. There's no need to turn child rearing into a competition in which your child must be the best academically, best athletically, best dressed, best all-'round camper. You will gain endless

> *If expectations are too high, the child's self-confidence may be undermined.*

rewards from your child in respect, love, and consideration if you delight in her accomplishments and minimize her shortcomings as they surface. Forget the presidency. It's one of countless options open to the only child.

Everyone, including a child, needs something to strive for. When goals are attained, self-esteem is enhanced. But, if expectations are too high, the child's self-confidence may be undermined when she cannot reach parental goals, and her desire to succeed may vanish. Only children expend great amounts of effort and energy to satisfy their parents. "Onlies" can be very hard on themselves and rarely need additional pressure from their parents. Andrea Balfour endured the pressure for years before she got out from under it. In grade school, she recalls, "Once I asked my father to listen to a poem that I had to memorize for a class. The first time I went to him, I really didn't know it, and he told me not to come back until I had it perfect. Only perfection was allowed. I performed perfectly until I left Tennessee to go to college. I almost flunked out after my first semester. Away from the constant observation of my parents, I felt free. I wanted to have fun, and I did."

By age 16, Jennifer Walsh's parental expectations were absorbed into her personality. "Ever since I was very young, I have always been in the top classes and involved in so many activities that I can't stop now. Even if I was under a lot of pressure, I couldn't stop, because that is the kind of person most people know me to be. Half of what I do is for myself; half is for my parents. I don't want to let them down, and I don't really think I want to break out of that mold." When asked if she thought they would love her any less, she hesitated before responding, and then said, "I suppose they wouldn't, but they would be disappointed, very disappointed."

Doing one's best does not seem to be good enough for many parents of onlies. One child only recalls never living up to his parents' ideal: "If I got a 98, they said, 'Why didn't you get a 100?' When the basketball team didn't win, my father said, 'Why didn't you get the extra point?' They demanded an improved performance for everything. I was not permitted any mistakes in any area."

Warnings Signs: Too Much Pressure

Overemphasis on excellence is easy to spot in the school-age child. You can tell you are being too demanding when your child begins to turn to your spouse on a regular basis for entertainment, consolation, or affection. A young child will walk away from the parent who insists that a dive be executed precisely or a book be read without errors. She will march to the parent who accepts her skills at her level.

A drop in the quality of schoolwork, extreme sensitivity to mild or constructive criticism, and a lowering of his own standards are also indicative of an overstressed child. If he feels—or says—he's lazy or dumb, if he appears to have stopped trying, you may be driving him too hard, expecting too much.

If this happens, pull back. Join forces with your spouse or significant other to start fresh and ease up. Block time so that the three of you can be together doing something enjoyable or sharing a task (work in the garden, clean a closet, paint a room or piece of furniture) to remove the focus from whether your child is doing well.

Look at Your Child Realistically

Make an honest evaluation of your child's talents and abilities, then offer opportunities to expand her strengths. If she's only a mediocre gymnast and she says she doesn't like it, let her stop training. Take your child's age and developmental level into account. Your 5-year-old probably doesn't have the muscular development and coordination to swim a perfect crawl—wait until she's older before you critique her strokes. She still has plenty of time to make the Olympic team. If you must address failures, do so in relationship to successes, emphasizing the latter.

Look at Yourself

Parents impose unrealistic expectations on their children for various reasons. Parents face their own childhood when they watch their children grow, and in doing so, they want their children to have the successes that eluded them in childhood. Evelyn Hanna spent long periods of time agonizing before she understood. "The first blow came when my son entered second grade. The teacher put him in the slowest reading group. I was sure she had made a mistake and insisted that Neil be retested. I had convinced myself that he was going to outshine anything I had ever accomplished in school. In my head he was going to be the academic fireball I had dreamed of being. With the help of the school principal, I learned to focus on his positive attrib-

There is a pronounced tendency on the part of the parents of only children to take responsibility for how a child turns out instead of accepting that that's how the child is.

utes—his popularity, his athletic abilities and warm personality. Those should have been enough for me from the beginning."

There is also a pronounced tendency on the part of the parents of only children to take responsibility for how a child turns out instead of accepting that that's how the child is. "She's not reading because I didn't spend time with her each evening teaching her the sight words." "He's not slamming the ball out of the park because I didn't have batting practice in the backyard twice a week." "If I had taken him to visit the Stock Exchange or to the bank with me more often, he would have been a financier."

Easing Up/Backing Off

Pressure intensifies when both parents excel because the parents, not siblings, are the only child's performance models. To ease the burden of living up to your level, make it clear that your child should make his own path by choosing something that particularly interests him. Tell him you understand that his choice may be quite different from yours. When you don't explicitly give a child room to be himself, the situation can appear hopeless and impossible to the child.

You can't help but have high hopes for your only child, but they can be tempered. Try to be very low-key and quiet about your aspirations. One school-age child talks about his parents' prudence: "My parents expect me to get good grades, but they realize that I'm not an Albert Einstein. As long as I maintain B's, they're pretty happy." Whether or not your child excels academically, she probably has strengths you can encourage and in which you can take pride. Being proud is very different from living vicariously through your child. Being a role model by expressing contentment with your own pursuits is more effective than expressing your hopes for your child or being a tough taskmaster. Demanding performance from a child who may not be capable of meeting your expectation or may not be interested in it is frustrating for everyone and could create a backlash whose effect might not be seen for years.

Parents of onlies would be wise to have other activities and interests so that there is less time to focus on every inch of their singleton's progress. It's a step in the right direction just to be aware that putting all your energy into your child may not be the best thing for her.

Understanding and Coping with ADD/ADHD

David Nylund

Author of *Treating Huckleberry Finn: A New Narrative Approach to Working with
Kids Diagnosed ADD/ADHD*

My comments will be directed to parents of children and adolescents with emotional and behavioral problems. During the past decade, our psychiatrists, psychologists, therapists, teachers, and even friends, family, and neighbors have been captured by a fascination with medical diagnoses. Increasingly, problems are described with medical labels and treated with medication. Currently, the most popular childhood diagnosis is ADHD (attention-deficit hyperactivity disorder).

I understand the popularity of this diagnosis. Parents and kids struggle with extremely hard problems and are frequently subjected to intense pressure from schools, physicians, friends, and family to consider ADHD as the explanation. Many children and parents experience a diagnosis of ADHD as having a very positive influence or turning point in their lives. Being diagnosed with ADHD means that your child has a so-called biological problem and can receive specialized medical treatment—stimulant medication treatment (Ritalin). Parents do not have to blame themselves for their child's medical condition. This is welcome relief for parents who have been feeling guilty for their kids' problems. Plus, some people find taking the medication helpful.

However, I have concerns when parents uncritically accept the notion that ADHD is a medically proven fact. It is my opinion that consensus has created the label ADHD, not science. In fact, no medical researcher or geneticist has proven that ADHD has a biological basis. The limited medical evidence that does exist has been hotly contested. Believing that children need special treatment interventions for ADHD blinds parents to their own long histories of parenting abilities, resources, and knowledge. Parents can get duped into thinking that they do not have the skills to parent children with special needs and must submit to the so-called experts. If there had been no invention of ADHD, would parents be hampered in helping children overcome problems? My hypothesis is no.

If there had been no invention of ADHD, would parents be hampered in helping children overcome problems? My hypothesis is no.

In addition, ADHD is a psychiatric label, which can have a totalizing and negative effect on the child. Many children who are labeled ADHD believe they are sick or stupid. Kids who are labeled often make excuses that inhibit them. Parents and teachers can easily get recruited into focusing on deficits. The ADHD label can limit the range of possibilities and options that people might otherwise have available. Deficit descriptions can often make the problem worse by magnifying it so that the situation seems hopeless. As family therapist Linda Metcalf, author of *Parenting Towards Solutions*, says, a diagnosis often becomes a "barbed-wire fence" that keeps kids and parents "stuck."

So what's a parent to do? Challenging the biological basis of ADHD does not mean that problems don't exist. Parents, teachers, siblings, and caretakers can feel overwhelmed with such problems as hyperactivity, aggression, and impulsivity. In my book *Treating Huckleberry Finn*, I describe an approach to thinking about and working with problems such as hyperactivity, aggression, and impulsivity. The approach is useful to parents, teachers, therapists, and even people who are committed to the existence of the ADHD diagnosis. My central thesis is that the ADHD diagnosis and Ritalin treatment paint an incomplete picture of children. To treat the whole child, I think the first thing parents can do is place the ADHD diagnosis in a context. When you place the problem in a broader sociocultural context, you realize that ADHD is more of a cultural problem than a disease that exists in your child's brain. Here are some of the contextual factors:

- *The increasing power and influence of pharmaceutical companies.* In fact, use of Ritalin has increased 700 percent since 1990. There is now a whole industry centered on ADHD, and many people profit from the popularity of the diagnosis.

- *The awareness that some children, particularly boys, are vulnerable to reproducing violence and aggression.* This reproduction may be due to learning men's ways of being, rather than some chemical imbalance or genetic imbalance.

- *The realization that many kids experience emotional distress through behavior.* Problems such as hyperactivity and inattention may be due to underlying stressors and environmental factors (such as trauma, abuse, divorce, poverty, racism, etc.)

- *The knowledge that we are living in a short-attention-span culture where media images, video games, and music videos are increasingly quicker and quicker paced.* Given that kids today are raised on TV, computer games, and the Internet, no wonder there has been an increase in ADHD diagnoses! Furthermore, society as a whole is increasingly hectic, stressful, and fast paced. People are working longer hours and are busier, leaving less time for rest, relaxation, conversations, and relationships. ADHD-like symptoms in widespread numbers may represent less a medical disorder than the natural consequence of our kids' brains adjusting to rapid-fire culture and a short-attention-span media.

• *The recent changes in the educational system including oversized classrooms, decreased funding for special programs, and increased emphasis on standardized testing.* Teachers are increasingly teaching for high test scores. The standard method of teaching is very linear and privileges rote memorization, categorizing, worksheets, and extensive homework. This standardization of teaching is based on the idea that students need to master the requirements and skills to become successful in corporate America and the global economy. Made over in the interest and the values of corporate culture (commercialization, technical job skills, and materialism), schools are no longer valued as a public good that teach kids about social responsibility or democratic life. Rather, schools are now informed by values that are consistent with the market economy.

With the increased trend toward homogeneity, children who learn through more creative and alternative methods are left behind. Many of these kids are not engaged or interested in this mechanical and market-driven learning process. Rather, these children learn through a more active, nonlinear, and multisensory manner. When not engaging their abilities, multiple intelligences, and creative knowledge, children are likely to be inattentive or hyper—and more likely to earn an ADHD or learning disorder label.

Imagine how Huck Finn or Thomas Edison would have managed in today's school? I believe they would have been extremely bored. Unfortunately, they probably would have been written off by the school system as underachievers and school failures. Moreover, they most likely would have been labeled ADHD for not fitting into the current-one-size-fits-all educational program. And many other creative people have possessed an ability—artistic, musical, literary, or scientific—that would be seen as irrelevant in today's school setting. Some of these influential people include Henry Ford, Agatha Christie, Maya Angelou, Pablo Picasso, and Leonardo da Vinci. What would have happened if any of these great people would have been labeled with a disease such as ADHD?

Imagine how Huck Finn or Thomas Edison would have managed in today's school? . . . They most likely would have been labeled ADHD.

Once ADHD is located in a broader context, creative solutions become available to parents of ADHD kids. For example, I think it is possible to assess and name your child's learning difficulties without labeling or inventing new deficit-based categories. And, if you choose to take your child to a psychiatrist or therapist, make sure that the professional is collaborative and strengths-based. Here are some

practical solutions:

• Remember who your child is apart from the ADHD label. What are your child's skills and talents?

• Avoid making excuses for your ADHD child.

• Do not view ADHD as an illness or disease that exists in your child's brain. Rather, view ADHD as something separate from your child that has effects on your child. ADHD is the problem, not your child.

• Look for times when your child is successful over the problem. Create a context for recognition for success and achievement. Do not accept the fact that your ADHD child will have to settle for less in life.

• Help create a slower pace of life for you and your family that will hopefully transform your child's exposure to rapid-fire culture and high-paced media images. Watch less TV and encourage your child to cut back on video games and other high-paced imagery.

• Help identify and nurture your child's unique learning styles. Once your child has discovered his own distinct learning style, he will become engaged in the learning process. When engaged in a learning process that celebrates his own learning styles, he will become more attentive and less ADHD-like. Advocate for your child in his school. Encourage schools to look beyond a standardized and deficit approach to education and embrace a more holistic view of the student—one that includes teaching to individual learning styles and multiple intelligences.

• If your child takes medication, give her credit for contributing to the success.

In summary, be suspicious of labels. Overcome the cynicism of the ADHD model and embrace a more hopeful stance. Trust in your own expertise as a parent. Provide an environment in which your child can solve his or her own problems. This means identifying exceptions to problems and stimulating a new view of the problem. By doing so, you will help nurture your child's special abilities and talents. When children have access to their unique capabilities, problems such as ADHD lose their strength.

～ *Lesson 63* ～
Age: All

A Wonderful Parent

Karyn Seroussi
Author of *Unraveling the Mystery of Autism and PDD:*
A Mother's Story of Research and Recovery

When I was 15, I was the most popular babysitter on my street. I could get rowdy triplets to bed in 10 minutes flat. To a healthy teenager who cared for small children only one night a week, the recipe for success was simple: Treat them like great kids. Expect them to be their very best. Be sure there is no payoff for a lack of cooperation or negative behavior. Even when being firm, be playful—a little humor goes a long way. Kids are eager to please if you can make them laugh.

I was confident that I would, one day, be a wonderful parent.

Skip ahead 10 years, to 3 weeks *after* I became a mommy, during a horrible afternoon when my colicky daughter wouldn't let me put her down, and wouldn't stop screaming and fussing. I had slept perhaps 4 hours in the previous 2 days. I stood at the top of the stairs and thought, *If I just chuck her down these stairs I can go to bed and get some sleep.* This was immediately followed by abject horror that I could think such a thing, and relief that I wasn't so far gone as to act on such a dreadful thought. Then I had another realization: *When a person is pushed to the limits of her endurance, there is no way to be a functional human being—let alone a great parent.*

With this in mind, I made a decision: For my daughter's sake and my own, I would always take care of my own basic needs. She got lots of love and attention, but if I needed a shower, I let her play in her crib. If I was hungry, I ate. If I needed rest, I sat with my daughter in a childproof room and let her watch sing-along videos while I closed my eyes. If I needed to get out of the house, I asked my husband for help or got a sitter. I started a regular support group for new moms and satisfied my social needs. As a result, for the next 18 months I achieved my goal of "wonderfulness," and my daughter was living proof. She was the happiest, smartest, most adorable toddler I had ever seen.

And then my son was born.

Two babies were certainly harder than one. But I stuck to my credo—"ain't Momma happy, ain't nobody happy." I tried to keep myself healthy so that I could be at my best for them.

But we had student loans to pay off and I went back to work part-time. Most of my salary went to a babysitter, I came home to piles of laundry and dishes, and there just weren't enough hours in a day to keep up with the housework. I began to sacrifice my own basic needs, one by one. I gave up reading, movies, socializing, exercise, and other kinds of personal care. I ate on the run, kept my hair in a ponytail, and wore baggy, frumpy clothes. My husband and I were too tired to go out on dates. This life was stressful, but I knew it was temporary. Parents have to make these sacrifices for a few years, and then things settle down. Usually.

But my son didn't sleep. He didn't nurse well. He was always sick—the poor child had ear infection after ear infection. I adored him with every ounce of my motherly love, but caring for him was much harder than for his sister. We were simply exhausted. Then, when he was 15 months old, things became far, far worse. He began to have chronic diarrhea and began screaming night and day. He lost the language he had been using, lost the ability to point and play interactive games, and withdrew into his own little world. At 18 months, our lives were shattered by a single word: *autism.*

Wonderful parenting no longer seemed like an option. We were told autism was a severe, lifelong disability that would seriously impair social and language development. Little was known about cause or treatment. Our life, as we knew it, would never be the same.

My husband and I were overwhelmed by anxiety, and what remained of our own time went completely by the wayside. My daughter was virtually left to her own devices while I became obsessed with researching autism and working with my son, and while my husband struggled to hold the rest of our lives together.

> **Parents of every type of special-needs child go through an initial shock and mourning period after the diagnosis.**

Parents of every type of special-needs child go through an initial shock and mourning period after the diagnosis. We mourn for the children we had always planned to raise, but who are not to be. We mourn for our child's own losses, and the struggles he or she will have to face. We are also angry to find ourselves in lives we did not ask for—lives that we do not feel we deserve. We worry constantly—how will we cope? How can we afford treatment? Are we missing something that might help our child? Will our marriage survive? Often, with a diagnosis of a lifelong disability or serious illness, the fact that there is no end in sight creates a kind of stress that can be all-consuming.

It was simply an awful time for us, and the strain of each terrible day just seemed to sap my energy right down to my toes. My daughter, now 3, was not concerned about her brother—he was who he was, and she adored him, rejoicing in his progress and insisting that he interact with her. But overall, she was becoming a sad, anxious little girl. She had been betrayed by her own mother, who had changed from a laughing, good-natured kindred spirit into a frightened, exhausted, impatient dictator. I watched helplessly as a gulf formed between us, not knowing how to make things right.

I was aware of what was happening to her, and also to my husband, who had become withdrawn and anxious. Yet I didn't realize what was happening to myself. I had forgotten what I had once learned: *When a person is pushed to the limits of his endurance, there is no way to be a functional human being—let alone a great parent.*

Still, I was missing the point of that lesson. Along the way I had lost touch with who I was "before autism"—letting go of my needs, my hopes, my pleasures, my very self. Worrying about my son had changed me into someone very different from the person, and the mommy, I had always meant to be.

One day, after dropping my son off at his special-ed nursery school, I trudged through crunching autumn leaves on the way to my car, fighting back the tears that threatened to invade every waking moment. Suddenly, I stopped before an old, beautiful maple tree with a wide, gray trunk. This tree was like the ones I had loved as a child in summer camp—big and leafy, with wavy vertical patterns in the bark and little seedpods that twirled as they fell to the ground. I stared at the trunk of the tree. Suddenly, I became a little girl again, with dreams of a glorious life, exciting adventures, the love of a wonderful man, and the joy of raising my own children.

She had been betrayed by her own mother, who had changed from a laughing, good-natured kindred spirit into a frightened, exhausted, impatient dictator.

A voice seemed to speak to me from nowhere, a soft voice that crept into my soul. "You are, above all else, the very self you have always been. Your son's troubles are *his* troubles. You will love him, you will help him in every way you can, and you will leave no stone unturned. But your own life is also sacred, also worth fighting for. To *your* mother, it is a life as precious as his life is to you. Sacrificing your happiness because of his illness is an insult to the magical force within you, to the gift of life itself."

The tears began to flow then, but they were no longer tears of help-lessness and grief. I knew at that moment—regardless of what happened to my child—that I deserved my own love and protection as much as my children did. And it was clear to me that only by being whole, by letting pleasure and laughter and joy back into my life, could I ever hope to be a wonderful parent to my own children. Perhaps I couldn't choose *not* to be the parent of a disabled child, but I still had the power to choose what kind of parent I would be, and what kind of *person* I would be.

I leaned on that marvelous old tree and let the tears flow, and with them I let go of my fear and the numbing worry that had gripped my heart for so many weeks. My son and I had a difficult road ahead of us, but we were going to be okay. I was going to be okay.

Our story had a happy ending. On that October morning, I gained strength, confidence, and determination. I would help my son in every way I could, but I was going to be at peace with whom he turned out to be. It was still my life to live, and it didn't have to be a life marred by tragedy. Even with an autistic child, I could choose a life full of love, joy, adventure, and celebration.

I don't know if this knowledge gave me the courage to persevere, to break free of the fear and worry that had held me back, but something wonderful happened soon afterward. My husband and I were able to find a treatment for my son, and then to help many other parents treat their children's autism. My son came back to a family filled with joy and laughter, a sister who was a delightful playmate, a remarkable father whose worry lines had left only faint creases, and a mother who could set an example of true happiness by giving her family the kind of precious love that radiates from within.

The Anxious Child

John S. Dacey, Ph.D.
and Lisa B. Fiore, Ph.D.

Authors of *Your Anxious Child: How Parents and Teachers Can
Relieve Anxiety in Children*

At one time or another, most parents attempt to alleviate their child's anxiety. This is not surprising, since between 8 and 10 percent of American children and adolescents are seriously troubled by anxiety that interferes with the basic functions and enjoyment of day-to-day living. Parental support and understanding are essential ingredients for empowering a child to develop coping strategies and tactics. As a result, both parents and children will become active participants confronting the challenges posed by anxiety.

All anxious children face four central problems:

1. They find it harder than other children to calm themselves when they are in a stressful situation.

2. Although many of them are highly creative, they seldom use this ability when making plans for coping with their anxiety.

3. Even when they do have a plan, they become discouraged with it after a while and often quit trying.

4. Even when they are making progress in reducing their anxious feelings, they fail to recognize their success.

As a parent of an anxious child, the challenges are often complicated because the cause of the anxiety is uncertain, or the child is able to hide her anxiety. By recognizing that a child is anxious, learning coping skills, and working to empower a child, parents can help relieve these feelings of anxiety.

Parents often want to know what has caused the anxiety in their child. They debate the potential sources:

- "It's because she was potty trained too early/too late."
- "It's all my fault. This type of thing runs in the family."
- She's heavily influenced by friends and television.
- She feels that she can't make the grade socially/academically.

There is no single cause of a child's anxiety, nor is there one solution or "cure" that will eliminate the problem. However, there are some common physiological reactions to anxiety that can trigger, accompany, and reinforce anxious feelings. Accordingly, one of the most important factors to consider is the biological component of anxiety in children. Specifically, calming the nervous system is one of the first steps that parents can take with their child.

There is no single cause of a child's anxiety, nor is there one solution or "cure" that will eliminate the problem.

Physiological symptoms of anxiety include, but are not limited to, shallow breathing, increased heart rate, sweaty palms, and tense muscles. These symptoms result when a child experiences *the alarm reaction.* This reaction is innate—that is, it is built into the human body as an evolutionary response to a perceived threat. When a child perceives that she is in danger, the alarm reaction is activated, resulting in the physiological symptoms. For an anxious child, her perception may not accurately reflect a given situation, and so her reactions could be considered unwarranted by others' standards. For example, a child who is scheduled to give a speech in front of a large audience may perceive the audience as a threat. She may begin to sweat, her palms may feel clammy, and she may feel thirsty yet have a hard time swallowing. These are all physiological reactions to the perceived threat, and the easiest way to alleviate these feelings is to avoid the situation completely.

Parents recognize that it is not possible, or desirable, for children to develop a pattern of avoidance associated with anxiety, for this could generalize to other situations. It is therefore important to teach a child how to cope with her anxious feelings by first calming her nervous system to a point where she can effectively evaluate the situation and make appropriate decisions.

Although there are numerous ways to calm the nervous system, what seems to work best with children and adolescents are methods that incorporate mental and physical activity. Interestingly, girls tend to gravitate toward the mental techniques, such as visualization, whereas boys tend to prefer the physical techniques, such as deep breathing. Parents, who know their child best, should try various techniques until they arrive at the ones that most fit their child's temperament and style. The following activities have been used by parents nationwide and have been determined to be successful at reducing children's anxiety.

Visualization: Pictures in Your Mind

Begin by asking your child to close her eyes and imagine up to five scenes that she finds particularly tranquil. Next, ask that she write a phrase describing each scene on an index card and arrange the cards in descending order in terms of their degree of tranquility. With a younger child, have her dictate her ideas to you, or let her choose scenes from pictures in a book or magazine that appeal to her. Your child's list may include waves on the shore, flowers in a meadow, puppies sleeping on a pillow.

Choose one of the scenes and ask your child to describe it in greater detail. Go through the list of scenes until she has described each one. Suggest that she memorize the list and practice visualizing each scene. Later, when she feels anxious, she can visualize each place on the list, and each step down the list will help her calm down. Her list also helps you understand her idea of tranquility; use her descriptions as a vocabulary to draw from as you're trying to understand her.

Abdominal Breathing

Talk with your child about teaching her body to cooperate and help when she feels afraid. Ask her to sit in a comfortable position with her back straight and pressed into the chair for support, or have her lie down on a mat or pad. Loose clothing is a good idea. Have your child take her pulse rate; with younger children it is fine to take their pulse rate for them. Press your fingers into the side of your child's neck, count the beats for 15 seconds, then multiply that number by 4 to find the number of beats per minute.

Have your child inhale slowly to a count of 5, then slowly exhale. After she has practiced several times, ask her to place her hand on her stomach and watch her hand move out as she breathes deeply into her abdomen. Young children can think of a beach ball or watermelon in their bellies. Tell her to breathe in slowly while counting in her head for 4 seconds ("one Mississippi, two . . ."), and up to 6 seconds for teens. She should exhale the same way and then hold her breath for 4 seconds. Repeating this sequence creates the maximum relaxation. Breathing must be done slowly.

Calming the nervous system is merely one step in the process of alleviating a child's anxiety, yet it is fundamental to success. Other steps include originating an imaginative plan, persisting in the face of obstacles and failure, and evaluating and adjusting the plan. These steps help parents help their children control the way they think about things, and ultimately empower them to cope with anxious feelings.

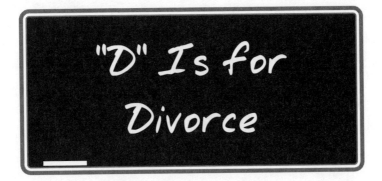

"D" Is for Divorce

"The greatest assault to our children's self-esteem today is hearing one parent criticize the other. Unfortunately, since more than half our marriages end in divorce in this country, this occurs with startling regularity.

You may have an ex-spouse, but there is no such thing as an ex-parent. Please allow your children to enjoy having two parents to love."

—*Leslye Hunter, M.A., L.P.C., N.C.C.*
Family, Marriage, and
Stepfamily Counselor,
Contributing expert on family and
marriage to Parents *magazine*

Helping Your Children Cope with Divorce

Edward Teyber, Ph.D.
Author of *Helping Children Cope With Divorce*

Nearly one of every two couples marrying this year will be divorced in 10 years. As a result, over 1.1 million children will go through a parental divorce every year. Most divorcing parents are guilty about the breakup and worried about how their children will adjust. Divorce is painful for children and parents alike, but by following the five lessons below, you can help your children successfully adjust.

1. *Shield children from parental conflict.* Divorce engenders enduring problems for children when they are exposed to ongoing parental battles. Most children are distressed during the initial breakup, often feeling sad, mad, and anxious during this tumultuous period. However, children are almost certain to suffer long-term adjustment problems when they are exposed to chronic or ongoing parental

wrangling such as arguing, yelling, threatening, demeaning the other parent, and so forth.

In contrast, parents of children who make a secure adjustment, while they may not like or trust each other, have the good sense to shield children from parental conflicts. Further, they don't undermine the other parent to the child (e.g., "Your mother's an idiot; you don't have to listen to her," or "Your father's a liar. Why do you want to see him?"). In particular, successful parents do not embroil children in adult conflicts (e.g., "Tell your father the next time he's late with the support check . . . "). There

> *By exercising restraint and buffering children from parental wrangling, you can do a great deal to help your children feel safer, worry less, and adjust more securely.*

is often a great deal of anger and hurt between ex-spouses that cannot be resolved. However, by exercising restraint and buffering children from parental wrangling, you can do a great deal to help your children feel safer, worry less, and adjust more securely.

2. *Provide continuity in parent-child relationships.* By 2 years after the divorce, over one-half of all divorced fathers have no regularly scheduled contact with their children. Many see their children infrequently and inconsistently, and some not at all. Fathers are most likely to disengage after their ex-spouses remarry, and researchers find that they are more likely to fall away from their daughters than their sons. When a mother or father disengages and fails to fulfill an active part-time parenting role, many children assume responsibility for the parent's lack of involvement and blame themselves. Sadly, these children often come to believe that they do not matter and are not love-worthy. They often become depressed, suffer a loss of self-

esteem, experience a decline in school performance, and cannot follow through on plans for their own future.

Children who are better adjusted, in contrast, usually maintain physical and emotional access to both parents following the breakup (children lose emotional access to parents who becomes depressed, preoccupied with their own personal problems, or cope with the breakup through drugs or alcohol). Although the divorce brings about far-reaching changes for everyone, children who make a successful long-term adjustment do not usually suffer the loss of a parent through the divorce. Beginning at the time of the breakup, divorcing couples need to make specific plans for when each parent will be with the child and follow through reliably on these visitation schedules.

3. *Avoid loyalty conflicts.* Virtually all children who have long-term problems adjusting to divorce (i.e., more than 2 years) feel they have to take sides and choose between their parents. These children do not have permission to love and be close to both parents at the same time. Instead, parents give children the message (often nonverbally or in subtle and covert ways) that they have to choose to be close to one parent at the expense of closeness to the other. For example, a mother may look sad or hurt when her son expresses how eager he is to visit his dad, or a father may feel mad when his daughter expresses how much she misses her mother. Almost every child wants to be close to both parents—no matter how limited or superficial that relationship may seem to the other parent. Children feel torn apart inside (e.g., stomachaches, headaches, peptic ulcers) when they are pressured to take sides. Divorcing parents can avoid loyalty conflicts by giving children overtly spoken permission to love and be as close to the other parent as possible.

4. *Maintain effective parenting practices.* Divorce can seem commonplace because it occurs so frequently, but it is still an earth-shaking crisis when it occurs. Most parents do not fully anticipate how stressful the divorce will be both for themselves and their children, and underestimate how much time and effort it will take to recover

emotionally. Researchers find that it often takes parents 2 to 3 years to fully regain their equilibrium, and that parents often reach a psychological low point 1 year after the separation.

As a result of their prolonged personal distress, most adults' parenting competence declines markedly following the breakup. That is, most parents are not able to (a) nurture and communicate, (b) discipline, and (c) provide an organized household as effectively as they did before the divorce. This is especially unfortunate since children are distressed by the breakup and have heightened needs for these effective child-rearing practices. For example, children feel more secure when their parents can be in charge and discipline effectively by providing clear limits and regularly enforcing rules. When so many other things in their lives are changing, children also are reassured by predictable daily routines (e.g., having dinner together at the table without the TV or telephone). The biggest problem for single-parent mothers in the aftermath of divorce is disciplining sons. Things soon go badly for everyone in the family when children gain the upper hand in parent–child relations.

5. *Give children explanations for the divorce.* Almost all parents feel painfully guilty about the divorce. Most parents want to do the best they can for their children, and they worry that their marital failure will hurt their children in some unknown but irreparable way. One of the many problems with excessive parental guilt is that it serves to keep parents from talking to their children about the divorce, as well as from giving children a basic explanation for the divorce and realistic expectations for what is going to happen. In the absence of effective parental explanations, children fill the void with their own

> Children need to be prepared in advance for departures and reassured repeatedly of the continuity of parent–child relationships.

311

problematic explanations in which they typically blame themselves for the divorce. If you ask preschool and school-aged children if they ever feel responsible or to blame for their parents' divorce, the majority of them will say yes! These children, who carry an unnecessary burden of blame and guilt, often feel responsible for their parents' divorce because they have heard their parents arguing over how to discipline or manage them.

Especially for young children under 6 years of age, the principal concern that divorce arouses is separation anxieties and fears of being left. Indeed, from children's eyes, their worst fear often comes true. For example, if Dad can suddenly pack up and move out on Saturday morning without any forewarning, and without telling children specifically when and where they will see him next, it is understandable that children worry—"Won't mom go away, too?" Children need to be prepared in advance for departures and reassured repeatedly of the continuity of parent–child relationships. For example, parents can say:

"Mom and Dad have decided we are not going to be married anymore. We are going to get a divorce. We are going to live in different houses from now on, but we will still always be your mom and dad. That is never going to change. Dad is going to move to a new apartment on Saturday, and you will be with him at his house on Tuesday. Even though we are not going to be married anymore, you will always live with one of us. We will both always love you and work together to take care of you until you are grown up. We are going to need to talk together a lot about this, but are there any questions we can answer for you right now?"

I have suggested a parental contract for divorcing parents to read aloud to each other and sign.

Finally, children also need an explanation for the divorce that does not assign blame. Parents often give ineffective explanations that demand children see only one parent's reality as "truth," embroil children in parental conflicts, or draw children into adult conflicts and concerns that are beyond their understanding. This occurs, for example, when one parent explains the divorce by saying, "Your father is leaving us for another woman!" or "Your mother is destroying our family because she just wants to meet her own selfish needs." Such explanations undermine the parenting authority of the other parent and diminish that parent as role model to the child. In effect, such explanations cause the child to lose a parent through the divorce. There are two truths to every marriage, and divorcing parents want to give explanations that allow children to have the best relationship possible with both of their parents.

In closing, I have suggested a parental contract for divorcing parents to read aloud to each other and sign:

"I agree to try to support (ex-spouse) in his/her parental relationship with our children. I will not try to undermine his/her relationship with our children, make the children choose between us, or involve the children in our disagreements. Although I probably will not be able to do this all of the time, I realize that this is in the best interest of our children and I will try to follow these guidelines as best I can."

These lessons are not a cure-all, but they will go a very long way toward helping your children successfully adjust to divorce.

I'm a Bonus Mom

Jann Blackstone-Ford, M.A.

Author of *My Parents Are Divorced Too* and *Mid-Life Motherhood,*
A Woman-to-Woman Look at Pregnancy and Parenting for
Women Approaching 40 and Older

Besides having two biological children, I'm a bonus mom. Not a stepmom, a *bonus mom.* I never liked the label "step," and when my kids came up with my new title, I was elated. Anything other than "...and this is my stepmom, Jann." Please. That word conjures up pictures of evil cat-eyed women staring into magic mirrors. I'm not like that at all.

I have to admit, my son—a.k.a. my bonus son—feels a little uncomfortable using the word *bonus,* but he tells me he feels even more uncomfortable using the word *step,* so it's a good compromise.

He used to get teased a lot when he was younger. "Hey, Steve," his friends would chide, "there's your bonus mom." I would just thank them for referring to me as bonus. Many of them had bonus parents. I thought their parents might also appreciate the upgrade. After all, a bonus is something positive—something extra you get when you purchase, say, laundry soap: ". . . and, as a bonus, the new whitening and brightening formula . . . " I hope I brighten my kid's lives a little.

My husband and his ex-wife have joint physical custody of their two kids, which means the kids live at our house for 2 weeks and then at their mother's house for 2 weeks. When the children were younger, the time spent away from each parent was a week, but as they grew older, they opted for the 2-week transition.

In order for children to successfully live in two different houses, all parents, bonus and bio, must do their best to communicate. We thought we were doing just fine until my bonus daughter mentioned that her brother went crazy while at their mother's house because they were out of fruit cocktail.

> *In order for children to successfully live in two different houses, all parents, bonus and bio, must do their best to communicate.*

"Fruit cocktail?" I asked. "Since when does Steven like fruit cocktail?"

"He loves fruit cocktail at my mom's house."

"Huh?" I was mortified.

You have to understand—Steven has been my bonus son for 12 years. I see him just about every day. I feed him just about every day. Even if he's at his mother's house for her 2 weeks, since we live less than a mile away, he still raids our refrigerator. So how could I have missed that he liked fruit cocktail? It made me feel terrible that I had overlooked something as important as my bonus son's favorite food, so I decided to ask his mother about it. That's when we started to compare notes.

It seems Steven has very different likes and dislikes at each home. Since he is 15, most of these likes and dislikes center around food. At his mother's house he snacks on fruit cocktail, but at my house he likes frozen bean and cheese burritos. His favorite dinner at his mom's house is stuffed green bell peppers. At mine, it's a Japanese udonlike soup I make. I think he likes the ritual that goes along with the soup as much as he likes the soup. You dip little pieces of chicken into bubbling broth, let them cook, then using chopsticks, dip the cooked chicken into various sauces—all the while you are chatting and talking about your day. It takes a long time to eat, and Steven likes to be the center of attention.

Since everything was now out in the open, with his mother and I comparing his newly discovered likes and dislikes, Steven took it upon himself to invite his mother over for dinner the next time I made his favorite soup. He didn't want her to learn the recipe. That would be crossing the line. Each favorite dinner must stay at the proper house. He just wanted his mother to taste the soup so that she would understand why he liked it so much. What a life.

While writing our book, *My Parents Are Divorced, Too*, my children and I compared notes with lots of other kids to make sure we were including the real issues, the important kid topics. Most kids felt the transition from living with married parents to living with two single parents was the hardest thing to accept. They discussed their parents dating new partners and accepting new siblings, but very few mentioned the little coping mechanisms that children develop over the years in order to live comfortably in two homes.

Why did the kids never mention this subject? I think it was because many of the children we consulted were living with newly divorced parents and they had not yet established a new pattern of living after divorce. A child who has lived for years with divorced parents settles into a pattern that is different from the way it was when Mom and Dad lived under the same roof. Some children cope, as Steven had, by emotionally separating Mom's house from Dad's house. Other children can never make the distinction, so the fact that their parents divorced continues to be a problem issue for the rest of their lives.

Keeping all this in mind and wanting to make Steven's life as easy as possible, I decided to stock up on fruit cocktail the next time my local supermarket was running a sale. Five cans, complete with extra cherries, have been sitting on my pantry shelf for over 2 months. When Steven is hungry, I tell him we have fruit cocktail to eat, but he just looks at me like I'm nuts.

"What?" he asks. "No bean burritos?"

I guess fruit cocktail just doesn't taste the same at my house.

So, my best lesson for parents to help their children deal with divorce is to make things as positive as possible. Divorce is a very painful experience for all concerned, and it's our job as parents to help our kids find solutions for the chaos that divorce adds to their lives. If we nurture their individual likes and dislikes, instead of trying to make them fit into the way we think things should be, it will be much easier for them to adjust to the changes.

Fun and Games

"You can discover more about a person in an hour of play than in a year of conversation."

—*Plato*

"It is paradoxical that many educators and parents still differentiate between a time for learning and a time for play without seeing the vital connection between them."

—*Leo Buscaglia*

∾ *Lesson 67* ∾
Age: All

The Wonder of Play

Cheryl L. Erwin, MA, MFT
Author of the *Positive Discipline* series

As I was driving home one bright spring day, I saw something that brought a smile to my face. Two young boys were walking single file along the top of a rock wall, grinning and holding their arms out for balance. Right behind them, smiling just as broadly, came their father.

The sight reminded me of the professor who taught my college child psychology class. This particular professor—a man who obviously loved and understood children—had an interesting theory. He believed that the reason we adults so often struggle to get along with our youngsters is that we've forgotten something very important. We've forgotten how to play.

Play is truly a child's "work." An infant learns about the permanence of people and things by playing peek-a-boo with her parents. She learns about her body by being bounced and tickled. As children grow older, play becomes the laboratory in which they explore their world.

They develop social skills and acquire manners and the complicated concept of sharing.

Children learn about gravity; they run, jump, and fall down. They try on new roles and personalities by dressing up and playing all the familiar "let's pretend" games: house, army, and the good guys against the bad guys. And, all too often, adults merely watch from the sidelines.

All too often, adults merely watch from the sidelines.

Oh, we're good at taking children places where they can play. We drive them to play group, to child care, to gymnastics and soccer. But we sometimes find it hard to get involved ourselves. When was the last time you played dress-up with your child? When have you gotten down on the floor and participated in a vigorous game of Legos or Chutes and Ladders? When did you last play hide-and-seek with all the lights turned off or have a real water fight with squirt guns, hoses, and water balloons?

Being an adult these days is serious stuff. It's hard work—a real 24-hour job. There's a living to be earned, which usually takes two parents—if you're lucky enough to have two. There are meals to be prepared and a house to be cleaned. When we think of parenting, we think of driving kids hither and yon, of learning effective discipline and building self-esteem. And those things are very important.

What will our children remember of us?

But where, in all the things we have to do and learn, is there time for relationship? When is their time for laughing until your ribs ache? By the end of the day, most of us are weary and longing for nothing more than a quiet moment. The request to "Read to me, Mommy" or "Play with me, Daddy" can feel more like a burden than an opportunity.

What will our children remember of us? I remember sitting in my little wading pool with my father (who must have had "more important" things to do), pouring cold water and grass cuttings on his stomach with a frosty aluminum cup. I remember the time he went to court for a traffic ticket with a black eye because I'd accidentally kicked him during an especially rowdy tickling match.

Do you want to get into your child's world? Do you want to understand how he thinks and feels, and what he dreams about? Then learn to play—really play. Get muddy; get rug burns on your knees; walk along rock walls; or go in-line skating. Learn to pretend and to play video games. Laugh—a lot. Play is good for parents, too.

Look inside yourself and find the kid you used to be. These precious moments of our children's lives will never come again. Enjoy your life with your children by rediscovering the importance of play. The bills and the housework will wait for you—I promise.

Lesson 68

Age: All

Creating Creative Kids:

Turning Boredom into Brightness

Charles Fay, Ph.D.

Author of *Love and Logic Magic for Early Childhood:*
Practical Parenting from Birth to Six Years

How many times does the average parent hear "This is *boooooring!*" or "I'm *booooored.*" before the kids grow up and leave home? And have you ever known a kid (or an adult for that matter) who seemed to exist in a vacuum of perpetual boredom?

Have times changed! Years past, kids really knew better than letting anyone know they were bored. Most believed beyond a shadow of doubt that uttering the words "I'm bored" or "This is boring" was an open invitation for some adult to say, "Oh goodie!" and hand them a rake, shovel, dust cloth, broom, or some other instrument of childhood despair.

In boredom are the seeds of creativity. Wise parents allow their kids some boredom from time to time, and they help them channel this boredom into creative discoveries.

323

A major shift in thinking has taken place in America. It wasn't long ago when the vast majority of people believed that it was their own personal responsibility to find happiness in life. Nobody else was expected to make it happen for them. They understood that contentment is an inside job. When a person was bored, he had to find something to keep himself busy. It was just that simple.

Today, many hold a vastly different mindset. Their logic seems to follow the opposite course. *People should entertain me. It's not fair if things are dull. Somebody needs to make sure that I don't get bored. If I'm unhappy, it's somebody else's fault.* Sadly, people holding these beliefs spend most of their time feeling frustrated.

Where have these new beliefs come from? Reading the newspaper, I came upon an advertisement describing a summer program for kids. It read something like this: "Only you [meaning parents] can prevent a boring summer!" The add went on to describe the wonderful things your child should be doing instead of sitting around being bored with you.

More and more, parents are being sent the message that it is bad if their kids get bored.

More and more, parents are being sent the message that it is bad if their kids get bored. Advertisements, the yuppie parents across the street, and misquoted research sends the same message: "You are a bad parent if you don't keep your kids immersed day-to-day, hour-to-hour in a highly entertaining environment." Hogwash! Where would we be today if someone had made sure that Ben Franklin or Thomas Edison never got bored?

The more we entertain kids, the more they will start to believe they need to be entertained.

It is clear from good, solid research that kids' brains do develop better when they are exposed to a wide array of stimulating experiences. Unfortunately, our society seems to have confused healthy stimulation with entertainment. Healthy stimulation encompasses a variety of activities that encourage kids to think. Some of these activities include reading your children books, telling them stories about your childhood and their ancestors, asking them questions about their day, playing games with them, and so on. And stimulation doesn't always require adult participation. Some of the most valuable activities involve children playing alone with materials or toys that foster creativity. The common characteristics of these materials or toys are (1) they don't have batteries, and (2) kids are encouraged to use them in a variety of interesting ways. Here are some examples:

Examples of Materials and Toys That Foster Creativity

1. Sand box
2. Clay
3. Dolls and toy animals (without batteries)
4. Books
5. Crayons, paints, markers, and paper
6. Toy cars and trucks that don't move or make noises on their own
7. Wood and safe hand tools for woodworking (for older kids)
8. The cardboard box that once surrounded the most expensive toy you purchased for your child's birthday

Using the materials and toys listed above requires active thought and creativity. Entertainment, in contrast, is passive in nature. In small doses, entertainment is healthy and important! How many of us occasionally go to the movies or watch a TV show just to get away from the daily grind or from something that's worrying us? Unfortunately, too many children are bombarded with entertaining toys and activities on a daily basis. What effect is this having? Across the country, teachers continually report that more and more kids are hyperactive, expect to be entertained, and have difficulty with self-directed thought and creativity. In my own work as a therapist, I've seen many children who've never really learned to play! One 5-year-old walked into my office full of the toys and materials suggested above, picked up a rag doll, pushed on it, and began to shake it. In disgust, he threw it on the floor, plopped down in a chair, and complained, "Booooring! Batteries dead."

Listed below are examples of toys and activities that should be limited by parents. In small doses, they are healthy and fun. When they become a way of life, they are harmful!

Examples of Toys and Activities That Discourage Creativity (and Encourage Boredom!)

1. Video games
2. Television (even watching educational shows or videos does not require *active* thought and participation)
3. Toys that talk too much and have too many flashing lights
4. Too many days that look something like this:

> Morning: Get dressed, eat breakfast, go to soccer practice.
>
> Mid-Day: Grab fast-food lunch on the way from soccer practice to the swimming pool.
>
> Afternoon: On the way to karate class, go by the store to pick up brownie mix for tomorrow's Boy Scouts meeting.
>
> Evening: Get home from karate and get ready for dinner with neighbor family.
>
> Night: Have dinner, go home, watch television, and pass out.

If this schedule looks familiar, give yourself and your kids a break!

More is not always better. Exciting, entertaining activities are great fun, but wise parents also know that quiet times are just as important!

Most adults will admit that parts of their jobs are pretty dull. Life can be fairly boring at times, particularly when we're trying to complete a rather long task or reach an

Because many children have been exposed to a constant barrage of stimulating activities, they are unable or unwilling to tolerate this delayed gratification or unwilling to tolerate "boredom."

important long-term goal. Because many children have been exposed to a constant barrage of stimulating activities, they are unable or unwilling to tolerate this delayed gratification or "boredom." They have no patience for it. These are the kids who find it extremely difficult or even painful to complete book reports and other more lengthy school assignments. They find the boredom of initial planning stages difficult, and they often lack the creative problem-solving skills necessary to jump hurdles as the task unfolds. What can parents do to avoid this trap? Listed below are some suggestions.

Tips for Encouraging Creativity, Problem-Solving Skills, and Patience in Your Home

1. Limit television viewing, watching videos, and playing video games to 30 minutes per day total.
2. Fill your home with materials and toys that foster creativity.
3. Purposefully develop boredom training sessions.

The ability to tolerate boredom and to entertain oneself are essential life skills. Like any other abilities, practice makes perfect.

1. Limit television viewing, watching videos, and playing video games. Nothing can compete with the constant audio and visual stimulation provided by the latest video games, fast-paced television shows, and special effects clogged–movies! Even the most energetic and well-trained teachers on the planet find it practically impossible to compete with the sheer entertainment value and momentum of these electronic wonders. What price are we paying here? What type of an impact must excess exposure to these activities be having on children's attention plans, their ability or willingness to tolerate boredom, and their overall ability to succeed in less consistently entertaining settings such as school or the workplace?

There are no sensible reasons for children to spend more than 30 minutes each day engaged in these activities. Even the viewing of educational television shows or videos does not require *active* participation, frustration tolerance, or creativity.

Wait a minute! Aren't watching *Mutant Death Squad* on TV and playing video games both civil liberties protected for children by the US Constitution? Not really, but have you noticed how some kids act as if they are?

2. Make your home rich with materials and toys that foster creativity. Listed above are some examples of toys that foster creativity. Some really nice things about them is that they are typically less expensive, tend to make a lot less noise, and don't require batteries! Even more importantly, they give children essential opportunities to create their own entertainment and learn by doing rather than merely watching. Research has clearly documented that this type of active learning is essential for healthy brain development and visual-motor coordination.

3. Purposefully develop boredom training sessions. What in the world is a boredom training session? Exactly what it sounds like! Purposefully provide a very dull period of time during each day, during which your children are forced to stimulate themselves. They should not have access to television, video games, or other highly entertaining toys or activities. Simply put, children need practice learning how to stimulate themselves in creative ways. Kids who never get this practice tend to become easily bored, unhappy, and rather difficult to be around when things get "boring." A boredom training session (BTS) is a *planned* opportunity for children to find themselves in a dull situation, get bored, and create their own excitement.

Provide a very dull period of time each day, during which your children are forced to stimulate themselves.

When the types of materials recommended above are made available, many kids quickly enter their own world of creativity and imaginative thought. It is through this process of being in a dull situation, becoming uncomfortable, and creating one's own enjoyment that children develop many of the self-control and problem-solving skills necessary for success in school, interpersonal relationships, and work.

Some kids seem to adapt pretty easily to these sessions. They go off by themselves and play without much of a struggle. Unfortunately, other children don't make it quite so easy! For any child, the key to success is planning. Listed below are some tips.

Basics of Planning a Boredom Training Session or BTS

1. Provide a dull period of time when it is convenient for you.
2. Don't give in or get sucked into an argument when your kids say, "This is boring!"
3. Watch your child learn and grow!

1. Pick a time that is convenient for you. Obviously, some days and times are better than others for a boredom training session. Which of the options below sounds best to you?
    (a) When you're exhausted with a terrible head cold?
    (b) The evening of April 14 while you're trying to finish your tax return?
    (c) When you are paying bills and the checkbook won't balance?
    (d) When you're well rested, relaxed, and have time to supervise the session?

All but the most adventurous parents typically choose option "d!"

2. Don't get sucked into an argument! What do average red-blooded American kids do when they first fall within the dreaded grips of boredom? Most start dragging. They drag on over to one toy. They drag on over to another. They drag outside. They drag inside. Finally, they drag over to one of their parents, frown, and complain, "I'm bored. There's nothing to do. Can I watch TV?" When the caring parent responds with a simple "no," the whine intensifies and becomes something like, "But this is *booooooring*. There's nothing to *dooooooooo*."

I've never met an honest parent who didn't have some fantasies about what they'd like to say to their kids in response. Unfortunately, many kids seem to be masters at the art of arguing for fun and profit. As soon as we respond with anger and get sucked into the fray, our kids are no longer bored! What could be more exciting than an entertaining display of parental frustration?

Listed below are some ideas for responding to. "This is boring!" Which one fits with love and logic?

(a) "I'm sick and tired of this whining. When I was a kid, we had to make our own toys out of worn-out shoes."
(b) "Go tell your mother."
(c) "Well . . . okay. You can watch TV . . . but just this one time . . . and stay off the cable channels!"
(d) "It's hard to be bored. What are you going to do?"

Obviously, idea (d) fits best with love and logic! The most essential tool for a successful BTS involves handing the problem back in a loving way.

Wise parents hand the boredom problem right back to their kids in a loving way. In response to "This is boring!" smart parents ask with empathy, "What are you going to do?"

Every time we expect our children to solve their own problems, and provide loving guidance as they struggle, we give a priceless gift! Each time we resist the urge to jump in and fix their problems, or entertain them, they walk away with a little more wisdom and self-confidence. Every time they encounter a problem, struggle, and succeed, they can look back and reason, "I did it! I've got what it takes!"

The art of turning any problem into a wisdom and self-confi-

Every time we expect our children to solve their own problems, and provide loving guidance as they struggle, we give a priceless gift!

dence builder involves sending two very powerful messages through words and actions. The first message communicates *You are such a bright kid! I know you can solve this problem. That's why I'm not going to.* The second one says *I love you, and I'm here if you want any ideas or suggestions.*

3. Watch your child learn and grow! There is nothing more exciting than watching your children engrossed in thoughtful play or some other creative activity! Sneak up on them sometime and watch for a while. When children begin to realize the joy of quiet, creative activities, we begin to see calmer and happier kids. We also begin to see how our own lives are much fuller without the constant distraction of electronic activities and hectic entertainment schedules.

~ *Lesson 69* ~
Age: All

The Importance of Humor in Parenting

Joseph Anthony Michelli, Ph.D.
Author of *Humor, Play and Laughter: Stress-proofing Life with Your Kids*

It has been said that the truly happy person can enjoy himself on a detour. As parents, we all know that family life is filled with unexpected turns. Unfortunately, most parenting books fail to temper their sage advice with the reality that for every rule of parenting there are at least two exceptions. Realizing that much of parenting involves a best-guess approach, parents must maintain a robust sense of humor to aid in the endless moments of uncertainty. Humor in the life of a parent does not function as a bulldozer clearing away family problems; rather, humor serves as shock absorbers for the bumpy roads that families travel.

Using humor not only serves the needs of parents but children as well. Charles Schulz, creator of the Peanuts comic strip, is credited with saying, "The greatest gift we can give the next generation is the ability for them to laugh at themselves." A household filled with humor, play, and laughter assures fluid coping skills for America's next generation and a more enjoyable journey for all.

> *Humor and play also serve to enhance children's intellectual development and expand their overall flexibility in dealing with problems.*

Many parents fear the experience of playing at their child's level. I believe that effective parents overcome such fears and laugh and play without worry about maintaining their adult image. They color, play hide-and-seek, and experience the world of make-believe. It is clear to these parents that play lures children into learning. Kids are drawn to activities that pleasure them and help them to master essential skills.

Humor and play also serve to enhance children's intellectual development and expand their overall flexibility in dealing with problems. Humor skills enhance divergent thought, assist in decreasing stress, and reduce interpersonal conflict. If only humor could help kids clean their rooms.

Many parents are too busy to engage the quality and quantity of time necessary to play with their children. I believe all parenting can be reduced to four basic rules:

1. Show up.
2. Pay attention.
3. Tell the truth.
4. Focus more on the process than on the outcome.

Many parents do not comply with either rule 1 or 2. I fear that these types of parents do not appreciate the benefits both they and their children derive from absorption in a humorous and playful experience.

As parents, our children offer us their delight in the simple things in life. Where can you make more time available to enjoy this simplicity through play with your children? How can you develop a ritual around this time? What will you do to make sure that other time pressures don't encroach on your ability to play and find humor in your experiences with your children?

Humor is not a sense like taste, touch, and smell. It is a skill that is either exercised or underutilized.

Do humor, play, and laughter abound in your home? If not, tomorrow is a new day. I contend that a commitment to a playful household assures that the families that laugh—last.

❧ *Lesson 70* ❧
Age: Young Children to Teens

Kids and Sports:
What's a Parent to Do?

Darrell J. Burnett, Ph.D.
Author of *Improving Parent–Adolescent Relationships, Raising Responsible Kids: 5 Steps for Parents, Parents, Kids, & Self Esteem: 15 Ways to Help Kids Like Themselves,* and *It's Just a Game! (Youth, Sports, & Self Esteem: A Guide for Parents)*

In this lesson of *Parent School,* we're going to discuss the role of parents in youth sports.

Each year, over 20 million boys and girls between the ages of 6 and 16 play one or more sports a year. And each year, the parents of those youngsters face decisions and questions: *Is my child old enough to play? Is my child big enough to play? Is my child good enough to play? Should my child play a team sport or an individual sport? Will sports build my kid's self-esteem or tear it down?*

There are no easy answers for parents. Most sports organizations set age and size limitations to ensure safety for the youngsters participating. As for whether to sign up for a team sport (baseball, softball, soccer, basketball, soccer, volleyball, hockey, etc.) or an individual sport (tennis, golf, swimming, track, gymnastics, wrestling, karate, etc.), there are several considerations.

Many kids initially shy away from team activities because they don't feel comfortable with a lot of kids. However, after their initial hesitation, they participate because of the friends they make through the sport. Some kids shine by competing in individual sports, competing against themselves, striving to improve their own records. Others need the excitement and social stimulation of team interaction and competition to keep them involved.

Once we register our kids and expose them to different opportunities, they will eventually show us where they fit—it's often a matter of trial and error. The important thing is to get children involved in youth athletics or youth activities.

Kids, Sports, and Self-Esteem

As a dad, a youth league coach, and a psychologist, I have a strong bias toward involving kids in sports. During my 20-plus years of dealing with problem kids and their families, I've noticed one thing: Most of the troubled kids have not been involved in sports. Many started in sports at an early age, but dropped out because of negative experiences (too much pressure, too much criticism, and not enough fun). I see this as a tragedy, because sports can and should be a positive experience and a self-esteem enhancer. In fact, I see youth sports as contributing to the four basic cornerstones of self-esteem:

1. A sense of belonging (team identity, team uniforms, etc.)
2. A sense of feeling worthwhile, regardless of looks, talent, wealth, etc. (everyone plays in youth sports, regardless of skills)
3. A sense of dignity, being treated with respect, without humiliation, sarcasm, etc. (Positive coaching is at the heart of youth sports philosophy)
4. A sense of being in control (as a child learns rules and skills in a specific sport, he or she begins to feel confident and in control)

A Behavior and Attitude Checklist for Sportparents

We as parents play a central role in making youth sports a positive experience. Our attitude and behavior as a "sportparent" is pivotal. One of the top reasons kids continue to participate in sports is *positive parent interaction.* It's no secret that Mom and Dad have the power to make or break a kid's enjoyment of sports. But how do we know if we're doing the right thing with our kids? Unfortunately, there isn't a manual with all the answers. However, there are a few guidelines we can keep in mind to help us stay on track as we interact with our kids during those wonderful years of youth sports.

It's no secret that Mom and Dad have the power to make or break a kid's enjoyment of sports.

Here are some sample items from the Sportparent Behavior and Attitude Checklist:

1. *I remember to look for and make a big deal out of positives with my kids, on and off the field.* It's important to remember that kids' self-esteem is often based on what they *hear* about themselves from others. It makes sense, then, to try to make sure they hear lots of positives. And, to make sure they hear it, it's important to use lots of action, commotion, and emotion when we praise our kids, because that's what they remember—the action.

2. *I praise my kids for specific behaviors, keeping a four-to-one ratio of positives to negatives, on the field and off.* It's been estimated that in a healthy relationship there are four positive interactions for every negative interaction. Likewise, in sports, although our kids may give us lots of opportunity for negative remarks as they gradually learn from their mistakes, it's important to heap the positives on them so that they can handle negatives without feeling overwhelmed. Moreover, if

we want our kids to remember positive remarks, we have to make them *specific,* so that they can visualize them. For example, if youngsters (sons or daughters) are on the losing end of a 10–1 defeat in baseball, and parents simply say "Good game!" it isn't enough. But if a parent says something like, "Hey, you were really flying down to first on that grounder you hit. I'm impressed with your speed!" that night, when the child puts his head on his pillow, he may not be thrilled with the defeat, but chances are he'll say to himself, "I *am* pretty fast. I really *did* hustle down the line to first!" He will visualize it, and he'll remember it.

> *If we want our kids to remember positive remarks, we have to make them specific, so that they can visualize them.*

3. *I praise my kids just for participating in sports, regardless of their athletic skills.* When it comes to youth sports, in spite of the "everybody plays" philosophy, one of the dangers is that all the attention usually goes to the kids with the superior skills (i.e., all-star teams, newspaper articles, team balls, etc.). As parents, we need to remember to praise our kids just for participating, just for being there, regardless of their batting average, their shots on goal, their free-throw percentage, their tackles, their aces, their backhand, their spikes, and so on. Simply participating in athletics should be an opportunity for positives in any youngster. Moreover, if the praise comes only when the performance is super, a youngster may place all of her value on performance and miss out on the joy of just playing.

It's also important for families not to get caught up in the trap of identifying the "athletic" son or daughter as the one who gets all the attention, while the siblings of "average" skills go unnoticed. Another concern is that a youngster may come to identify himself or herself as worthwhile only to the extent of his or her athletic abilities. I once spoke with a teenager who was a superb athlete and had signed a letter of intent to attend a major university on an athletic scholarship. In his senior year, he injured his knee and lost the scholarship. He attempted suicide. His entire identity had been as an athlete. He somehow felt he had not lived up to his parents' expectations for him to get a college athletic scholarship.

4. *I help my kids recognize even their smallest progress in youth sports activities.* One of the reasons many kids stop playing sports is because they don't see themselves as getting any better at the sport, and it stops being fun. As parents, we can help our kids focus on their *progress* in any of three areas: (1) *frequency* (they're doing the right thing more often, or they're making less mistakes); (2) *duration* (they're doing the right thing for a longer period of time, or the wrong thing for a shorter period of time); (3) *intensity* (they're showing more energy in their effort).

5. *I remain calm when my kids make a mistake, on the field or off, helping them learn from their mistakes.* If we remain calm when our kids make a mistake, we can teach them some valuable life lessons. We can teach them that mistakes happen and mistakes can help us learn.

   Many youngsters live in fear of making a mistake because they see the mistake as an unforgivable failure. They then live in anticipation of the next mistake, full of tension and fear. Consequently, they make more mistakes because they can't concentrate on giving it their best effort. If we scream, yell, or threaten, every time our kids make a mistake, we miss a chance to teach them that mistakes are stepping stones for growth.

6. *I keep my expectations reasonable when it comes to my kids, on the field and off.* A poignant cartoon shows a mother speaking to a sports psychologist, saying, "Doctor, I think my 11-year-old has the potential to be a professional athlete. What should I do?" The psychologist replies, "Get a second opinion!"

   It is very important for us as parents to keep a perspective on youth sports. A survey by the Athletic Footwear Association surveyed over 20,000 kids on the top ten reasons why they participate in sports. The top reason was "to have fun." The bottom reason was "to win." If the kids are in it mainly for the fun, we need to put our emphasis in the same place. Let the kids have fun, and let them enjoy the youthful years, building positive childhood memories. They will have enough pressures just growing up. Don't add pressure in an area that should be just fun and games. We've all seen the misguided parents who tend to live vicariously through their children in sports, overidentifying, interfering with coaches, challenging the officials, taking the entire youth sports experience too seriously. Let's remember that only a small percentage of the kids in youth sports will go on to play in high school, a smaller percentage will play in college, and a miniscule percentage will play professionally.

As we parents participate in the youth sports experience, let's think ahead. Let's plan on having our kids, at age 25, look back on their youth sports experience and thank us for making it a time of fun, a time of learning some skills and a time of feeling good about themselves.

To help keep the proper focus on youth sports, whether as a coach or simply as an involved parent, here are some reminders. Think of the phrase:

KIDS IN SPORTS
• Keep it positive.
• Instill laughter and humor.
• Develop team spirit.
• Step into their shoes.
• Involve yourself.
• Notice any and all progress.
• Show excitement and enthusiastic praise.
• Praise specifics.
• Offer a good example.
• Remember to have fun.
• Teach skills.
• Set reasonable expectations.

Raise a Child Who "Plays Smart"

Susan K. Perry, Ph.D.

Author of *Playing Smart: The Family Guide to Enriching, Offbeat Learning Activities for Ages 4–14; Writing in Flow: Keys to Enhanced Creativity;* and *Catch the Spirit: Teen Volunteers Tell How They Made a Difference*

Child's play can be so much more than child's play. Playtime offers you a great opportunity to pass along some of the most important lessons of learning and life to your child. When your child is intensely focused on any activity, she is likely to be in "flow," or "in the zone." These terms describe how we feel when time seems to stop and nothing else matters as much as what we're doing right now. It's a state that not only feels wonderful but that produces the most creative work and the most motivation to stick with challenging activities. Here are some pointers on encouraging your child to spend time "playing smart":

1. *Discuss the concepts of flow, focus, and challenge.* Learn the signs of flow and point out to your child when she seems to have been most deeply engaged in an activity. For instance, when your child is playing with her friends so intently that she forgets to stop for lunch, you might say, "Honey, you were really involved just now, having fun with your friends. When you're in flow like that, it's hard to get back to ordinary stuff, isn't it?" If you like tough personal challenges, share your experience by saying something like, "Wow, that was really hard! I think that's why I enjoyed it so much. It feels great to stick with something long enough to see results!"

2. *Offer time and space to concentrate.* Make a point of not filling every moment of your child's day so that she has more time to follow her own interests. If she's focused intently on reading or doing a puzzle, let her finish. When it's time for school or bed, acknowledge her frustration at the need to stop. Encourage a longer attention span by not having the TV on during homework time. Make it a family habit to put away one thing (or place it out of sight) before beginning another.

3. *Learn and teach self-monitoring.* Show your child how to monitor her own attention by becoming more aware of your own limited attentional resources. For instance, say, "I'll have to read this later. I'm so tired right now that I don't know what I'm reading." That way, your child will recognize that it's a good idea to stop when her focus flags. Perhaps all that's needed is a change of pace or a rest break. Or does she need some help to get over a difficult spot? Suggest that your child note her daily energy levels. Is doing her homework the moment she comes home the best use of her energy?

Suggest that your child note her daily energy levels. Is doing her homework the moment she comes home the best use of her energy?

4. *Offer challenging pastimes.* Encourage hobbies that grow more complex with play, such as drawing, story writing, photography, cooking, and kite making—all activities with infinite options.

5. *Emphasize activities for their own sake.* Encourage your child to do things because he enjoys them, rather than focus on how he's doing. Rather than, "You did a good job," say, "You certainly are having a lot of fun learning about dinosaurs, aren't you?" When you're tempted to say, "If you draw a picture for me now, I'll play with you later," resist resorting to rewards and bribes. It's been found that the primary effect of rewards is to reduce long-term interest in whatever it is kids have to do to get the reward. It's less manipulative to say, "If you draw a picture or play by yourself a little while so that I have time to finish paying these bills, then I'll have more time to play with you later."

6. *Experiment and find the novelty.* Teach your child to experiment with tasks in order to add novelty, thus raising his interest level. For instance, ask your child to choose the simplest everyday chore and find a way to make it more enjoyable. How might your child make straightening his room more interesting? He could put music on, dance from location to location, try to beat the clock, decorate storage boxes, and so on. When something new doesn't work as well as you'd hoped, point out that it's a learning experience anyway.

Help! I Have a Toddler!

Excerpt from The Toddler's Busy Book

Trish Kuffner

Author of *The Toddler's Busy Book, The Preschooler's Busy Book,*
The Children's Busy Book, and *Picture Book Activities*

> "A toddler, according to the dictionary,
> is one who toddles, which means 'to
> walk with short tottering steps . . .'
> Regardless of what the experts or the
> outsiders say, those tiny steps will
> plunge you into one of the most exas-
> perating periods of your adult life."
> —*Jain Sherrard*

Toddlers are at an interesting stage of development. They can get around on their own, but they need constant supervision. They understand most of what they hear but are usually unable to effectively communicate their wants and needs. They want to do everything for themselves, but their skills and abilities are limited. They want to try everything, and most of what they do is motivated by an interest in cause and effect ("Let's see what happens when . . . ").

Toddlers also have an abundance of energy. As children enter the toddler stage, some will still be having two naps per day, but by the end of toddlerhood, many will not be napping at all. It means that a parent or caregiver must occupy the toddler for many hours each day, often without a break. It can be a challenge for most adults, whether they are encountering life with a toddler for the first time or experiencing toddlerhood for the second, third, or fourth time. It's no wonder that parents at home all day—every day—with a toddler often entertain the thought that "professionals" (early childhood educators or trained and experienced day care workers) could do a better job of occupying and stimulating their child.

Whether they know it or not, parents usually have enough of what it takes to keep their toddler happy and stimulated.

Would your child be happier, better occupied, and more stimulated if he were cared for by professionals? In certain extreme situations, the answer may be yes, but generally most parents lack only experience and confidence. Whether they know it or not, parents usually have enough of what it takes to keep their toddler happy and stimulated. Keep in mind that most of the activities in preschools and day care centers imitate what can naturally occur in the home on a day-to-day basis: talking, singing, reading, exploring, having a snack, playing out-doors, playing with friends or siblings, napping, and so on. Some may feel that the group setting of a preschool or day care center will bene-fit their child, but toddlers do not learn well, if at all, in group situa-tions. Cynthia Catlin, in her book *Toddlers Together: The Complete Planning Guide for a Toddler Curriculum* (Gryphon House, 1994), says, "Toddlers learn best through their independent explorations and interactions with their caregivers, who can promote their learning by initiating activities based on the children's play behaviors and interest."

Parents and caregivers are instinctively doing things that stimulate their children to learn. Talking on a toy telephone, asking, "Where are your ears?" as you change him, playing hide-and-seek or peek-a-boo, letting him bang about with pots and pans in the kitchen—you've done these activities countless times without even thinking you're providing a rich learning environment. You are. Running, sliding, swinging, and playing outside encourage physical development. Playing with clay, paints, and crayons develops small muscle skill and promotes creativity. Washing hands before meals teaches health. "Hot! Don't touch!" teaches safety, and a short playtime with friends helps your child learn social skills.

Toddlers need a stimulating environment and a variety of experiences to help them develop.

Simply put, toddlers need a stimulating environment and a variety of experiences to help them develop. Activities that emphasize the senses and physical activity will be the most successful. A consistent daily schedule will help your child know what to expect and help him become more independent. He will enjoy repetition of the familiar in songs, books, arts and crafts, and simple games, and he will also be interested in anything new. Try to make a short walk or some outdoor play a part of every day. Be sure to allow your child plenty of free time with interesting things to discover and explore. We all learn best when our interest motivates us to find out about something, and toddlers are no exception.

Organizing for a Toddler

In many cases, toddlers know how to create their own fun when given the proper materials. Although they require constant supervision, there are things you can do and materials you can provide that will encourage creative and independent play. In all cases, be sure your home is properly toddler-proofed with regards to safety. Many small items interesting to toddlers, such as coins and beads, pose an extreme choking hazard. Make sure these items are well out of reach—an especially difficult task if you have older children in the house.

The following suggestions will help you better organize your home to meet your toddler's changing needs:

1. *Keep a baker's box in the kitchen.* Dealing with kitchen tasks can be extremely difficult when combined with keeping an eye on an energetic toddler. At times, 1-year-olds may be happy just to sit in their highchair or at their own little table with a few toys or snacks to keep them occupied while you work. At other times, they will want to be right there with you, underfoot and into everything. Kitchen cupboards and drawers are full of interesting things that may prove irresistible to your child.

    Provide your child with his very own baker's box. Put together a collection of unbreakable kitchen tools in a plastic crate or small storage box. Store it in a spare cupboard that is low enough for your child to reach. He can use his tools (cookie cutters, mixing bowls, spoons, measuring cups, and so on) for play or for helping you do some "real" cooking or baking.

2. *Have a busy box handy.* Since much of our time at home is spent in the kitchen, a spare kitchen cupboard low enough for your child to reach is an ideal spot for her very own busy box—a small storage box or plastic crate containing things he can do on her own anytime. An older toddler or preschooler will appreciate many craft-type items in his busy box: crayons, markers, coloring books, paper, tape, stickers, glue, inkpad and rubber stamps, claydough, and so on.

    Filling a busy box for a younger toddler is more of a challenge. Most of us don't want our 1-year-old to have tape and markers without close supervision! Items for a toddler busy box must be safe for him to play with even when relatively unsupervised, and they should be things that will not make a mess (at least not much of a mess). Watch what types of things interest your toddler and include those in the busy box. For example, if he loves playing with plastic bottles and lids, put some in the box (be sure the lids are big enough to pass the choke test). Most toddlers love to build, so add an assortment of stackable things. Items that work well are empty cereal boxes, covered yogurt containers, and individually wrapped rolls of toilet paper. Vary the contents of the busy box from day to day so that your toddler will always find something fresh and exciting to keep him busy and happy.

3. *Set up a tickle trunk.* A tickle trunk full of dress-up clothes and props will not only foster your child's imaginative play but will keep her occupied with all the wonders it contains. Fill a trunk, toy box, large plastic container, or cardboard box with adult clothes, shoes, hats, scarves, gloves, and costume jewelry to use for dress-up. Old suits are great, as are Hawaiian shirts, vests, baseball hats, bridesmaid dresses, nightgowns, wigs, boots, slippers, and purses. Great items can be found at garage sales or local thrift shops, or stock up on princess gowns and animal costumes at post-Halloween sales.

   Toddlers may have trouble with zippers and small buttons, so consider replacing the zippers or buttons with Velcro, or enlarge the button holes and replace small buttons with large ones that are easy for little fingers to grasp.

4. *Rotate your child's toys.* In the first few years of life, most children receive many wonderful toys as gifts for birthdays, holidays, or other occasions. While parents appreciate the good intentions of the givers, most children have more toys than they can possibly play with. Also, even the most creative toys will fail to hold your child's interest if they're always around. When rotated every 4 to 6 weeks, toys will seem new to him and will be interesting and exciting all over again.

   Separate your child's toys into piles (if your child has a favorite toy, keep it out all the time). Keep one pile in your child's play area and pack the others away in boxes, marking dates for when they are to be brought out. If you have friends with children the same age, why not try a toy exchange? Keep a list of what's been exchanged and be sure to agree on the terms beforehand (how long, who's responsible for breakage, and so on).

5. *Make a Crazy Can.* Someone once referred to the dinner hour as "arsenic hour." Once you've had a toddler or two hanging around at that time, you'll know why! This is usually the time when you are at your busiest and they are at their crankiest. In the midst of the chaos, you yearn for a distraction to keep them busy. It's not a great time to brainstorm for creative activities, so plan ahead with a crazy can full of ideas for your toddler.

   Make a list of on-the-spot activities that require no special materials, no time-consuming preparation or cleanup, and no serious adult participation or supervision. Write these ideas down on index cards or small pieces of paper and put them in an empty coffee can. If you like, cover the can with cheerful contact paper, or cover it with plain paper and have your child decorate it with paints, markers, or crayons. When things start to get crazy (or when there's just nothing to do), choose a card from the can for an instant remedy.

6. *Take along a busy bag.* A busy bag will help you be prepared for those times when you just have to wait—at the doctor's office, hairdresser's, restaurant, and so on. Turn a drawstring bag or backpack into a take-along busy bag that can be filled with special goodies to keep your child amused. Borrow the portable items from your busy box, or take along items such as dolls and their associated clothing, blankets, bottles, and accessories; an edible necklace (cereal or crackers with holes in the middle strung on a piece of shoestring licorice; a favorite toy, stuffed animal, or blanket; magnets and a small metal cake pan; matchbox cars; simple wooden puzzles; special snacks.

7. *Look for new activities and experiences.* While children need free time for creative play and unstructured time in which to explore and discover the world around them, they also rely on you to introduce them to new projects, activities, and adventures. This is sometimes hard to do on the spur of the moment, so planning ahead is a good idea. Try to schedule one or two fun, challenging, creative activities

each day (not necessarily major projects—sometimes a 5-minute game will do). Decide on the activities ahead of time and have all the necessary supplies assembled in advance.

Planning Your Activities

Failing to plan is planning to fail. That applies to the big stuff (like saving for your child's education) as well as the little stuff (like a new art project or playing a game with your child). Preschools and day care centers plan their curriculum carefully to ensure that children have a variety of experiences each day. Parents at home can be somewhat less structured, but the importance of planning new and creative activities should not be overlooked. Children's activity books and resources abound and can be easily purchased or borrowed from the local library. However, the ideas these books contain are only valuable if you use them. If you don't do a little planning, chances are you won't use them. Here are some helpful guidelines for planning your activities:

1. Read through a children's activity book and create a weekly planner with activities you'd like to try each day. Include a few alternate activities for bad-weather days or when things just won't work for what you've planned.

2. Use your weekly activity plan to make a list of supplies you'll need, and assemble or purchase them beforehand.

3. Make a list of what you need to prepare before your child becomes involved in the activity—mix paint, assemble supplies for a game, and so on.

4. Plan special activities for your babysitter, and have all the necessary materials handy. This will let your sitter know that watching TV all day is not an option.

5. Make a list of ideas that would be fun to do anytime you can fit them into your schedule. Have this list ready when you have some unexpected free time.

What About Television?

The influence of television on children has been much debated over the years. While your child may still be young enough that television is not yet an issue, be assured that it is something you will need to think about carefully in the months and years to come.

The key to the whole children and television issue for me is not so much what the children watch, because we can control that. I am more concerned about how parents use television and what children do not do when they watch television. It's easy to use television as a babysitter on occasion, but it can be habit-forming to both parent and child. The few short years of early childhood are better spent playing, reading, walking, talking, painting, and crafting—in other words, doing things together.

But, whether we like it or not, television is here to stay. It's up to parents to use it in a way that will be beneficial to their child's development and their parent–child relationship. How should parents do this? First, be selective in what your children watch. Good television programs can make learning fun and can expand your child's knowledge of the world. As your toddler gets older, programs like *Sesame Street* can help her get ready for school. Choose wisely. Look for programs or videotapes that instruct, entertain, and reinforce the values and principles you wish to develop in your child.

Second, limit your child's viewing time each day. Remember, time spent watching TV is time that your child does not spend on other, more valuable activities such as playing games, reading (or being read to), or using his imagination in countless other ways.

Third, watch television with your child whenever possible. Most programs move at a very fast pace in order to hold the attention of their young audience. But young children often have a hard time keeping track of the content, and it is almost impossible for them to stop and ponder what is being presented. By watching with your child, you can provide connections that would otherwise be missed. And by reminding your child of related events in his own life, you help him make sense of what he sees.

Finally, set an example for your child. Show him that you would rather read a book or play a game or talk to him than watch TV. It's hard to expect your child to learn to limit his viewing and choose programs wisely when you do just the opposite. Remember, children learn from our actions more than our words.

Set an example for your child. Show him that you would rather read a book or play a game or talk to him than watch TV.

A Word of Encouragement

Raising a child is a monumental task that brings countless rewards, most of which will be realized only after many years of hard work. But there are also many "warm fuzzies" you receive daily as a parent: the first time your baby smiles at you, his first word, his first step, his warm hugs, and that irresistibly cute thing he did that you can't wait to tell Grandma and Grandpa about. As your child moves through the various stages of early childhood, from infant to toddler to preschooler, you will also see the changes that parenting is bringing about in you. You will stretch and grow as a person, you will learn new things (many of them about yourself), and you will develop more patience than you ever thought possible.

If you are parenting a preschooler and a toddler, or a toddler and an infant, or all three (or more) at the same time, the daily challenges you face are even greater. You may not be able to get out as much as you want, or do as many fun and interesting things one-on-one with each child as you'd like, but chances are, if you care enough to read a book such as this, you're already doing a great job. Treasure what you've been given, keep a positive outlook on life, and do the best job you can each day. (They will grow up—I promise!)

Is there only one way to raise happy, healthy, confident, and capable children? Of course not. But by providing your child with daily activities that are simple and fun, by placing more importance on your child's happiness and learning than on the appearance of your home, and by talking to your child on a level he or she understands, you are well on your way to achieving this goal. Not only will your children be better prepared for preschool, kindergarten, and the world beyond, but, in the process, you help to make many happy memories of childhood.

∽ *Lesson 73* ∾

Age: All

Quality Time—Anytime!

How to Make the Most of Every Moment with Your Child

Penny Warner, M.A.

Author of over 30 books including *Preschool Play and Learn, Baby Play and Learn Book, Baby Birthday Parties, Kids' Outdoor Parties* and *Giant Book Of Kids' Activities & Games*

Time spent with your child is precious. As any parent of a grown child will tell you, the time flies by too quickly. Looking back, most would say, "I wish I'd spent more time with my kids."

Instead, we seem to waste a lot of time, running errands, waiting for appointments, and doing chores, when we could be sharing quality time with our children.

A lot has been written by child development experts about *quality time*. The term was created when they found that parents were too busy working, taking care of the house, juggling careers and parent-hood duties, to spend much worthwhile, meaningful, or significant time with their kids. Parents increasingly found they had to grab a few minutes whenever they could if they wanted any time at all with their fast-growing young ones.

Since then, we've discovered that quality time can be any time—it's what you make of the time that gives it quality. There are many moments throughout the day that we fritter away—standing in line, waiting for the doctor, walking the kids to school, getting ready for bed—that we could turn into quality time, filled with intellectual challenges, physical tasks, sensory stimulation, social skills, and just plain fun. Here are a few examples:

All it takes is a little imagination and a few minutes to turn downtime into quality time.

1. During bath time, gather some items for the tub, and have your child guess which ones will sink and which ones will float.

2. At bedtime, read a story to your child, and have her try to guess the ending before you finish the book.

3. While you're riding in the car, play rhyming games, make up rap songs, and play the alphabet game.

4. As you prepare dinner in the evening, have your child help you cook, or let him create his own kitchen concoction.

5. At mealtime, while the family is gathered, play word games, tell jokes, and share funny stories.

6. While you're shopping, pretend you're aliens, spies, or invisible.

7. When your child is sick in bed, spend time coloring pictures together, putting on a puppet show, or playing name that tune.

8. If you're just waiting someplace, sometime, such as in the waiting room at the doctor's office or in line at the amusement park, try to guess people's names, imagine their occupations, or predict their futures.

All it takes is a little imagination and a few minutes to turn downtime into quality time, no matter where you are or what you're doing. Each moment you spend with your child will enhance that special bond between you—a bond that will last the rest of both your lifetimes.

Tips and Tricks

"As a parent, you learn to listen to everyone's advice, and to quietly use only that with which you agree."
—*Jerry and Lorin Biederman*

～ Lesson 74 ～
Age: All

Tools for the Trade

Lisa Whelchel
Author of *Creative Correction*

I sincerely wish parenting were easy, but it's not. It is my hope, however, that this *Parent School* lesson will, in some way, make your journey a little easier. And if I can't help in that area, then I'll shoot for "more enjoyable" at least.

Over the years, I have gathered a variety of creative ideas from moms all across the country. I have also come up with many tips of my own in an effort to make my role as a parent both effective and fun-loving. Raising three unique children, including one diagnosed with ADHD, has required a mixture of approaches.

As you well know, the parenting adventure is different with each child—and it's vital to recognize and adapt to your children's various temperaments, strengths, and weaknesses. Think of yourself as a sculptor as you shape and mold the lives of your young ones. With each child, you may be working with a different medium. Each raw material requires a distinct combination of tools to strike the balance between respecting its uniqueness and steadfastly pursuing the potential for beauty within.

The following ideas are samples from the "Toolbox" sections of my book, *Creative Correction*. Peek under the lid and pick out a couple of new tools to try. You may be surprised to discover that there's no reason discipline has to be boring to be effective!

• Do you have to constantly remind your children to feed their pet? Mount a little box on top of the pet's house or cage and put their lunch money or lunch bag in it. If they want their lunch that day, they must make sure their pet gets his lunch first.

• When one of my children is acting disrespectful, disobedient, or defiant, I will instruct him or her to choose a chore from the job jar. The jobs include scrubbing the toilet, organizing the pots and pans, moving and vacuuming underneath the furniture, weeding the garden, matching up odd socks, defrosting the refrigerator, and cleaning the closet, garage, or under the bed. And those are just a few possibilities. You could add ironing (if the child is old enough), scrubbing the inside of small wastebaskets, polishing the silver, cleaning the window wells, brushing the animals, cleaning the fireplace, vacuuming the couch, alphabetizing the spices, and so on. Not only does the job jar help to get my house clean, but it also keeps my little ones from complaining they're bored! They know that with the job jar, Mom will always have an antidote for boredom. (The job jar isn't all chores, though. I've added into ours one grace slip in which no job is required.)

• I have a friend whose son's morning chore was to get the pooper-scooper and clean up the doggie gifts that littered the backyard. The boy was not doing this job with much diligence, so his father came up with this creative solution: After the boy had completed the task, he would be required to run through the yard barefoot! Their lawn is now perfectly clean.

- Tucker is the only boy in our household. Therefore, whenever I find yellow water in the toilet without any paper floating around, I know he's the culprit who did not flush. The same is true for leaving the toilet seat up. Whenever I discover the bowl in either state of male insensitivity, I grab the toilet bowl brush and go looking for the offender. He is then required to scrub the toilet clean.

- If your children are constantly turning in sloppy schoolwork, keep a few photocopied pages of printing or cursive exercises around. (These can be found at any teacher's supply store.) Then ask your haphazard child this: What takes longer, a report done neatly in 15 minutes or one you've sped through in 10 that must be redone and warrants a page of handwriting practice?

- Next time your child "forgets" to put something away, like the video game stuff or sports equipment, put it away for him. When he asks where it is, tell him that he'll just have to look for it. Believe me—he will learn that it's a lot more trouble to find something that Mom has hidden than it is to put it away in the first place.

- If you have younger children who are messy, try this: Put their toys in a rainy day box to bring out later. This has the added benefit of making an old toy seem new again. Or set the toy somewhere out of reach but within sight for a predetermined number of days. This increases the impact of the correction by keeping the forbidden toy fresh in their minds.

- Having a struggle at bedtime? Try this: Next time you're dealing with the usual bathroom trips, cups of water, giggling, and talking, call off bedtime. Declare, "Nobody has to go to bed tonight!" Then stand each child in another part of the house, all alone. Inform them that they may stay up as long as they choose—the operative words being *stay up*. Their warm, comfy beds will look awfully good after a few minutes of standing alone in the cold!

- My kids seriously dislike running errands. I usually hear complaining throughout the grocery store, dry cleaners, and department store. In order to make them aware of how often they had something negative to say, I gave them each a dollar in nickels before our next afternoon errand crusade. Then I informed them that the last errand would be to the drugstore, and whatever change they had left in the bag, they could spend on candy. In the meantime, they had to give me a nickel for every negative word spoken while running errands.

- I have a friend who offered her daughter one ingredient to her favorite cookie recipe every time she had her backpack ready by the door the night before school. By the end of the week, she'd earned all the ingredients, and they baked the cookies and enjoyed them together.

- I kept a large container of jellybeans on the kitchen counter that I named "Good Manner Beans." Whenever one of my kids remembered to say "please, thank you, yes sir, no sir, yes please," and so on, I would let them grab a jelly bean. They would also get a "Good Manners Bean" for having nice table manners and for displaying good manners when meeting new people. They would suddenly become even sweeter than the candy, and because they only received one at a time, I could offer them anytime without worrying about spoiling their appetite.

- Get an old pickle jar, clean it out, and call it the "Pickle a Privilege" jar. Fill it up with little slips of paper with a variety of fun, extra-special privileges written on them. This "Pickle a Privilege" jar is for when your children make great choices. When it's time for them to pick a slip from the jar, have them close their eyes and pick a privilege. Here are just a few ideas: having soda with dinner, sleeping with Mom and Dad for one night, going to a Saturday matinee, choosing the next pizza topping, having a pillow fight, going to work with Dad, eating dessert first, or a "get out of jail (correction) free" card.

• Tucker loves Legos, but those things are expensive! So we bought the Lego Pirate Ship kit and informed Tucker that he could earn it several pieces at a time. He was allowed to open the box and put the first ten pieces together according to the instruction booklet. After that, every time he showed initiative, he was allowed to add the next five pieces. This could be whenever he chose to pick up the toy on the floor instead of stepping over it, or clean the toothpaste off the sink after brushing, or even put his sister's shoes away for her. The result was that he not only built a really cool ship but an important character trait as well.

If you've tried grounding or time-outs and nothing seems to be working, don't get frustrated—get creative. I like my son, Tucker's, response to challenges. I reprimanded him for fooling around during a home-school kindergarten lesson. Exasperated, I told him, "Tucker, the more you goof around, the longer this is going to take."

"And the funner it's going to be!" he responded with a grin.

When it comes to parenting, I agree. Goof around a little. It will make the journey "funner"!

~ *Lesson 75* ~
Age: All

Drive Time

Excerpt from
Survival Tips for Working Moms

Linda Goodman Pillsbury
Author of *Survival Tips for Working Moms*

Driving with the children can be so unpleasant you want to scream. There is practically nothing worse at the end of a demanding day at work than to pick up tired, hungry kids and listen to them scream and fight all the way home. On the other hand, car rides can offer a time to actually talk with your children without distractions, listen to music, or just sit and think (and drive). How do you reach the point of having more good car rides than bad ones?

Planning

Have snacks in the car ready for your children when you pick them up at school or day care.

Either pack extra in the lunchbox or have food and a juice box in the car. For me, this is a necessity. I have endured many screechy, exhausting, unpleasant rides home. The days the kids have a snack, they cheerfully munch and even share! I consider car snacks so important on the pick-up that now I will usually stop and get something (yogurt, fruit, bagels) if I've forgotten.

Have a small bin or bag of toys and books in the car at all times. It really keeps toddlers occupied. Therese has her older children bring along books any time they load up for a long ride.

Have several "special" blankets, and leave one in the car. If your child can't live without her flannel "B" or "fringie," buy several and leave one in the car. When you pick her up at day care and she forgets it, when you are halfway to the sitter's, or when you visit a friend, you won't have to go back to get her

Cut up the favorite blanket into portable pieces.

special blanket. We once endured an hour of screaming from our 3-year-old on a trip. We finally figured out what was wrong, stopped at a mall and bought a new fringed blanket, and she immediately calmed down. It was not, of course, exactly the same as the treasured "fringie," but it was good enough. On busy workdays the last thing you want to do is lose time by going back or endure the screaming (not to mention wanting your child happy). We have found that three to five of the blankets give enough flexibility so that you can wash them.

Cut up the favorite blanket into portable pieces. If your child has only one special blanket and cannot be consoled by any other, Cynthia suggests cutting the treasure into two or four pieces and leaving one in the car.

Buy a cassette player with headphones for each child. Lesley finds this brings peace to car rides. Each child can hear what he wants and the grown-ups don't have to listen. Younger children love the taped stories that go with picture books and older children like the longer books on tape. Lots of kids love listening to music; it just may not be what you want to hear. This is especially good for long trips.

Get tapes you don't mind listening to. This is a must if you are going to put the kids' tapes on the car tape deck. For toddlers, Hope highly recommends the Discovery Toys tapes with all kinds of noises—violins, dogs, cats, baby crying, man laughing, and so on.

Buy some relaxing tapes to play on the drive home from work. Lee reports that it helps with the transition.

Train your kids to like what you like. Cynthia likes oldies. She's trained her kids to like the oldies station by offering valuable prizes when they recognize favorite songs or recording artists: 10 cents for the Beatles, 25 cents for the Four Tops—it's a great way to keep the radio on a station you like and have fun with your kids. Try this with classical, jazz, or whatever music you like.

Use drive time to tell stories. Every day, sometimes twice a day, Holly tells the kids stories that she thinks up on the spur of the moment.

Keep a book in the car for you. When you get to the store and your baby or toddler has fallen asleep and you don't want to wake him, at least you can relax and read. Hope has read a lot this way.

Behaving

Set up drive time rules ahead of time.

Let your children know what the rules are and what the consequences are. I expect my children to wear their seat belts, use indoor voices, keep their hands to themselves, and not distract me when I have to concentrate on the driving. Many parents also have rules about radio use.

If your kids squabble through car rides, just calmly pull off the road and stop the car. Don't say anything—just look out the window, flip through papers in your briefcase, whatever. Pretty soon they will notice you've stopped and question you. Simply say, "When you are quiet, we will continue." I once did this when I was driving a car full of 6-year-olds on a school field trip. Boy, were they surprised. They behaved the rest of the way back to school.

Play the "Quiet Game." Whoever can be quiet the longest wins.

Lolita finds that her kids think it is hysterical when she loses.

Stop the fighting over who sits where. Do your kids argue over who gets to sit in the front seat? When the bickering got to be too much, Judy told her kids that for several weeks neither could sit in front. Afterward they were only allowed in the front seat if they did not argue. The arguments ended.

∽ *Lesson 76* ∽
Age: All

Positive Discipline Techniques

Nancy Samalin, M.S.

Author of *Loving Your Child Is Not Enough, Love & Anger: The Parental
Dilemma,* and *Loving Each One Best: A Caring and Practical
Approach to Raising Siblings*

All parents and teachers want the best for their children and are
concerned with their self-esteem. But when children tune us out
and won't do what we want, or defy us, it is normal to become annoyed
and frustrated. Here are some positive discipline techniques for
encouraging kids to listen and cooperate without threatening/brib-
ing/yelling/punishing/commanding/attacking/namecalling/arguing/cr
iticizing/spanking.

1. *Be brief:* Say what you want in *one word.* "Rob, jacket!" or "Jill, teeth!"
   or "Maria, shoes!"

2. *Describe:* Make an impersonal statement. "Books belong on the shelves." "The coat needs to be hung in the closet." "The dishes have to be put in the sink." "It is bath time."

3. *Put it in writing:* Make a sign or write a note to your child. "Dear Jo, reminder. Here is what has to be done before TV today. Clean clothes in the drawer. Dishes washed and dried. Dog fed and walked. Thanks. Love, Mom."

4. *Offer limited choices:* "Do you prefer toast or a bagel?" "Would you like to hear a story or play a game?" "Do you want a shower or a bath?" "Which do you want to put away first, the blocks or the cars?"

5. *Point out the positive:* Whenever a child does something that is helpful, caring, cooperative, or an improvement, give words of appreciation. "Thanks, Joey, I like the way you helped Amy put away her toys." "I was impressed with the way you solved your homework problem." "Grammy was touched by the card you made for her."

6. *And an important tip when you are feeling angry or frustrated: Use I not YOU.* Talk about *your* feelings; do *not* attack your child: "I get mad when you are late and I'm not called." "I won't be spoken to like that." "I am irate at the sight of this room." It is better to say, "I'm mad" than "You're bad."

Enjoy the Ride

Maureen A. O'Brien, Ph.D.
Author of the *Watch Me Grow* series

Parenting is the journey, not the destination. Too often in life, we worry about the endpoint and ignore how we get there. But it is precisely in the smallest details of the journey that the true essence of parenting emerges, and it is in the detours that we often discover our greatest treasures. Along the way, it's helpful to have a bit of a road map:

1. *There is more than one way to get there.* Try not to get hung up on someone else's directions. Parenting books and helpful advice both have their limitations, since no one-size-fits-all parenting style exists. While certain basics are always true ("make sure you have plenty of gas"), there's lots of room to create your own itinerary.

2. *You will get lost.* No matter how much you rely on your instincts or how detailed the map, there are no guarantees you will reach your destination directly. Even if you've traveled these roads before, life

will throw you curve balls in the shape of closed roads, stormy weather, and unexpected delays. It's how your family handles these unforeseen detours that matters to you and your child.

3. *Slow down for a better view.* In the rush to arrive, be careful not to lose sight of what's in front of you right now. You don't want to look back and realize that you never noticed or appreciated a moment with your child that may not be there next time. How fast you get somewhere is not the point; in fact, speed can be your enemy as it shortens time spent traveling together.

4. *Pay attention to the signs.* Your child will present you with lots of signs in your shared travels. Some will be clear as day ("Stop," "One-way street"), but others will require you to assess carefully what's coming ("Danger ahead," "Yield"). Whatever the message, such cues allow you to make informed decisions about how you may need to steer differently as a parent.

5. *Watch out for potholes.* Anticipate, especially after stormy seasons, that the road will not always be smooth. As you maneuver around the inevitable dips, bumps, and puddles that your child is bound to send your way, try to remember where they are. Odds are you'll encounter them again.

6. *Keep your eyes on the road.* You are not the only driver around, and it can be dangerous to ignore others or to get overly distracted by your surroundings. Your child is relying on you to be a steady influence in the driver's seat and to be always on the lookout for what lies ahead. Let her gaze out the window for now; she'll be getting her own license soon enough.

7. *Beware of shortcuts.* Everyone loves a shortcut. But often what starts out looking like a faster, more convenient way to go may not turn out that way. Indeed, the abbreviated trip may be a bumpier, less well-traveled, or otherwise unpredictable road. Sometimes we need to fully experience the trials and tribulations of parenting so that we

can better appreciate the smooth stretches. And longer journeys allow us the opportunity to unwind.

8. *Talk to fellow travelers.* You can always learn something from individuals who've been there before. Perhaps they will merely confirm the direction you're heading in, or they may caution you to try another route. Their advice may help you determine what necessities to bring or how long a delay might last. Keep your ears open to their guidance, but keep your mind open as well, as your child's course may be different.

9. *Use your horn sparingly.* If you want to be taken seriously and have your child (and others) heed your concerns, keep your road rage in check. It is better to be on quiet alert and save the horn for when you really need it than to be seen as the parent who cries wolf. Your child will pick up on your message that your warnings are worth paying attention to.

10. *Share the driving.* Don't travel alone if you don't have to. The journey will be more fun if you can share the moments together, and taking turns at the wheel allows you the luxury to sit back once in a while, observe your child, and reflect on your trip so far.

Without a doubt, life as a parent is going to be a bumpy ride, so do fasten those seat belts. But be sure to enjoy the trip, keep souvenirs, and let your child know that you couldn't have better company along for the ride!

∽ *Lesson 78* ∽
Age: All

Tips We've Learned While Attending Parent School

Jerry and Lorin Biederman
Editors of *Parent School*

As new parents, we know we still have much to learn and we will be students of *Parent School* for a long time to come. Here are some of the tips taken from our own real-life, hands-on experiences that we've picked up along the way:

Necessities for Mom During Pregnancy:

1. *Sea Bands.* These are wristbands you can buy at the drugstore. They really do help with nausea and overall aches. We knew a woman in our childbirth class who was sick for 7 months—throwing up every day, sometimes three times a day. We told her about these and for the rest of her pregnancy she was nausea-free. A must!

2. *Baby oil with vitamin E.* It helps to prevent stretch marks and itching.

3. *Tums.* Don't be without these! Keep them in your purse and on your nightstand! They help with heartburn and they're a good source of calcium. Also for heartburn, sleep on your left side as much as possible.

4. *A pillow between your legs when you sleep.* This is important not only for comfort but it keeps your hips even and gives the baby room to grow.

5. *Don't wear tight clothing!* This can add to nausea. Make sure you are as comfortable as possible at all times.

6. *Something to keep in mind.* On the day your baby is born, whatever happens will be your story. Imagine years from now telling your child how he or she was born. It won't matter whether it was naturally or by cesarean, whether you went through 30 hours of labor or 2. It will be an amazing story—your story—which you will always keep in your heart and mind. So try to enjoy every moment—you will never again be pregnant with this child and you will never again go through labor with this child. And don't be a hero—if you're in pain, your doctor can make recommendations. God had people invent painkillers for a reason. (Remember the man in the ocean? Boats kept coming by to rescue him, but he refused to be helped, saying God would save him, Then, when he got to the Pearly Gates, God said, "Why didn't you get on any of the boats I sent?")

Necessities For Baby

1. *Rubbing alcohol.* Use with cotton balls or swabs to clean the umbilical cord.

2. *100 percent pure corn starch.* We found this to be better than baby powder. It keeps the baby dry and can even be used in addition to ointments.

3. *A&D Ointment.* The original, not the cream. The ointment is used when the baby gets red and irritated from diaper rash. It's the best! Tried and true!

4. *Pacifiers.* We were one of those couples who said *never!* But these are actually good for babies. We really just used them when the kids were sleepy. The best way to pacify babies is to hold them and take care of their needs (food, warmth, diapers), but this did help (especially in the movies).

5. *Bottles.* We tried all different kinds. Whether you're breastfeeding or using formula, you may have to try a few different types of bottles and nipples, so don't buy too many until you know which your baby likes.

6. *Baby bathtub.* It doesn't hold as much water as the regular bathtub. The one we got had a hammock for the newborn that you can take off when the baby is able to sit up.

7. *Mustela.* This is baby shampoo and soap. Our kids never got cradle cap (white stuff on the scalp), because of this shampoo. The benefit is that it smells great and doesn't dry baby's skin.

8. *Vaseline:* Good for dry skin on face or lips.

9. *Infant Tylenol or Motrin.* Get the one with the dropper. If your baby has a fever and you're worried, the best thing to do, in addition to Tylenol or Motrin, is to put him in tepid or warm water in the tub and let him sit there while you sponge water over his shoulders and on his forehead. Of course, always consult your doctor.

10. *Hylands Teething Tablets.* They sometimes sell these at the drugstore or grocery store, but mostly at health food stores. They are tiny, harmless, dissolving pills that have chamomile in them, and they are really soothing for the baby.

11. *Mylecon Drops.* Very important. Our kids never spit up, and we think it was because of this miracle potion. It's a little pricey but worth it, because it's great for stomach upset. When Jennifer was fussy and didn't need food or diapers, we gave her some Mylecon and she was fine. Whenever she has a sore stomach now, she asks for it.

12. *First-aid kit.* Make sure you include Ipecac Syrup (the stuff that makes you vomit). Also make sure you have the number of Poison Control near the phone. Call them first.

There are, of course, so many other necessities. These are just some things you may not think of.

General Tips

1. *Love.* Our Papa (the kids' great-grandfather) said that, in his day, they thought it was better for the baby to "cry it out." Now, seeing how well behaved his great-grandchildren are, he realizes that you should pick them up and give them as much love as you can. According to many experts, you can't spoil a baby, and physical contact promotes overall health.

2. *Enjoy every moment.* It does go very fast, so even if you haven't slept in 3 nights, someday you'll be lying on a beach waiting for a call from your kid at college . . . and you'll probably be dreaming of these days.

3. *Discipline.* This starts around 8 or 9 months.

4. *Advice.* When you get advice from people, remember you can take what you want and leave the rest.

5. *Let the baby fall asleep on his or her own.* Just feed them until they're a little drowsy and say, "I'm going to put you in your bed now." Then, lay them in their crib and let them fall asleep on their own (without

rocking them to sleep). One interesting trait for a baby is that sleep is learned. They may come out with a natural ability to fall back to sleep on their own after waking up, but then they forget because us moms, dads, grandparents, and great-grandparents like to hold them and rock them to sleep. If they become used to that, they have a harder time on their own later.

6. *Talk to your baby.* From the day they are born (if not before), tell them everything you are doing. "It's diaper time." "Did you go peepee?" "Oh, are you hungry? Do you want food?" If you talk to them, they begin to understand quickly and learn key words. We noticed if the baby was crying and we said, "Oh, are you hungry?" she would look at us and stop crying for a moment. This made communication easier for both of us. There seems to be less frustration, and they may even begin talking sooner. Also, Joseph Garcia's book, *Sign with Your Baby* is very helpful with nonverbal communication. As they grow up, from very early on, it helps to talk to your child as you would talk to an adult. For example, by using the word *horse* instead of "horsie," your child will learn the correct word from the start.

7. *Tickle, tickle.* When we asked our cousin, David, who has two amazing boys, for advice, the only thing he said was, "Tickle them." That was it. Now, although we haven't had much experience with different types of personalities, we do believe that tickling releases serotonin (a happy chemical in the brain). The lack of this chemical is being blamed for ADD and other depression in children. It may sound odd, but Jennifer and David have been such happy kids and we believe tickling helped.

8. *Don't give up and don't give in.* These are words to live by. You may have to constantly pull your toddler away from the stereo after telling him no many times. Then, suddenly, when you're just about to give up, he'll walk up to the stereo, shake his head, say, no, and then walk away all by himself. It's very rewarding, so hang in there. And try to find humor in an otherwise stressful situation whenever

possible. Our 9-year-old neighbor, Kayla, was over when our kids were acting up. She heard us say to them, "You know what happens to kids who don't behave in this house?" Our neighbor looked at us with fright in her eyes. We continued, "They get *tickled!*" And we ran up to our kids and began tickling them. Soon, the misbehaving turned into fun and everyone was happy. (Our little neighbor was a little stunned, though.)

9. *The magic of home videos.* Like many parents, we have an ever-growing library of home videos. We noticed that our kids enjoy watching these films that star them, as much as those staring such bigger-than-life characters as Dorothy, Areielle, Belle, and Tarzan. You don't have to wait for years to pass before you can appreciate these family archives. In fact, showing your child's birthday party as soon as the day after the party can give him a unique perspective of the day and reinforce his memories. Also, just like a sports team can improve their skills by watching films of previous games, we discovered that home videos can be used to help your children see themselves as others see them, and thus serve as a catalyst to positive behavioral changes. And we have learned that the best use of the camera isn't necessarily in capturing the big events like the school play. The most precious moments you can capture on tape include the ordinary events or everyday life (those you might not even think of recording). Try candidly taping a conversation between your 3-year-old daughter and her grandmother, bath time, a typical Sunday dinner, or your kids playing together when they don't think anyone else is watching.

10. *Ask your child questions.* When you think about asking questions, you naturally think of the child asking the parent: "Why?" "Are we there yet?" "Do I have to?" We have learned the value in turning the tables and asking our kids to answer a variety of questions: "How would your day be different if you were a fish?" "Do you think the person in this magazine is happy or sad?" "Why do you think the sky is blue?" "Do you think ants have families?" "If you could fly an airplane, where is the first place you would go?" The imagination

has no boundaries, and it's important to explore this unchartered territory of the child's mind. Having fun with questions (venturing beyond the standard "What color is the ball?" "What do cows say?" "How was your day?") stimulates curiosity and creativity, and ultimately increases knowledge.

11. *Boredom.* A doctor's waiting room reveals a lot about how differently children are raised. The longer the wait, the more you learn. As Charles Fay, Ph.D., mentioned in his *Parent School* lesson, "Creating Creative Kids: Turning Boredom into Brightness," we believe you can teach your children to never be bored (a lot of adults could use this lesson, too). Children should know that their imagination is a magical weapon that can easily slay the Boredom Dragon (anywhere, anytime). But you don't always have to resort to the imagination to rescue you. Children can be raised to see the real world around them as a land of mystery and adventure—yes, even a doctor's waiting room. Condition your child with questions, such as: "See that boy over there with the cast on his arm? What do you think happened to him?" "Would you ever want to be a doctor?" "What's your favorite fish in the aquarium?" "Let's guess who's going to be called next!"

12. *Mutual respect.* Giving respect teaches respect. Just because you're the boss doesn't mean you should always take full advantage of that role; it doesn't mean saying no and ordering your kids around simply for the sake of flexing your muscles (or getting back at *your* parents). You can be respectful of children without giving up your position of authority. Being respectful of your children could include listening to them when they want to talk to you (for looking them in the eyes, you get bonus points); not making promises that aren't intended on being kept; telling them what you have planned for the day, instead of dragging them through it blindly; and giving them choices whenever possible.

13. *A little tip for Mom.* Be easy on the man. Most men can't do two things at once, so talking on the phone and changing the baby's

diaper may be out of the question. (It's just not in their nature.) Also, the two of you may do things differently. As long as the baby's shoes aren't on the wrong feet, or the diaper isn't backward, or the baby isn't dangling from the changing table, let it be. Variety is good for the baby. It teaches her to be adaptable. Jennifer would say, "Daddy do it," or "Mommy do it," and it was usually an even amount of times. And if you do need to give him advice, instead of saying, "Don't do it that way," or "You're doing it wrong," begin your sentences with "I usually do it like this . . . " or "I read in *Parent School* that this way is even better . . . " Just keep in mind that men want to help and do things right (they just don't have the same instincts as women do), so give them room and appreciate the things they do without being asked.

14. *Take care of yourself, too.* Kids want and need their parents to be happy, relaxed, and fulfilled. Taking care of yourself means taking care of your family—just like when you travel in an airplane and the flight attendant explains that when the oxygen masks come down, put yours on first and then your child's. You need enough oxygen to help your child. If you take care of yourself first, you will have enough energy to take care of your family. It's not selfish to give yourself time to do whatever you want. Of all the things to do (outside of being a mom or dad), time to do nothing in particular belongs at the top of your list! Being a good parent does not mean being a martyr. Contrary to popular belief, never-ending struggle and fatigue are not parenting requirements. While loving and protecting are, indeed, full-time jobs of all moms and dads, there should always be plenty of time left over for living a life beyond the role of parent. If you lose your true self when performing the part of caretaker, if you don't maintain your other adult relationships (friends, family, and husband/wife), if you don't have time for a hobby, or if you're too tired and stressed to fully enjoy and participate in quality time with your spouse and children—then all is lost. You deserve a break—a walk in the park; a weekly yoga class; a round of golf; lunch with friends; a shopping spree (anywhere *except* the grocery store); a long, hot bath . . . and especially a

romantic dinner date with the mother or father of your children. The time and care you spend on yourself will be given back to your family tenfold.

We hope you are enjoying your parenting journey and that the lessons in this book help pave the way to more joyous and fulfilling experiences.

Much health, fulfillment, and love,
Jerry and Lorin

The Parent School Faculty

Penelope Leach, Ph.D. is a research psychologist, a favorite source of child development information and child care advice for parents all over the world, and a powerful advocate for the needs of families. Her best-selling books include *Babyhood; Children First: What Our Society Must Do and Is Not Doing—for Children Today; The First Six Months; Your Growing Child—From Babyhood Through Adolescence;* and *Your Baby & Child,* the most loved, trusted, and comprehensive book in its field. Translated into twenty-nine languages, and the basis for an award-winning cable-TV series shown on all five continents, a new version of *Your Baby & Child* was published in 1997. Rewritten for a new generation, it encompasses the latest research on child development and learning, and reflects the realities of today's changing lifestyles and new approaches to parenting. Penelope Leach was educated at Cambridge University, England, and at the London School of Economics, where she received her Ph.D. in psychology (for a study of the effects of different kinds of upbringing on personality development). Her research has included a 4-year study, under the auspices of Britain's Medical Research Council, of the effects of babies on their parents, and many aspects of adolescence for the International Centre for Child Studies at the University of Bristol. She is currently co-director of a 7-year study based within London University of the effects of different kinds and combinations of child care on 1,200 children from birth to first grade. Penelope is a fellow of the British Psychological Society, a founding member of the U.K. branch of the World Association for Infant Medical Health, and works on both sides of the Atlantic and in various capacities for parents' and children's organizations concerned with prenatal care and birth, family-friendly working practices, day care, and education in the early years. She is married to an energy and environment consultant and has two children and at least four grandchildren.

Becky A. Bailey, Ph.D., is an award-winning author, renowned teacher, and nationally recognized expert specializing in early childhood education and developmental psychology. She teaches a profound yet practical approach to parenting in her new book titled *Easy to Love, Difficult to Discipline: The 7 Basic Skills for Turning Conflict into Cooperation.* Her methods discipline both parents and children brilliantly and respectfully. Her experience includes 25 years as a university professor. She is the founder and currently the president of Loving Guidance, Inc., which is dedicated to creating positive environments for children, families, schools, and businesses. Dr. Bailey has authored numerous research articles, audio tapes, and six books, including the highly acclaimed *There's Gotta Be A Better Way: Discipline That Works!* Her book, *I Love You Rituals: Activities to Build Bonds and Strengthen Relationships with Children,* received the honorable 1999 Parent's Guide Award. *Shubert's BIG Voice,* Dr. Bailey's new children's book, demonstrates how children can resolve conflicts peacefully. Her award-winning audio tapes, *The Ten Principles of Positive Discipline, Preventing Power Struggles, Conflict Resolution,* and *Transforming Aggression into Healthy Self-Esteem,* have reached the hearts and souls of thousands, and are used throughout the country to help parents and teachers improve and renew relationships with children. She is nationally recognized for her methods of working with aggressive and difficult children. Dr. Bailey has appeared on CNN, PBS, and *Hour of Power* with Dr. Robert Schuller, among other programs. She is being featured in her own public television special. To see her speaking schedule and for a full list of her books, tapes, and instructional materials, visit Dr. Bailey's web site at www.beckybailey.com.

Jann Blackstone-Ford, M.A. received her master's degree from San Jose State University. Formerly a teacher, she is now a certified mediator who specializes in conflict resolution specifically in divorce and family issues. Understanding firsthand that divorce and remarriage are difficult on everyone in the family, Jann founded Bonus Families, www.bonusfamilies.com, a web site dedicated to support and reassure every member of your stepfamily. Bonus Families is a family-friendly web site, a place where everyone, from kids to grands can turn for help. It promotes a positive image for stepfamilies and prefers to use the word *bonus* rather than step. Why bonus? Most people say they hate to be called a step anything. Step implies negative things—wicked, evil, certainly not a contributing member of a family. But a bonus is something positive, a reward for a job well done. Using the word *bonus* instead of *step* is simply an acknowledgment of your hard work. It may not be the final word, but it's definitely a step in the right direction. Bonus Families not only deals with conventional stepfamily problems but offers advice on getting along with an ex-spouse and handling alternative lifestyle problems as well. On a more personal note, in 1989, Jann—a divorced single mother and 36 years old—remarried and began the midlife infertility chase. After 3 years, and operations for both her and her husband, she finally had a healthy baby girl in 1992. This experience made her realize the lack of literature and support for midlife mothers, and she began doing research and networking with other women her age who also chose to have babies at midlife. This research and networking became *Mid-Life Motherhood, A Woman-to-Woman Look at Pregnancy and Parenting for Women Approaching 40 and Older* (St. Martin's Press, 2001). Jann is the mother of two children, plus the bonus mom to two bonus children. She has written two books on the subject of divorce and parenting, *My Parents Are Divorced, Too*, a book about divorce for kids, by kids, and *The Custody Solutions Sourcebook*, for adults contemplating divorce and unsure of their custody alternatives. She also serves as an expert on stepfamily and custody issues for www.ivillage.com and she is co-authoring her next book, *Ex-Etiquette*, with her husband's ex-wife.

Michele Borba, Ed.D., is the author of more than 25 books, including *Building Moral Intelligence: The Seven Essential Virtues that Teach Kids to do the Right Thing*, and *Parents Do Make a Difference: How to Raise Kids with Solid Character, Strong Minds, and Caring Hearts*, which was selected by *Child* magazine as "one of the most outstanding parenting books of the year." Filled with step-by-step advice, practical ideas, and real-life examples, it shows parents and teachers how to teach kids eight indispensable skills—self-confidence, self-awareness, communication, problem solving, getting along, goal setting, perseverance, and empathy—they'll need for living confident, happy, and productive lives. Dr. Borba is an internationally recognized consultant who has presented workshops to more than half a million parents and teachers for more than two decades. She has been a frequent guest on television and NPR radio talk shows throughout North America, and her work has been quoted in publications such as *Newsweek*, *Parents* magazine, *Working Mother*, *Family Life*, *Redbook* and *First for Women*. One of her essays appeared in *Chicken Soup for the Soul*. She is a former teacher, recipient of the National Educator Award, and mother of three children. To find out more about her work, visit www.moralintelligence.com.

Mark L. Brenner, MFCC, has been a licensed marriage, family, and child therapist for over 18 years. His focus is on early childhood and adolescent development. He is a lecturer and published author of *When No Gets You Nowhere*. Mark Brenner's clinical experience over the past 18 years has included both normal and abnormal childhood development. He has worked with children and parents at the Children's Neurological Clinic, the Early Childhood Center at Cedars Sinai Hospital, and outpatient psychiatric services at the VA Hospital in Los Angeles. Mr. Brenner also coauthored an international children's magic program in three languages for Club Med USA, Children's Mini Club, for ages 7 through 13 years. He is currently working on a six-part video series on parent–child communication. In addition, Mr. Brenner has just completed two new parenting books on both child and teenage behavior. Mr. Brenner lives in California and is married with two children.

Martha M. Bullen is co-author, with Darcie Sanders, of *Staying Home: From Full-Time Professional to Full-Time Parent* and *Turn Your Talents into Profits: 100+ Terrific Ideas for Starting Your Own Home-Based Microbusiness*. Bullen has appeared on NBC's *Today*, *The Early Show*, CNN, *Roseanne*, and NPR. Her books have been featured in *Woman's Day*, the *New York Times*, *Time*, the *Christian Science Monitor*, *Working Woman*, *Good Housekeeping*, the *Chicago Tribune*, *Parenting*, *Parents*, and *American Baby*. She also edited and contributed to the recent book *Tales from the Homefront*, which features insightful stories from home-based moms about their daily lives. For more information on *Tales from the Homefront*, contact: 27956 Forest Garden Rd., Wauconda, IL 60084; (847) 526-4537; fax: (847) 526-2857; e-mail: writermb@aol.com; website: www.spencerandwaters.com. *Tales* is available online at amazon.com & barnesandnoble.com, and through the 24-hour toll-free order number 1-800-711-3627.

Darrell J. Burnett, Ph.D. is a clinical child psychologist, a marriage and family therapist, author, lecturer, and father of three. Dr. Burnett has specialized in positive parenting in his private practice for over 20 years in southern California. For his *family life* publications, Dr. Burnett has authored *Improving Parent-Adolescent Relationships; Raising Responsible Kids: 5 Steps for Parents* (audio tape and booklet); and *Parents, Kids, & Self-Esteem: 15 Ways to Help Kids Like Themselves* (audio tape and booklet). Dr. Burnett is also a youth sports psychologist, applying positive parenting to the field of youth sports. He was named as a national sports ethics fellow by the

University of Rhode Island's Institute for International Sport for his work in promoting ethics and fair play. He is popular on the lecture circuit, and has been involved with youth league clinics at the local and national level. Besides several journal articles, his youth sports publications include *It's Just a Game! (Youth, Sports, & Self Esteem: A Guide for Parents)*; "Hey, Mom & Dad, It's Just a Game!" and "Positive Coaching: The Art of Being a Successful Youth League Coach." His "A Coach with Soul" was published in *Chicken Soup for the Soul at Work* and "Challenger Baseball" appeared in *Chicken Soup for the Unsinkable Soul*. Most recently, he contributed several articles about the role of parents in youth sports in the *Gatorade Playbook for Kids: A Parent's Guide to Help Kids Get the Most Out of Sports*. Dr. Burnett can be reached at (800) 493-5943; e-mail: djburnet@pacbell.net; or visit djburnett.com.

Ross Campbell, M.D., is associate professor of pediatrics and psychiatry at the University of Tennessee College of Medicine. He is the author of *How to Really Love Your Teenager*, which has sold more than 300,000 copies and is an internationally acclaimed best-seller. His other books include the best-selling *How to Really Love Your Child* and *Kids in Danger*. Dr. Campbell and his wife, Pat, have four grown children.

John S. Dacey, Ph.D., is professor at Boston College in the Department of Counseling, Developmental Psychology, and Research Methods. An expert in child development, he is also the author of many books and articles on parenting, creativity, adolescent psychology, and human development. He has co-authored the following books with Lisa B. Fiore, Ph.D.: *Your Anxious Child: How Parents and Teachers Can Relieve Anxiety in Children*; *Understanding Creativity: The Interplay of Biological, Psychological, and Social Factors*; and *The Nurturing Parent: How to Raise Creative, Loving, Responsible Children* (Fireside).

Theresa Foy DiGeronimo, M.Ed., is adjunct professor of English at The William Paterson University of New Jersey and mother of three. As a team, Schaefer and DiGeronimo have co-authored several books including *How to Talk to Your Kids About Really Important Things* and *How to Talk to Teens About Really Important Things* (Jossey Bass Publishers).

Mimi Doe, M.Ed., is the author of *Busy But Balanced, 10 Principles for Spiritual Parenting—Nurturing Your Child's Soul*, which won the 1998 Parents' Choice Seal of Approval and was a finalist in the Books for a Better

Life Award. *Ladies Home Journal* called Doe "a parenting guru." She is the co-author of *Drawing Angels Near: Children Tell of Angels in Words and Pictures,* and she co-produced the award-winning children's video, *Concert in Angel-Land,* which aired on ABC. She holds a master's degree in education from Harvard. Her workshops have changed the way thousands of parents interact with the children in their lives and her weekly e-mail broadcasts, "Spiritual Parenting Thought for the Week," inspires many. Mimi Doe appeared on the *The Oprah Winfrey Show* (April 1999).

Roslyn Duffy is co-author, with Elizabeth Crary, of *The Parent's Report Card* and best-selling co-author, with Jane Nelsen and Cheryl Erwin, of *Positive Discipline for Preschoolers,* and *Positive Discipline: The First Three Years.* Duffy is a 17-year veteran director of a child care program in Seattle. She lectures and teaches classes for both parents and teachers, and is a counselor in private practice. She has presented talks to large and small groups. She has extensive credentials working with families, especially those with young children. She began one of the first all-day Montessori child care programs in the United States and directed it for 17 years. She has taught children of all ages and sees children as part of her counseling practice. Roslyn Duffy does a monthly question-and-answer program on the Internet for *MomsOnline* magazine, appears on local NPR radio, and teaches at various college programs in the Northwest. She is a mother of four children and lives with her family in Seattle, Washington. Her bimonthly column for *Childcare Information Exchange* magazine is titled "From a Parent's Perspective." E-mail: RainRoz@yahoo.com.

Meg Eastman, Ph.D., is a clinical psychologist with the Children's Program in Portland, Oregon. She enjoys teaching families "the tools of peacemaking so they can tame the dragon of anger within them." She provides family consultations, therapy, workshops, and community speaking regarding her book *Taming the Dragon in Your Child: Solutions for Breaking the Cycle of Family Anger* (John Wiley and Sons).

Cheryl L. Erwin, M.A., M.F.T., is a licensed marriage and family therapist with a practice in the Reno, Nevada area, a parenting consultant, and a popular speaker and trainer. She is the co-author, with Jane Nelsen, Ed.D., of four books in the best-selling *Positive Discipline* series and *Parents Who Love Too Much: How Good Parents Can Learn to Love More Wisely and Develop Children of Character* (Prima, 2000). For more information, visit www.robisonhouse.com or www.positivediscipline.com. Erwin can be reached at (775) 355-7722 or by e-mail at erwincl@aol.com.

Charles Fay, Ph.D., is a parent, author, nationally certified school psychologist, and consultant to schools, parent groups, and mental health professionals across the United States. His expertise in developing and teaching practical discipline and behavior management strategies has been refined through work with severely disturbed children and adolescents in school, hospital, and community settings. His interest in this field resulted from years of watching and learning from two internationally recognized experts: his father, Jim Fay, and their friend, Foster Cline, M.D. Dr. Charles Fay received his Ph.D. from the University of South Carolina School Psychology Program. He has also earned national certification from the National Association of School Psychologists (NASP). Dr. Fay has taken an active role in blending his unique psychological background and expertise with the "Love and Logic" techniques originally developed by his father and Dr. Cline. Charles Fay is the co-author, with Jim Fay, of *Love and Logic Magic for Early Childhood: Practical Parenting from Birth to Six Years.*

Jim Fay is one of America's most sought-after presenters in the areas of parenting, positive discipline, and classroom management. He is the co-founder, with Foster W. Cline, M.D., of the "Love and Logic" philosophy. Love and Logic teaches a way of working with children so that they would be responsible and prepared for the real world. Fay provides consulting and speaking presentations through School Consultant Services. He serves as a consultant to schools, parent organizations, , and the U.S. military. Fay began his career as a teacher, and for 31 years served in public, private, and parochial schools. He has also been a school principal and school administrator. In 1984, Jim Fay founded the Cline/Fay Institute, Inc., in Golden, Colorado, which publishes Love and Logic books, audio cassettes, CDs, and video cassettes. Fay co-wrote the best-selling book, *Parenting with Love and Logic* with Foster W. Cline, M.D., which launched a series that includes *Parenting Teens with Love and Logic, Teaching with Love and Logic,* and *Grandparenting with Love and Logic.* Fay is the parent of three children. His son, Charles Fay, Ph.D., has joined Jim in his work at the Love and Logic Institute.

Lisa B. Fiore, Ph.D. teaches courses in developmental and educational psychology at Boston College, Curry College, and Lesley University. Her background as an early childhood educator has fostered her research in HeadStart centers and her work in counseling parents of young children. She is the co-author, with John S. Dacey, Ph.D., of *Your Anxious Child: How Parents and Teachers Can Relieve Anxiety in Children and Understanding Creativity: The Interplay of Biological, Psychological, and Social Factors.* Fiore is the author of *In Adolescence in America: An Encyclopedia.*

Chris Fletcher's humorous essays on parenthood have appeared in a number of parenting publications and in the book *Tales from the Homefront.* This book features 110 insightful stories from home-based moms about their daily lives. Fletcher writes the regular "On the Homefront" column for the national newsletter of the nonprofit mothers' association, *Mothers and More* (formerly Employed Mothers at the Leading Edge; to learn more about *Mothers and More,* send a SASE to: *Mothers and More,* P.O. Box 31, Elmhurst, IL 60126). A former day care director and early childhood teacher trainer, Fletcher has also written on issues of early childhood education and development. For more information on *Tales from the Homefront,* contact: 27956 Forest Garden Rd., Wauconda, IL 60084; phone (847) 526-4537; fax (847) 526-2857; e-mail: writermb@aol.com; web site: www.spencerandwaters.com.

Judy Ford, LCSW is a nationally recognized family counselor and parenting coach, best-selling author, and speaker. She has worked for nearly three decades with children and families in various settings—from gang turf in the inner city to crisis intervention in hospitals. Her workshops—*Parenting with Love and Laughter* and *Positive Ways to Handle Conflicts, Complaints, Upsets and Little Annoyances*—have been attended by thousands. Judy is the best-selling author of the *Wonderful Ways* series (over 500,000 copies sold) which include *Wonderful Ways to Love a Child, Wonderful Ways to Love a Teen: Even When it Seems Impossible, Wonderful Ways to Be a Family, Wonderful Ways to Be a Stepparent, Wonderful Ways to Love a Grandchild.* Her other books are *Expecting Baby Between Mother and Daughter: A Teenager* and *Her Mom Share the Secrets of a Strong Relationship Getting Over Getting Mad.* Two of her titles were awarded the National Parenting Center's Seal of Approval and the Family Channel's Seal of Quality. Articles on her work have appeared in over 1,000 publications including *Family Circle Magazine, USA Today, Good Housekeeping, Women's World,* among many others. She has appeared on *Oprah,* CNN, *National Public Radio,* Canadian Broadcasting, and others. Judy has dedicated her life to family healing and wholeness and is currently in private practice in Kirkland, Washington. She can be reached at www.judyford.com.

Fred Frankel, Ph.D., a psychologist, is director of the world-renowned UCLA Parent Training & Children's Social Skills Programs. Dr. Frankel is professor of medical psychology at UCLA where he teaches and trains pediatricians, psychologists, social workers and child psychiatrists. His book, *Good Friends Are Hard to Find* (Perspective Publishing), is available at 1-800-330-5851, www.familyhelp.com, or at bookstores.

John C. Friel, Ph.D., and **Linda D. Friel, M.A.,** have written the popular book *The 7 Worst Things Good Parents Do* (more than 500,000 copies sold). This book was written for parents who are contemplating starting a family, have children who haven't entered school yet, or are empty-nesters wondering how you can be better parents to your grown children. The material in this book has been field-tested in the authors' own household, with hundreds of their clients, and thousands of their workshop and Clearlife Clinic participants. The Friels offer 40 years of combined experience as practicing psychologists, and 50 years of combined experience as blended-family parents. They are full-time practicing psychologists in the Minneapolis/St. Paul suburbs, where they do individual, couple, and family therapy, and ongoing men's and women's therapy groups. They also conduct the 3½ day *ClearLife/Lifeworks Clinic,* a gentle process to help people replace old patterns of living with more effective ones, in several U.S. cities. They are internationally recognized speakers and trainers and are the best-selling authors of *Adult Children: The Secrets of Dysfunctional Families, An Adult Child's Guide to What's "Normal," The Grown-Up Man, Rescuing Your Spirit, The Soul Of Adulthood,* and *The 7 Worst Things Good Parents Do.* To see their speaking schedules and for a full list of their books and tapes, as well as a schedule for the ClearLife/Lifeworks Clinic, visit their web site at www.clearlife.com.

Joseph Garcia, Ed.D., is an author, teacher, lecturer, and interpreter. He has taught courses in community development, grant writing, and American sign language. His best-selling book, *Sign with your Baby* (which advocates teaching sign language to hearing infants and toddlers to reduce the baby's stress and enhance early communication), is the recipient of the 1999 Parents' Choice Award, the Emerald City Award (ITVA Seattle Chapter), the 1999 Communicator Award, and the 1999 National Parenting Center's Seal of Approval. *Mothering* magazine reports, "For the toddler, signing can be an active step into the world; it breaks the early communication barrier that stands between gurgling infants and puzzled parents." His video, *Sign with your Baby,* was awarded the Telly Award 2000 and was given the Chris Award at the Columbus International Film Festival 1999 for Best Educational Video. Dr. Garcia is also the author of *Medical Sign Language*—a 726-page reference text that interprets medical terminology into American sign language. He received his doctorate at Nova Southeastern University. Dr. Burton White, the Director of the Center for Parent Education and one of the world's leading authorities on early childhood development, calls Joseph Garcia "a pioneer." Dr. Garcia lives in Bellingham, Washington. E-mail: seekorg@gte.net.

Catherine Musco Garcia-Prats and **Joseph Garcia-Prats, M.D.,** have been married for over 25 years and are the proud parents of ten sons ranging in age from 5 to 23. They are the authors of *Good Families Don't Just Happen: What We Learned from Raising Our Ten Sons and How It Can Work For You* and *Good Marriages Don't Just Happen: Keeping Our Relationship Alive While Raising Our Ten Sons*. Individually, and as a couple, they lecture nationally on family and parenting. They have been guests on *The Oprah Winfrey Show*, *The Gayle King Show*, *American Journal*, *Home Life*, and *Primer Impacto*, as well as many local radio and TV talk shows. Feature articles on the Garcia-Prats family have appeared in the *Houston Chronicle*, the *Houston Post*, the *Dallas Morning News*, *Becoming Family*, and the *Ladies Home Journal*, as well as stories in many newspapers throughout the United States. In 1998, the Garcia-Prats family was honored as "Houston Family of the Year" by Family Service Center at their annual "Celebration of Families" luncheon. **Dr. Joseph Garcia-Prats** is a practicing neonatologist at Baylor College of Medicine in Houston and holds joint appointments in the Department of Pediatrics and Center for Ethics, Medicine and Public Issues. He is originally from El Paso, Texas, where he went to Jesuit High School, after which he obtained his undergraduate degree at Loyola University in New Orleans. He received his medical degree at Tulane Medical School and did his pediatric training and fellowship in neonatology at Baylor College of Medicine. He is also a member of the board of directors of the Gulf Coast Chapter of the March of Dimes. **Catherine Musco Garcia-Prats** is a former first-grade teacher and received her bachelor of science degree from Loyola University in New Orleans. She has served on the board of directors of the Woman's Hospital of Texas, the board of the woman's Hospital Foundation, and the St. Francis de Sales School Board. She presently serves on the Galveston-Houston Diocesan Board of Education and the Board of the Family Service Center. The Garcia-Prats have been a sponsor couple for their parish marriage preparation program for 16 years. They volunteer with their church, the boys' schools and sports activities, as well as the community. Web page: www.garcia-prats.com; email: gp12tex@neosoft.com

William P. Garvey, Ph.D. is the author of *Ain't Misbehavin': The Ten Discipline Issues Every Parent Faces and How to Resolve Them.* Dr Garvey has been in clinical practice for 35 years and for most of that time has been a consultant to a large group of cooperative nursery schools in the San Francisco Bay Area. He was an associate professor of psychology at San Jose State University, where he was also the director of the Family Services Clinic and trained graduate students to work with families.

Susan Gilbert is the author of *A Field Guide to Boys and Girls* (HarperCollins, 2000), which explores the latest findings on differences between boys and girls and development, play, education, and health. She is also a co-author of *The Children's Hospital Guide to Your Child's Health and Development* (Perseus, 2001). She is a writer for *Harvard Health Publications* and a regular contributor to the *New York Times* science section.

Jessica B. Gillooly, Ph.D. is the author of *Before She Gets Her Period: Talking with your Daughter About Menstruation,* which won the NAPPA Parenting Resources Gold Award for 2001. She currently serves as associate professor at Glendale Community College. In addition to her teaching, she has been in private psychotherapy practice for over 20 years. Dr. Gillooly conducts workshops and seminars on women's issues, parent techniques, and family relationships. She has been interviewed by many newspapers and magazines including *Parents Magazine, Family Life, New Moon for Parents, Los Angeles Times,* and the *Boston Globe.* Dr. Gillooly often serves as a psychological expert for CNN and has appeared on numerous radio talk shows across the United States. She was the recipient of "Women Helping Women" award for both local and regional chapters of Soroptimist International, (Spring 1999). She is also a member of several professional organizations and is currently president of the San Gabriel Chapter of California Association of Marriage and Family Therapists. Dr. Gillooly can be reached through the www.family-help.com website.

Marilyn E. Gootman is the author of *Loving Parents' Guide to Discipline* and *The Caring Teacher's Guide to Discipline.* Gootman has had over 25 years of experience working with parents and teachers, as well as parenting her own three children with her husband, Elliot. Dr. Gootman is also the author of *When a Friend Dies, A Book for Teens About Grieving and Healing,* which she wrote when her teenaged daughter's friend died and she found that no books spoke directly and reassuringly to teens to help them through such a difficult ordeal. Her background includes teaching experiences ranging from elementary school to the university. She is known nationally for her advocacy efforts on behalf of children, parents, and teachers. Dr. Gootman has appeared on CNN, MSNBC, CBS, Public Radio, and on local radio and television shows throughout the United States and Canada. Publications as diverse as *Parents'* magazine, *Newsweek*, the *New York Times*, *Moneysworth*, and *Reader's Digest* have solicited Gootman's professional opinion. She is founder of Gootman Education Associates, an educational consulting company that provides workshops and seminars for parents and educators, focusing on successful strategies for raising and teaching children. She can be reached at Gootman@earthlink.net or (706) 546-0106.

John Gray, Ph.D., is the author of 10 best-sellers, including the runaway hit *Men Are from Mars, Women Are from Venus*, which has sold more than 10 million copies worldwide. In *Children Are from Heaven*, John Gray presents a brand-new approach to parenting, which shows parents how to give their children the freedom and direction to discover and express their true selves. An internationally recognized expert in the fields of communication and relationships, Dr. Gray has been conducting relationship seminars in major cities for 26 years. He is a certified family therapist (NACFT), a consulting editor of *The Family Journal*, a member of the Distinguished Board of International Association of Marriage and Family Counselors, a fellow and diplomat of the American Board of Medical Psychotherapists and Psycho-diagnosticians, and a member of the American Counseling Association. He lives in northern California with his wife, Bonnie, and their three children.

Michael Gurian is a family therapist, educator, and author of twelve books, including three major best-sellers: *The Wonder of Boys*, *A Fine Young Man*, and *The Good Son*, as well as poetry, articles in psychology and education, and a novel, *An American Mystic*. He travels to fifty cities a year to speak at conferences and lead seminars. He is co-founder and co-director of the Michael Gurian Institute at the University of Missouri–Kansas City, which trains teachers worldwide in educational innovation. Michael lives in Spokane, Washington, with his wife, Gail, also a family therapist, and their two children. Web address: www.michaelgurian.com.

Patricia Hersch is the author of *A Tribe Apart: A Journey into the Heart of American Adolescence*, which answers the question, "Why do teenagers so often seem like a different species?" In her powerful book, which the *Philadelphia Inquirer* dubs "a contemporary masterpiece," Hersch offers readers a fly-on-the-wall perspective as she spends 3 years submerging herself in the lives of eight teens in her hometown of Reston, Virginia. She observes that "adolescents have become strangers . . . a tribe apart, remote, mysterious, vaguely threatening." A journalist who writes frequently about teens, Hersch is a former contributing editor to *Psychology Today,* she has been published in the *Washington Post, McCall's, Family Therapy Networker,* the *Baltimore Sun,* and other newspapers and magazines. She was the editor of the "Women in Development" newsletter for the United Nations and conducted an ethnographic study of homeless adolescents in San Francisco and New York for the National Institute of Drug Abuse and Georgetown University Child Development Center. Ms. Hersch lives in Reston, Virginia, with her husband and three sons.

Julia Indichova is the author of *Inconceivable: A Woman's Triumph Over Despair and Statistics.* She is editor in chief of www.FertileHeart.com and the director of the Fertile Heart Learning Center in Woodstock, New York. Julia leads ongoing support groups and workshops on holistic approaches to fertility issues, parenting, and health empowerment.

Aaron Kipnis, Ph.D., teaches psychology at Pacifica Graduate Institute and is president of the Fatherhood Coalition, a nonprofit organization that supports positive male involvement. He is author of *Knights Without Armor, What Women and Men Really Want,* and *Angry Young Men: How Parents, Teachers, and Counselors Can Help "Bad Boys" Become Good Men.* For more information or to contact the author, visit www.malepsych.com.

Karen Kleiman, M.S.W., is co-author, with Valerie Davis Raskin, M.D., of the book, *This Isn't What I Expected: Overcoming Postpartum Depression.* She is a licensed clinical social worker and founder and director of the Postpartum Stress Center near Philadelphia, Pennsylvania, where she treats women with postpartum depression and their families. After graduating in 1980 from the University of Illinois at Chicago with a masters degree in social work, Kleiman opened a private practice with an emphasis on women's issues. After the birth of her second child and the unexpected medical complications that followed, she became profoundly aware of how often and how easily a new mother's needs can fall through the cracks of the medical system. It was then that she became committed to the treatment of women who experienced difficulties related to pregnancy, pregnancy loss, and postpartum-related illnesses. In addition to her practice, she provides training, supervision, and consultation to mental health professionals and frequently lectures on postpartum depression to medical students, health care practitioners, and groups of new parents. Her work has received national attention from *The Oprah Winfrey Show, Inside Edition,* and a variety of newspapers, radio shows, and parenting magazines. Kleiman serves as a postpartum expert for "Moms Online" (AOL), BabyCenter.com, and contributes articles to a number of other parenting web sites. For more information, visit her web site at http://www.postpartumstress.com or call the Postpartum Stress Center at (610) 525.7527.

Trish Kuffner is an author, wife, mother, home-schooler, and lover of good books (but not necessarily in that order). She lives with her husband and five children in Coquitlam, a suburb of Vancouver, British Columbia, Canada. Trish has written four books, all published by Meadowbrook Press: *The Toddler's Busy Book, The Preschooler's Busy Book, The Children's Busy Book,* and *Picture Book Activities* (from which the article in *Parent School* was excerpted). Trish's books are available at bookstores throughout North America. You can contact Trish or order her books through Meadowbrook Press by calling 1-800-338-2232, writing to 5451 Smetana Drive, Minetonka, MN 55343, or visiting their web site at www.MeadowbrookPress.com.

Lawrence Kutner, Ph.D., is the author of five books: *Parent & Child: Getting Through to Each Other, Pregnancy* and *Your Baby's First Year, Toddlers and Preschoolers, Your School-Age Child,* and *Making Sense of Your Teenager.* The Associated Press calls him "Dr. Dad." *Publisher's Weekly* says one of his most recent books "places him firmly in the pantheon occupied by Spock, Brazelton, and Leach." Dr. Kutner is a nationally known clinical psychologist who trained at the Mayo Clinic and teaches at Harvard Medical School. From 1987 to 1994, he was the author of the award-winning weekly *New York Times* "Parent & Child" column, which was also syndicated to several hundred other newspapers throughout the United States. His column won the 1990 American Psychological Association National Psychology Award as the best writing about psychology in the country. After spending 8 years as the child behavior columnist for *Parents* magazine and as the author of its "Ask the Expert" column, he recently left that position to become a columnist and contributing editor for three magazines published by Time Warner: *Parenting, Family Life,* and *BabyTalk.* He is also a featured writer for two online services: Pampers.com and ParentTime.com. He's an Emmy award–winning television reporter and documentary producer. For 2 years, he hosted a call-in program on parenting on KGO Radio (ABC) in San Francisco. He's been a consultant on child development, and a spokesperson for a wide range of foundations, universities, and corporations, including Microsoft, Disney, Procter and Gamble, and General Mills. During 1998, he toured the United States on behalf of Philips Consumer Communications on a project to promote better communication between young adolescents and their parents. He's a father who has done his share of diaper changes, tantrum taming, and managing adolescent angst. Dr. Kutner received his bachelor's degree from Oberlin College in Ohio and his Ph.D. in clinical psychology from the University of Minnesota. He divides his time between homes in Basel, Switzerland, and the United States.

Sandra E. Lamb is the author of *How to Write It, A Complete Guide to Everything You'll Ever Write* (Ten Speed Press), and is a frequent writer of parenting, women's issue, and relationship articles, which have appeared in such magazines as *Family Circle, Woman's Day, Working Mother,* and *Parents.* Sandra also writes literary fiction and nonfiction books on a variety of subjects. She has three grown sons, and lives with her husband in Denver. Check Sandra's web site, sandralamb.com, for more information and upcoming books.

William Martin is the author of *The Parent's Tao Te Ching, The Sage's Tao Te Ching, The Couple's Tao Te Ching, The Way of the Word,* and *The Art of Pastoring.* He is also a teacher, counselor, and retreat leader. He is a graduate of the University of California at Berkeley and of Western Theological Seminary. After spending 4 years as a research scientist for the Department of the Navy, he returned to graduate school and earned his master's degree in pastoral counseling. He served for 20 years as a counselor in private practice and as a college instructor in counseling. He and his wife, Nancy, now live in Chico, California, where they direct the Still Point, an educational center for spiritual and personal growth. He conducts seminars, workshops, and retreats around the country for schools, businesses, couples, and parent groups on themes such as "Peaceful Parenting," "Compassion Fatigue," and "Loving Couples." He is the parent of two grown children, Lara and John. Martin can be reached at Still Point, 1163 East Avenue, Suite 103, Chico, CA 95926; (530) 345-0542; e-mail: Stlpnt@aol.com.

Fred Mednick, Ed.D., is the author of *Rebel Without a Car: Surviving and Appreciating Your Child's Teen Years.* Recipient of the Johns Hopkins University Outstanding California Educator's Award, his book has been successful in America as well as throughout Europe. He has been working with adolescents for more than 20 years, in community service organizations and public as well as private schools, and is known for his unique theory on adolescence, which is articulated with humor. Dr. Mednick served on an Internet chat panel, sponsored by Time-Warner, with the late Doctor Spock and child development expert Penelope Leach. He is a nationally known speaker and has been featured on National Public Radio. He has served as a visiting lecturer and educational consultant in China, Thailand, India, and Russia. Dr. Mednick's most recent projects involve seminars on innovative new school reform models to meet the needs of "global teens." His international consultancy work has been endorsed by UNESCO and The World Bank. He is now president of Teachers Without Borders (teacherswithoutborders.org), a global consortium of educators committed to educational tools, resources, and collaboration for teachers worldwide.

Joseph Anthony Michelli, Ph.D., is the author of *Humor, Play and Laughter—Stress Proofing Life with Your Kids* and *Surviving Sibling Rivalry: Healthy Options for Managing Your Children's Conflicts.* Dr. Michelli is a licensed clinical psychologist; he runs Humor Profits, conducting keynotes, workshops, and training on parenting, humor, and corporate development. Web site: www.humorprofits.com; e-mail: joseph@humorprofits.com; and toll-free at (888) 711-4900.

Matthew J. Miller has been a primary grade teacher in Newton, Massachusetts, since 1993. He was nominated for the 1998 Massachusetts Teacher of the Year Award, and is currently a member of the Cabot School Council. Matt is the co-author of *A+ Activities for First Grade* and *A+ Activities for Second Grade.* He lives with his wife in Brighton, Massachusetts.

Marianne Neifert, M.D., better known as Dr. Mom, is an award-winning pediatrician, dynamic professional speaker, author of popular parenting books, columnist, wife, and mother of five grown children, who were born during her medical training. A fellow of the American Academy of Pediatrics, diplomate of the American Board of Pediatrics, and clinical professor of pediatrics at University of Colorado School of Medicine, Dr. Neifert offers readers the accumulated wisdom of decades of parenting skills and the latest medical knowledge. She is the best-selling author of *Dr. Mom: A Guide to Baby and Child Care, Dr. Mom's Parenting Guide: Commonsense Guidance for the Life of Your Child, Dr. Mom's Guide to Breastfeeding, and Dr. Mom's Prescription for Preschool.* She is a contributing editor for *Parenting* magazine and writes a bimonthly medical column, "Ask Dr. Mom," for *Baby Talk* magazine. For millions of parents, the name "Dr. Mom" is synonymous with practical, prudent, empowering advice, laced with empathic support and reassurance. A well-known child and family advocate, Dr. Mom makes frequent media appearances to educate the public about parenting and children's health issues and has inspired audiences in 45 states. She was chosen as one of *Glamour* magazine's *Ten Outstanding Young Working Women.* She is also a columnist for *McCall's.* She lives with her husband, Lorance, and their children in Denver, Colorado.

Jane Nelsen, Ed.D., is the best-selling author of *Positive Discipline.* She is a California-licensed marriage, family, and child therapist; she was an elementary school counselor and a college instructor in child development for 10 years. She is also the author or co-author of the following: *Positive Discipline A–Z, Positive Discipline in the Classroom, Positive Discipline: A Teacher's A–Z Guide, Positive Discipline for Teenagers, Positive Discipline for Single Parents, Positive Discipline for Preschoolers, Raising Self-Reliant Children in a Self-Indulgent World,* and *From Here to Serenity: Four Principals for Understanding Who You Really Are.* She has also co-authored training manuals for *Positive Discipline in the Classroom* and *Teaching Parenting the Positive Discipline Way.* Dr. Nelsen has appeared on *The Oprah Winfrey Show, The Sally Show, Twin Cities Live,* and as the featured parent expert on the *National Parent Quiz,* hosted by Ben Vereen. She is the mother of seven children and has thirteen grandchildren.

Susan Newman, Ph.D., is a social psychologist and author of many books relating to family issues, among them, *Parenting an Only Child: The Joys & Challenges of Raising Your One & Only* (Doubleday / Broadway); *Never Say Yes to a Stranger: What Your Child Must Know to Stay Safe* (Putnam); and a gift book series, each with hundreds of suggestions: *Little Things Long Remembered: Making Your Children Feel Special Every Day; Little Things Mean a Lot: Creating Happy Memories with Your Grandchildren;* and *Little Things Shared: Lasting Connections Between Family and Friends* (Crown). She teaches at Rutgers University and is often a featured speaker and workshop facilitator on family topics ranging from stranger abduction and drug use to raising only children and strengthening family bonds. Dr. Newman is a member of the American Psychological Association, the New Jersey Psychological Association, the Authors Guild, and the American Society of Journalists and Authors. She was the stepmother of four children before remarrying and now lives in New Jersey with her husband and son, where she is a court-appointed special advocate for abused and neglected children. For more information, contact Susan Newman by e-mail at snewman@susannewmanphd.com or visit her web page: http://www.susannewmanphd.com. Her books are available from amazon.com, bn.com, and bookstores.

David Nylund is the author of *Treating Huckleberry Finn: A New Narrative Approach to Working with Kids Diagnosed ADD/ADHD* and the co-editor of *Narrative Therapies with Children and Adolescents*. He has been a practicing family therapist for over 15 years and conducts workshops for parents and professionals throughout the United States and abroad on ADHD, couples/marital problems and narrative therapy. Currently, David is a doctoral student in cultural studies at the University of California–Davis, where he is studying the effects of the media on youth. He can be reached via his e-mail address: ddnylund@yahoo.com. Log on to his web site for further information: www.treatinghuck.com.

Irving Penn, M.D., received his medical education and his M.D. degree from the University of Leiden, the Netherlands. He then served a rotating internship and 2 years of a surgical residency at Cedars of Lebanon Hospital in Hollywood, California. In 1960, he went into general practice in the west San Fernando Valley and has practiced there ever since. Soon after starting his practice, Dr. Penn began to notice the role that obesity played in decreasing the quality of life, and it was then that he began developing his Penn Program. Recently, he put his program into a book called *The Penn Program for Weight Control* (1stBooks.com). Dr. Penn can be contacted via email at IrvingPenn@msn.com.

Susan K. Perry, Ph.D., is a social psychologist who has been researching and writing about psychological and family topics for more than two decades. Among her specialties are creativity and intellectual development, focusing on how parents can help their children achieve their potential while having fun. Her latest book for parents is the totally revised and updated edition of the award-winning *Playing Smart: The Family Guide to Enriching, Offbeat Learning Activities for Ages 4–14* (Free Spirit Publishing). Find out more about

Playing Smart, from which the article in this book was adapted, at www.BunnyApe.com/otherbooks.htm. Perry is also the author of the bestseller *Writing in Flow: Keys to Enhanced Creativity,* as well as *Catch the Spirit: Teen Volunteers Tell How They Made a Difference,* which won the honor of being named to the New York Public Library 72nd Annual Books for the Teen Age List. She has written hundreds of articles for publications including *Child, Parenting, Psychology Today, Seventeen, Woman's World, USA Today,* and the *Los Angeles Times.* She is a contributing writer for *United Parenting Publications* and judges their annual awards for parenting books. (To read her parenting book reviews, see www.BunnyApe.com/recommendedsue.htm.) Perry's work has won a First Place Award for Service Articles from the American Society of Journalists and Authors, as well as a First Place Award of Excellence in the Parenting Publications of America Annual Competition. She is often quoted as an expert on human development in magazine articles and books. Perry teaches psychology at Woodbury University and writing for *Writer's Digest's Online Workshops.* Previously, she founded and directed a unique and successful early childhood program called *Discovery House School,* and she developed innovative courses in creativity for young children for the Gifted Children's Association of Los Angeles. She is the mother of two grown sons. Her Internet home is www.Bunnyape.com.

Thomas W. Phelan, Ph.D., is a nationally renowned expert and lecturer on child discipline and attention deficit disorder (ADD). Dr. Phelan is the author of the following books and videos: *1-2-3 Magic: Effective Discipline for Children 2–12, All About Attention Deficit Disorder, Surviving Your Adolescents, Self-Esteem Revolutions in Children, Adults with Attention Deficit Disorder,* and *Medication for Attention Deficit Disorder.* As a registered clinical psychologist, Dr. Phelan has worked with children, adults, and families for more than 25 years. He is a member of both the Illinois and American Psychological Associations. In addition to writing and producing, Dr. Phelan manages his private practice and maintains an active schedule of national lectures, as well as radio and television interviews. Dr. Phelan received his doctorate from Loyola University in 1970 after completing his internship at the Loyola Child Guidance Center. He worked at the DuPage Country Mental Health Center until 1972 and then entered private practice. The father of an ADD child, he is the founder and past president of the Illinois Association for Hyperactivity and Attention Deficit Disorder (IAHADD), a support group for parents of ADD children. He has also served on the boards of directors for both ADDA and CHADD, two national organizations for the parents of children with ADD.

Linda Goodman Pillsbury is the author of *Survival Tips for Working Moms*. She is founder and President of Perspective Publishing, a former entertainment executive, and mother of two. She can be contacted through her web site at www.familyhelp.com.

Valerie Davis Raskin, M.D., is a psychiatrist practicing in the Chicago area. She is co-author, with Karen Kleiman, MSW, of *This Isn't What I Expected: Overcoming Postpartum Depression,* which was featured on *The Oprah Winfrey Show.* This book offers compassionate advice for the approximately 400,000 women who suffer each year from postpartum depression. It provides information on overcoming self-defeating thoughts, medical and therapy treatment options, self-esteem, depression, and a chapter on how husbands can help their wives when postpartum depression overcomes them. Dr. Raskin is also the author of *When Words Are Not Enough: The Women's Prescription for Depression and Anxiety* and *Great Sex for Moms: Ten Steps to Nurturing Passion While Raising Kids.* The mother of three, she is currently at work on a book about "above-average sex for average moms."

John Rosemond is considered "America's most widely read authority on child rearing and family life." His syndicated parenting column appears weekly in some 200 newspapers across America and has an estimated readership of 25 million parents. He is the best-selling author of eight parenting books, including *John Rosemond's Six-Point Plan for Raising Happy, Healthy Children,* and his latest, *Raising a Non-Violent Child.* His other titles include *A Family of Value, Because I Said So!, Ending the Homework Hassle, Making the Terrible Two's Terrific, Parent Power!, To Spank or Not to Spank,* and *Teen-Proofing: A Revolutionary Approach to Fostering Responsible Decision Making in Your Teenager.* Rosemond, a family psychologist, is also one of America's busiest and most popular public speakers, giving close to 250 presentations per year to various parent and professional groups. He lives in Gastonia, North Carolina, with his wife, Willie. They have two adult children. For more information on John Rosemond's books and presentations, see his web site at www.rosemond.com or e-mail him at jrosemond@aol.com.

Alvin Rosenfeld, M.D. is a child and adolescent psychiatrist in practice in New York City and Greenwich, Connecticut. He is co-author, with Nicole Wise, of *The Over-scheduled Child: Avoiding the Hyper-Parenting Trap* (Griffin/St.

Martins, 2001) and four prior books. Dr. Rosenfeld has served on the faculties of Harvard, Stanford, and Columbia Universities, and is the author of over seventy articles. He lives in Connecticut with his wife, pediatrician Dorothy Levine, M.D., and his three somewhat hyper-parented children.

Nancy Samalin, M.S., a pioneer in the field of parent education, has worked with parents, educators and health care professionals throughout the United States. and abroad since 1976. She has been giving speeches and offering introductory and advanced workshops for parents of toddlers through teens for more than two decades. Some of her most popular topics are positive discipline, expressing anger without insult, and solving sibling dilemmas. Married and the mother of two children, Nancy discovered first-hand how difficult it is to be a parent. She became aware of the self-defeating patterns many of us repeat with our children, despite our love and good intentions. Convinced that others could benefit from the parenting skills she had acquired, Nancy founded Parent Guidance Workshops and received her master's degree in counseling from Bank Street College. Nancy's many years of working with parents became the inspiration for her three highly acclaimed books, published by Penguin and Bantam: *Loving Your Child Is Not Enough: Positive Discipline That Works, Love and Anger: The Parental Dilemma,* and *Loving Each One Best: A Caring and Practical Approach to Raising Siblings.* Acknowledged as one of the most influential and widely respected parenting authorities in the field, Nancy is in great demand as a speaker and by the media, both nationally and internationally. Her appearances include the *Today show, 20/20, Good Morning America, Dateline/NBC, CBS This Morning,* and CNN. Nancy is a contributing editor for *Parents* magazine and Bottom Line/Personal, the nation's largest consumer newsletter. Find out more at www.samalin.com.

Darcie Sanders is co-author, with Martha M. Bullen, of *Staying Home: From Full-Time Professional to Full-Time Parent* and *Turn Your Talents into Profits.* As recognized authorities on at-home motherhood and self-employment, the authors have appeared on *Today, The Early Show,* CNN, *The Roseanne Show, The Montel Williams Show,* and NPR. Their books have been featured in *Woman's Day,* the *New York Times, Time,* the *Christian Science Monitor, Working Woman, Good Housekeeping,* the *Chicago Tribune, Parenting, Parents,* and *American Baby.* Sanders and Bullen also run their own publishing company, which publishes *Tales from the Homefront.* This book features 110 insightful stories from home-based moms about their daily lives. For more information about their books, visit www.spencerandwaters.com.

Charles E. Schaefer, Ph.D., is professor of psychology and director of the Center for Psychological Services at Fairleigh Dickinson University, New Jersey.

Inda Schaenen is a writer based in St. Louis, Missouri. She is a contributor to *salonmagazine.com*, and the *St. Louis Post-Dispatch*. Schaenen is the author of *The 7 O'clock Bedtime* (ReganBooks, May 2001), a parents' guide to helping children get the sleep they need. She lives with her husband and three children, ages 6, 9, and 12.

Martha Sears, R.N., is the mother of eight children, ages 8 to 33 years, and co-author, with her husband, William Sears, M.D., of nine major books on child care. Sears is a childbirth educator and certified lactation consultant for the International Board of Certified Lactation Consultants. She has been a guest on over one hundred television shows including *The Phil Donahue Show, Good Morning America, The Home Show, CBS This Morning, Today,* and CNN. She is a popular speaker for parenting organizations, such as La Leche League International, of which she has been a member for nearly 20 years. Along with "Dr. Bill," Sears co-hosts a bimonthly online program for Time Warner called *Parenttime,* and a 1-hour weekly America Online parenting program for *Parent Soup.* She currently works as a breastfeeding and parenting consultant in San Clemente, California.

William Sears, M.D., one of America's most renowned pediatricians, is the father of eight children, ages 9 to 34 years, author of twenty-four books on child care, and associate clinical professor of pediatrics at the University of California Irvine School of Medicine. Dr. Sears received his pediatric training at Harvard Medical School's Children's Hospital in Boston and The Hospital for Sick Children in Toronto, the largest children's hospital in the world, where he served as associate ward chief of the newborn nursery and associate professor of pediatrics. In addition to writing many celebrated books and scientific articles, Dr. Sears is a medical and parenting consultant to *Baby Talk* and *Parenting* magazines. Dr. Sears is a fellow of the American Academy of Pediatrics, and a fellow of the Royal College of Pediatricians. A pediatrician for 26 years, he currently lives and practices pediatrics in San Clemente, California. "Dr. Bill" (as his little patients call him) has been a guest on over a hundred television shows including: *20/20, The Phil Donahue Show, Good*

Morning America, The Oprah Winfrey Show, CBS This Morning, Today, Dateline NBC, and CNN. Dr. Sears and his co-author/wife, Martha Sears, host a 1-hour, twice-a-month online show for Time Warner called *Parenttime.* They also host a one-hour weekly America Online parenting program for *Parent Soup.* William and Martha are best known for their books, *The Pregnancy Book, The Birth Book, The Baby Book, The Discipline Book, Parenting The Fussy Baby, The A.D.D. Book, The Family Health and Nutrition Book,* and *The Breastfeeding Book.*

Karyn Seroussi is the author of *Unraveling the Mystery of Autism and PDD: A Mother's Story of Research and Recovery.* This book has been called a landmark in the understanding of autism spectrum disorders—marking the watershed between the old belief that autism is genetic and "hard-wired" and the newer understanding that many cases of autism are metabolic and treatable. Her article in *Parents* magazine, describing how her son's autism was resolved using biomedical intervention, helped thousands of parents to find effective treatment for their children. Karyn Seroussi is the co-founder of ANDI, the Autism Network for Dietary Intervention, and co-editor of the *ANDI News*: a quarterly newsletter providing support for parents of children using biological intervention for their children with autistic spectrum disorders. Karyn has spoken at conferences around the world, helping others understand what is beginning to be known about the nature of, and the treatments for autism. Her goal is to see parents and professionals working together; to have autism diagnosed early and treated appropriately. Her web site includes a worldwide parent support network, answers to frequently asked questions, her original *Parents* magazine article, links to other helpful web sites, sample articles from past newsletters, and subscription information.

Laurel Schmidt is the author of *Seven Times Smarter: 50 Activities, Games and Projects to Develop the Seven Intelligences in Your Child* (Three Rivers Press, 2001). She has worked for 30 years in the fields of art and education, as a teacher, principal, consultant, professional development specialist, and writer. She is the Director of Pupil Services for the Santa Monica–Malibu School District and an adjunct professor at Antioch University. She developed integrated curriculum based on multiple intelligence theory for the Galef Institute and conducted staff development programs nationwide. She presents lectures and workshops for parents, teachers and child care workers at local, state, and national conferences on education, gifted programs, and home-schooling. For more information about Laurel, her work, and publications, visit www.seventimessmarter.com. Laurel has been a guest on numerous radio programs discussing education and parenting. Her book, *Seven Times Smarter*, was featured in the *New York Post*, the *Santa Monica Mirror*, *Parents* magazine, *Parent Guide*, *Publishers' Weekly*, and *Better Homes and Gardens*. Laurel is also a consultant to the Museum of Contemporary Art (MOCA) in Los Angeles, and co-author of *Contemporary Art Start: A Guide to Contemporary Art and Culture*, published by MOCA in 1985. It is the centerpiece of a widely acclaimed, inquiry-based art education program. She trains gallery educators and teachers to use Contemporary Art Start (CAS). She is a member of the education and advisory board of the Natural History Museum and a Landmarks Commissioner.

Steven Shelov, M.D., M.A., is the editor-in-chief of the American Academy of Pediatrics' reference book, *Caring for Your Baby & Young Child: Birth to Age 5* (more than one million copies sold, *Parents* magazine "Best Bet"). Dr. Shelov received his B.S. from Yale University, his M.D. from Medical College of Wisconsin, and his master's degree in administrative medicine from the University of Wisconsin. His residency and subsequent chief residency in pediatrics was at Montefiore Medical Center. Until 1997, Dr. Shelov was professor and vice chairman of pediatrics, director, Division of Pediatric Education, at the Albert Einstein College of Medicine, Montefiore Medical Center. In 1997, he was appointed chairman of the Department of Pediatrics at Maimonides Medical Center and professor of pediatrics at State University of New York at Brooklyn. He has written more than a hundred scientific articles and reports, has written and edited two well-respected pediatric textbooks, and has been an active participant in all of the major pediatric academic societies, most notably being president of the Ambulatory Pediatric Association. He was honored as the recipient of that society's highest award for Outstanding Contributions to Pediatrics, the George L. Armstrong Award. In his capacity as chairman of the Department of Pediatrics at Maimonides, he is responsible for all educational, clinical patient care, and research activities for this large department. Under his initiative, the department will be developing a newly conceived Children's Hospital and Child Health Network throughout Brooklyn and the region, linked closely to a newly established women's health program. Dr. Shelov has had a parallel career in advocacy and education for parents and children and in leading broad educational efforts directed toward that audience. He has written a column for 6 years for *Healthy Kids* magazine, "Discover Play, Raising Your Type A Child." Most recently, Dr. Shelov co-edited two additional books for the American

Academy of Pediatrics for parents, *A Guide to Your Child's Symptoms* and *Your Child's First Year*. For 4 years, he was the pediatrician on WNBC's *Today* show and is a frequent child health expert on other television networks. He has an ongoing cable presence on *The Healthy Kids Television Show*, the official show of the American Academy of Pediatrics for parents and is currently working on a number of other television and video projects to educate parents.

Myrna B. Shure, Ph.D., a developmental psychologist, received her Ph.D. from Cornell University, and is professor in the Department of Clinical and Health Psychology at MCP Hahnemann University in Philadelphia. Her Interpersonal Cognitive Problem Solving (ICPS) programs, called "I Can Problem Solve" (also ICPS), and her pioneering work with George Spivack, have won four national awards. Dr. Shure is the author or co-author of six books and numerous book chapters and journal articles, including the *I Can Problem Solve* curriculum guides for preschool through grade 6 for use in schools. Her most recent books for parents are *Raising a Thinking Child, Raising a Thinking Child Workbook,* and *Raising a Thinking Preteen.* Both the *I Can Problem Solve* programs and *Raising a Thinking Child* (for families) were recognized by the Mid-Atlantic Region of Health and Human Services as among the top six violence-prevention programs in a six-state area. The *Raising a Thinking Child* book and audio are 1996 Parents Choice Honors Award Winners. In addition to her research, Dr. Shure has created and record-ed 1-minute parenting tips for WHYY-FM in Philadelphia, local affiliate, National Public Radio, which presently appear weekly in the column "Your Thinking Child" in the *Philadelphia Daily News.* Dr. Shure also speaks across the country on issues relating to America's youth.

Naomi E. Singer has been a teacher in Newton, Massachusetts, for more than 20 years. In her role as language arts and reading specialist, she teaches kindergarten through grade 5, and works with faculty and staff to coordinate and integrate the language arts program with all other areas of the curriculum. Naomi is the author of several literature units for grades 2 through 5, as well as the co-author of *A+ Activities for First Grade* and *A+ Activities for Second Grade.* She lives in Watertown, Massachusetts.

Mary Snyder is the co-author of *You CAN Afford to Stay Home with Your Kids* (Career Press, 1999), available from most major bookstores, Amazon.com, or by calling 1-800-Career1. In 1995, Mary Snyder traded her business suits for blue jeans and power lunches with CEOs for peanut butter and jelly sandwiches with her kids. This life-changing shift became the catalyst for her co-authored book, *You CAN Afford to Stay Home with Your Kids.* Since publication of the book, Mary has launched a successful freelance writing career. Mary's work has appeared in national print magazines and on a variety of web sites. She writes on subjects ranging from parenting and relationships to investing trends and retirement issues. Mary is currently at work on her second nonfiction book—a look at how the media impacts the way we raise our children. Mary lives in Remlap, Alabama, with her husband, Vaughn, and her two daughters, Charity and Paige.

Paula Statman, LCSW, is the award-winning author of *On the Safe Side: Raising, Careful, Confident Kids in a Crazy World* and *Life on a Balance Beam. On the Safe Side* was recently revised and retitled as *Raising Careful, Confident Kids* (available direct by calling 1-800-300-9800). Statman is founder of the KidWISE Institute, 484 Lake Park Ave., #101, Oakland, CA 94610, 1-888-KID-WISE; www.kidwiseinstitute.com. KidWISE offers an instructor certification program for qualified candidates who want to teach the popular workshop, "Raising Careful, Confident Kids in a Crazy World." Paula Statman is a sought-after speaker who presents parenting and women's programs at professional conferences and community events. Her views and articles appear regularly in such magazines as *Redbook, Parents,* and *Sesame Street.* She is frequent guest on television programs such as *The Oprah Winfrey Show* and *Today.*

Maureen Stout, Ph.D., received her doctorate in education from UCLA. She also has degrees from the London School of Economics, the University of London, and the University of British Columbia. Dr. Stout is currently teaching in the Faculty of Education at the University of British Columbia. For 6 years prior to that, she taught in the College of Education at the California State University, Northridge. Dr. Stout is the author of *The Feel-Good Curriculum: The Dumbing-Down of America's Kids in the Name of Self-Esteem,* published by Perseus (2000) in hardback and paperback (2001). She has also published papers in academic journals in education, presented at major conferences, and received a number of awards, including the Social Sciences and Humanities Council of Canada Doctoral Fellowship. In 1997, Dr. Stout was chosen as one of 167 "future leaders" to attend the United Nations University International Leadership Program in Amman, Jordan, where scholars and future leaders from around the world studied with international leaders such as Shimon Peres, Yasser Arafat, the King and Queen of Jordan, UN officials, and many others.

Edward Teyber is a clinical psychologist and psychology professor at California State University, San Bernardino. He is the author of the award-winning book *Helping Children Cope with Divorce*, which has now been translated into eight languages (Jossey-Bass: revised 2001). He has published numerous research articles on the effects of marital and family relations on child adjustment, and he regularly contributes articles on parenting and post divorce family relations to newspapers and magazines. Dr. Teyber is also the author of two counseling textbooks: *Interpersonal Process in Psychotherapy* and *Case Studies in Child and Adolescent Treatment*.

Christopher A. Thurber, Ph.D., is a licensed clinical psychologist and the co-author of *The Summer Camp Handbook: Everything You Need to Find, Choose, and Get Ready for Overnight Camp—And Skip the Homesickness!* The culmination of 6 years of camp-based research, *The Summer Camp Handbook* contains helpful information for families on preparing for camp, preventing homesickness, and getting the most out of the camping experience. Dr. Thurber grew up in Maine, where he attended day camp before mustering up the courage to attend overnight camp in nearby New Hampshire. He has been working at camps ever since, and now consults to the American Camping Association and conducts camp staff training workshops nationwide. Dr. Thurber earned a B.A. from Harvard University and a Ph.D. in clinical psychology from the University of California at Los Angeles. It was during his graduate work at UCLA and during a postdoctoral fellowship at the University of Washington that he conducted his landmark studies on homesickness. In addition to *The Summer Camp Handbook*, Dr. Thurber is the author of a dozen scholarly articles on homesickness and children's adjustment to separation from home. Summaries of this research have been featured by *CBS News*, National Public Radio, *US News & World Report*, the *Wall Street Journal*, the *Washington Post*, *Parents*, *Parenting*, and numerous web sites including www.familyhelp.com. When he is not at camp, Dr. Thurber teaches and works as a psychologist at Phillips Exeter Academy, a boarding high school in Exeter, New Hampshire. He can be reached at cthurber@exeter.edu.

Cynthia Ulrich Tobias, M.A. is a motivational speaker and best-selling author of six books, including the classic *The Way They Learn*. She was a public high school teacher for 8 years, served 6 years in law enforcement, and more than 12 years as a business owner. She holds a master's degree in learning styles. A lifelong strong-willed child herself, she also has her own strong-willed son, and has talked to and worked with hundreds of strong-willed children and adults. Contact: AppLe St. LLC, P.O. Box 1450, Sumner, WA 98390; (253) 862-6200; e-mail: Applest@aol.com; web sites: www.applest.com and www.cantmakeme.com.

Rae Turnbull is a mentor teacher, author, designer, and calligrapher who uses a wide range of professional experience in her successful teaching strategies. She is a syndicated columnist whose poetic essay feature, "Friend of the Family," appears in five major newspapers in the West and Midwest. The essays offer heartwarming views of everyday events that reflect the richness of family life. Her limited edition books, collections of her essays, are *Echoes in the Corners of My Heart, When Wildflowers Are in Bloom,* and *When the Heart Most Clearly Speaks.* Her essays and short stories have been published in magazines such as *First for Women, Good Housekeeping,* and the quarterly *Becoming Family.* Rae Turnbull is also the creator of the intensive ten-session seminar series, "Forum for Parents: The Parent as a Teacher." Her most recent book, *Be the Parent Your Child Deserves,* published by New Page Books, a division of Career Press, is based on the forum and is designed to help parents understand that their primary parental role is to teach. The book offers a new vision. Parents find the power to lead, motivate, and inspire their children to become self-reliant adults. Parents gain the courage to face up to the changes they may need to make in their own lives, in order to be the parent their children deserve. Rae Turnbull's extensive teaching career spans 40 years. It includes a variety of teaching experiences at prominent eastern college preparatory schools, a school for exceptional children in Los Angeles, as well as small rural schools in the West. Her teaching credits also include California State University, Long Beach, and California State University, Chico. Students of Hamilton Union High School (twice awarded California Distinguished School honors) voted her Teacher of the Year in 1990. Listed in *Who's Who Among America's Teachers,* Rae Turnbull was inducted into the Glenn County Educator's Hall of Fame in 2001. These exceptionally varied credentials as an author and a teacher allow Rae Turnbull to offer unusually keen insights into the rightful role of the parent as a child's first teacher.

Jackie Waldman began her career teaching special needs children in Dallas Public Schools. She was living "the perfect life with three healthy children, a loving husband, and a thriving business" when she discovered she had multiple sclerosis. Instead of dwelling on her physical pain, she began a new career in volunteerism. She inspires others to give through volunteering—no matter what—and to discover that they, too, can triumph over tragedy to make a difference in the world. Waldman co-founded Dallas' Random Acts of Kindness Week. She is the author of four books, *The Courage to Give, Teens with the Courage to Give, Teachers with the Courage to Give,* and *America, September 11th: The Courage to Give* (all proceeds from the sale of *America, September 11th* are being donated to the American Red Cross and the New York Firefighters Fund). She was chosen by CNN as one of their Millennium Heroes, and has appeared a number of times on the Oprah Winfrey Show. Waldman's *Finding Your Courage to Give* is a workshop program specifically designed for corperations, schools, and non profit organizations. The process allows an individual to discover his/her "giving style" and provides the necessary tools to create an action plan to volunteer, according to each individual's uniqueness. She lives in Dallas, Texas, with her husband of 29 years, three children, and a miniature dachshund. For more information about Jackie Waldman, volunteer opportunities, and the subject of her books, visit her web shite at www.couragetogive.com. For speaking and workshop inquiries, please call Karen Frost at 703-836-3770.

Penny Warner, M.A., has written over thirty books for parents and kids featuring child development, parties, games, activities, and snacks. Her books include *Slumber Parties, Preschool Play and Learn, Baby Play and Learn Book, Baby Birthday Parties, Kids' Outdoor Parties, Travel Fun for Two, Kids' Pick-a-Party, Big Book of Party & Holiday Fun, Games People Play, Great Games for Kids On the Go, Kids' Party Cookbook, Giant Book of Kids' Activities & Games, Splish Splash— Water Fun for Kids, Birthday Parties for Kids, Kids' Holiday Fun, Healthy Treats & Super Snacks, Contemporary Kids' Party Games and Activities, Best Party Book, Penny Warner's Party Book, Happy Birthday Parties, Super Toys, Super Snacks for Kids, Healthy Snacks for Kids,* Coming soon: *Quality Time, Anytime, Storybook Parties, Baby's First Year—Week by Week, First Year Baby Care, Learn to Sign the Fun Way, Dance Parties, Office Parties,* and a new series for middle-grade girls: *Troop 13 Mystery of the Haunted Caves, Troop 13 Mystery of the Missing Mustangs.* Warner has a bachelor's degree in early childhood education and a master's degree in special education. She teaches child development courses at Diablo Valley College, and has taught special education, infant/toddler development, and sign language. Warner appeared on several San Francisco TV talk shows for 4 years, and on national TV, presenting tips for parents and kids. She was recently featured on HGTV's *Smart Solutions* and *Later Today.* Warner also wrote a weekly newspaper column for 11 years on family life. She lives in Danville, California, with her husband and has two children.

Lisa Whelchel is the author of *Creative Correction—Ideas for Everyday Discipline* for Tyndale House Publishers, *The Facts of Life and Other Lessons My Father Taught Me* for Multnomah Publishers. Lisa Whelchel played the part of Blair Warner on NBC's *The Facts of Life* for nine seasons. You can view her web site at www.LisaWhelchel.com.

Dr. Burton L. White is considered among the world's leading authorities on early childhood development. He is the author of *The New First Three Years of Life: The Completely Revised and Updated Edition of the Parenting Classic* and *Raising a Happy, Unspoiled Child*, which was deemed as the most valuable guide to a child's development on the market by the *Detroit Free Press*. Dr. White is the director of the Center for Parent Education in Newton, Massachusetts, and the designer of the Missouri New Parents as Teachers Project. The father of four (now grown) children, he lives in Waban, Massachusetts.

Valerie Wiener, M.A., M.A., started her career in communications in 1964 as a commercial radio talk show host in Las Vegas, Nevada. Wiener is a nationally recognized author, magazine writer, consultant, and speaker in both corporate and youth markets. She has written five books, including *Gang Free: Friendship Choices for Today's Youth, The Nesting Syndrome: Grown Children Living at Home*, and *Winning the War Against Youth Gangs: A Guide for Teens, Families and Communities*. Wiener is also a Nevada state senator. E-mail: Vwiener@aol.com; web sites: www.ValerieWiener.com and www.PowerMarkPublishing.com.

James Windell, M.A., is a juvenile court psychologist, an author, and a psychotherapist in private practice. He has worked in the juvenile justice system for almost 25 years. For the past 9 years, he has been a psychologist in the Oakland County Juvenile Court, in Oakland County, Michigan. In the last 7 years he has done group therapy with delinquents, and prior to that, he developed a discipline training program for parents of delinquents. His first book, *Discipline: A Sourcebook of 50 Failsafe Techniques for Parents*, was published in 1991. Since then, he has written *8 Weeks to a Well-Behaved Child, Children Who Say No When You Want Them to Say Yes, Six Steps to an Emotionally Intelligent Teenager*, and is co-author of *What You Need to Know About Ritalin*. Windell is also a columnist; his "Coping with Kids" has appeared in the *Oakland Press* for the past 14 years. He was the mental health columnist for the *Detroit Free Press*, was the "Coping with Kids" columnist for *Working*

410

Mother magazine, and has written numerous booklets and journal articles. Windell has appeared on more than 150 radio and television shows, including CNN, *Kelly and Company*, *Gerry Spence*, and *Donahue*. In addition, he is a parenting expert who is frequently sought for quotes in all of the leading parenting and women's magazines. His books and his research with parents have been featured in many leading newspapers, including the *Chicago Sun Times*, the *Detroit News*, the *Detroit Free Press*, and the *New York Times*. His web site features his books and columns and can be found at www.Jameswindell.com. He welcomes questions from readers and is happy to give parenting advice by e-mail: JWIND27961@aol.com.

Nicole Wise is an award-winning journalist who has written about health and family life for more than 15 years. Her work has been featured in a wide range of national and international publications, including the *New York Times*, *Parents*, *Woman's Day*, *Good Housekeeping*, *Redbook*, *Parenting*, *Child*, and others. Life at home in Connecticut, where she lives with her husband and four children, is richer and happier than it used to be—before she began working on, and living, *The Over-Scheduled Child: Avoiding the Hyper-Parenting Trap* (Griffin/St. Martins, 2001), co-authored with Alvin Rosenfeld, M.D.

Bettie B. Youngs, Ph.D., is former teacher of the year, university professor, and author of twenty books published in nineteen languages, including the Pulitzer-nominated *Gifts of the Heart*; *A String of Pearls*; *Taste Berry Tales*; and *Values from the Heartland*. She is co-author of the national best-seller *Taste Berries for Teen* series and a frequent guest on television and radio talk shows. Contact Bettie B. Youngs, 3060 Racetrack View Drive, Del Mar, CA 92014; e-mail: byoungsint@aol.com.

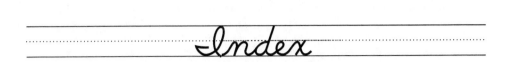

acceptance, 182, 187
accidents, 66
accountability, 147
active listening, 122. see also *listening*
activities, 10
ADD/ADHD, 285, 291
adjustment problems, 308
adolescents, 2, 22, 27
  and accountability, 141
  and ADD/ADHD, 291
  and anger, 39
  and anxiety, 302
  and autism, 297
  challenges of parenting, 13
  and conflict, 181
  and control, 141, 164
  conversations with, 263
  and creativity, 323
  and discipline, 132, 154, 160
  and divorce, 308, 314
  and encouragement, 266
  and family values, 254
  and fathers, 222
  and foundation stones, 34
  and giving, 274
  and giving thanks, 268
  good parenting of, 8, 19, 31
  and gratitude, 261
  health care of, 48, 65
  intimate conversations with, 61
  letters to, 98
  listening to, 106
  and multiple intelligences, 210
  and only children, 286
  and perfect mother myth, 90
  and play, 320, 341
  and positive memories, 271
  and power struggles, 119
  and praise, 136
  protecting, 114
  and reading, 216
  and self-belief, 238
  and self-esteem, 233
  and self-reliance, 242
  and separations, 55
  and sleep, 51
  strong-willed, 172
  and teasing, 228, 247
  viewpoints of, 6
  and weight problems, 70
  and youth sports, 335
adoption, 264
adult-onset diabetes, 67
affection, physical, 139
aggression, 293
alarm reactions, 304
alcoholism, 264
aloneness, 189. see also *loneliness*
alpha-speech, 132
ambivalence, 87, 283
American Academy of Pediatrics (AAP), 48
anger, 37, 87
anorexia, 68. see also *eating disorders*
askable parents, 264
aspirations, 290
attachment parenting, 7
attention, positive, 136, 151
attitudes, 239
authority, 111, 173. see also *leadership*
autism, 297
availability, 191

babies, 2, 22, 27
  and anger, 39

and autism, 297
challenges of parenting, 13
and control over food, 70
and divorce, 314
and encouragement, 266
and family values, 254
and fathers, 222
and foundation stones, 34
good parenting of, 8, 19, 31, 80
and gratitude, 261
health care of, 48, 65
letters to, 98
and multiple intelligences, 210
and only children, 286
and perfect mother myth, 90
and play, 320
and power struggles, 119
protecting, 114
and reading, 216
and self-esteem, 233
and self-reliance, 242
and separations, 55
and sleep, 51
and trust, 61
viewpoints of, 6
badgering, 166
Bailey, Becky A., 181, 382
bedtimes, 11, 53, 209
Bemelmans, Ludwig, 216
Biederman, Lorin Michelle and Jerry, xix, 357, 372, 417
Blackstone-Ford, Jann, 314, 382
bonus parents, 314
Borba, Michele, 238, 383
boredom, 323
Brazelton, T. Berry, 285
breast development, 63
Brennan, Heidi, 95
Brenner, Mark L., 129, 383
bulimia, 68. see also *eating disorders*
Bullen, Martha M., 93, 384
Burnett, Darrell J., 147, 335, 384
Buscaglia, Leo, 18, 319
Bush, George, 269
buttering up, 167

Campbell, Ross, 34, 385
carbohydrates, 73
Catlin, Cynthia, 345
Center for Research on Women, 93
challenges, 9, 77
Chambers, Suzanne, 97
charity, 255
Cheney, Ron, 224
child roles, 98
child spacing, 81
choices, 14, 29, 72, 122, 131, 282
chores, 11
co-sleeping, 7
communication
    and discipline, 110, 132, 138, 193
    and divorce, 311
    and sign language, 76
    tips for, 264
comparisons, 234, 240
compassion, 23
competition, 336
confidence, 233. see also *self-esteem*
conflict, 74
consequences
    of actions, 9, 154
    of choices, 29
    and empathy, 278
    and responsibilities, 148
control, 31, 68, 72, 107, 143, 174
cooperation, 106, 120, 155, 176
coping skills, 59, 229, 248
    and anxiety, 302
    and humor, 333
crime, 223
criticism, 214

Dacey, John S., 302, 385
Dalgleish, Alice, 219
death, 264
decisions, 9
defiance, 173
depression, 52, 67
    and perfect mother myth, 88
determination, 173
development, stages of, 32
diabetes, 67

difficulties, 9
DiGeronimo, Theresa Foy, 263, 385
discipline, 28, 32, 124, 132
    and anger management, 41
    and creative correction, 359, 367
    and divorce, 311
    and foundational stones, 36
disconnection, 8, 88
distraction, 121, 349
Dobson, James, 173
Doe, Mimi, 261, 385
Deicers, Rudolf, 122
Duffy, Roslyn, 124, 386

Eastman, Meg, 39, 386
Eastman, PD, 216
eating disorders, 68
emotional
    control, 40
    health, 8, 52
    maturation, 62
    needs, 36
    swings, 64
    tones, 155
empathy, 101, 234
encouragement, 352
equality, 255
Erwin, Cheryl L., 320, 386
expectations, 157, 162, 179
    and only children, 287
    and self-esteem, 234
    and youth sports, 339
    of parents, 11, 16
    eye contact, 262

failures, 21, 25, 199, 234
faith, 17. see also *spirituality*
family
    crest, 207
    meetings, 120
    planning, 81
    read-in, 206
    values, 16 see also *values*
Fay, Charles, 323, 387
Fay, Jim, 141, 228, 387
feminism, 96

fertility, 82
Fiore, Lisa B., 302, 387
Fletcher, Chris, 90, 388
flexibility, 23, 108
follicle-stimulating hormone (FSH)
tests, 82
food testing, 71
Ford, Judy, 266, 282, 388
forgiveness, 103
foundation stones, 35
fragmentation in families, 8
Frankel, Fred, 247, 389
Frankly, Viktor E., 203
freedom, 116
Frill, John C. and Linda D., 8, 389
From, Eric, 14
fruits, 72
frustration, 52

Garcia, Joseph, 76, 389
Garcia-Parts, Catherine Masco and
Joseph, 13, 390
Gardner, Howard, 212
Garvey, William P., 154, 391
gender inequities, 65
generational contact, 190
Gilbert, Susan, 65, 391
Gilroy, Jessica B., 61, 391
goals
    and self-reliance, 245
    of parents, 95
good lives, 254
Goodman, Marilyn E., 160, 391
Gray, John, 106, 392
Greenwood, Jacqueline, 224
guilt, 166
Gurian, Michael, 2, 392

happiness, 99, 245
Hearne, Betsy, 218
Hirsch, Patricia, 189, 392
Holmes, J. A., 227
home schooling, 94
homosexuality, 264
honesty, 265
hunger, 71

Hunt, Gladys, 219
Hunter, Lesley, 307
hyperactivity, 293

inattention, 293
independence, 55, 115, 242
Indichova, Julia, 82, 393
individuality, 15
infants, 2, 22, 27
   and anger, 39
   and autism, 297
   challenges of parenting, 13
   and control over food, 70
   and divorce, 314
   and encouragement, 266
   and family values, 254
   and fathers, 222
   and foundation stones, 34
   good parenting of, 8, 19, 31, 80
   and gratitude, 261
   health care of, 48, 65
   letters to, 98
   and multiple intelligences, 210
   and only children, 286
   and perfect mother myth, 86, 90
   and play, 320
   and power struggles, 119
   protecting, 114
   and reading, 216
   and self-esteem, 233
   and self-reliance, 242
   and separations, 55
   and sign language, 76
   and sleep, 51
   and trust, 61
   viewpoints of, 6
inner resources, 77
interactions, 155
interpersonal bonds, 55
interpersonal styles, 155
intimidation, 166
involvement, 191

Kennedy, Rose, xiv, 1
Kinas, Aaron, 222, 393
Kalian, Karen, 86, 393

knee injuries, 66
Kuffner, Trish, 216, 344, 394
Kutner, Lawrence, 31, 394

labels, 240
Lamb, Sandra E., 268, 395
Landers, Ann, 105
Leach, Penelope, xv, 381
leadership, 106, 132
   roles, 8, 28
learning, 213
life, meaning of, 2
limits, 10, 107, 154, 160
listening, 101, 106, 197, 214
loneliness, 3. see also *aloneness*
love, 91, 99. see also *unconditional love*
   choosing, 14
   and discipline, 182
   as a family value, 255
   and positive memories, 272

macronutrients, 74
manipulation, 165
manual communication, 78
marriages, 9
Martin, William, 22, 395
martyrdom, 166
Marx, Groucho, 85
masturbation, 264
McCloskey, Robert, 216
Mednick, Fred, 197, 395
memory, 52
menstruation, 62
mentors, of parents, 96
Metcalf, Linda, 293
Michelli, Joseph Anthony, 332, 396
Miller, Matthew J., 204, 396
misinformation, 264
mistakes, 10, 108
money, 107
Mothers and More, 96
Mothers at Home, 95

name-calling, 247
naps, 52
National Institute Mental Health, 9

natural consequences, 158
natural virtues, 24
Neifert, Marianne, 27, 396
Nelsen, Jane, 119, 397
Newberger, Eli H., 285
Newman, Susan, 286, 397
nicknames, 239
Nixon, Brenda, 253
non-verbal messages, 122, 229
normal behavior, 32
Nylund, David, 291, 398

O'Brien, Maureen A., 369
obedience, 106
obesity, 67
onliness, 287
only children, 286
overexposure, 117
overprotecting, 114
overscheduling, 10, 68, 326

parental
    involvement, 49, 62, 337
    roles, 94, 98, 153, 244
    styles, 155
patience, 101, 214
pediatricians, 49
Penn, Irving, 70, 398
perfect mother myth, 87
perfectionism, 68
Perry, Susan K., 341, 398
perspective, of child, 7
Phelan, Thomas W., 164, 399
physical maturation, 62
physical tactics, 168
pick-up deals, 56
Pillsbury, Linda Goodman, 363, 400
Plato, 319
play, 53, 333
pleasure, 255
pornography, 264
positive intent, 185
positive memories, 271
power, 109
    assertion of, 279
    struggles for, 144, 154, 182

practice, 126
praise, 136
pressures, 288
preverbal infants, 76
priorities, 3, 14, 16, 28, 89, 102
problem solving, 76, 120, 278, 327
puberty, 63
punishment, 109, 119. see also *discipline*
    differs from discipline, 33, 36
    and empathy, 279

quality time, 16, 20, 27, 80, 107, 123
questions, 214

Raskin, Valerie Davis, 43, 400
Reagan, Ronald, 269
rebellion, 173
reflective listening, 122. see also *listening*
Reiser, Paul, 75
resistance exercises, 66
respect, 15, 112
responsibilities, 101, 120, 148, 179, 234
revenge, 165
Ritalin, 292
rituals, 186. see also *traditions*
Rosemond, John, 132, 400
Rosenfeld, Alvin, 254, 400
Rothenberg, Michael B., 47
routines, 53, 120, 292
rubbing alcohol, 373
rules
    and discipline, 154, 160
    and driving, 365
    and structure, 11

Samalin, Nancy, 367, 401
Sanders, Darcie, 93, 401
satisfaction, 93
Schaefer, Charles E., 263, 402
Schaenen, Inda, 51, 402
Schmidt, Laurel, 210, 403
Schulz, Charles, 332
Sears, Martha and William, 6, 402
Security Dads, 224

self-care, of parents, 9, 29, 43, 298, 379
self-confidence, 25, 233
self-control, 41
self-discipline, 120, 136
self-esteem, 8, 20, 27, 108
    from accomplishment, 56
    and divorce, 310
    undermining, 115
    and youth sports, 336
self-images, 239
self-reliance, 199
self-respect, 243
self-worth, 14, 16, 120
separations, 55, 312
Seroussi, Karyn, 403
seven intelligences, 212
sexual
    maturation, 62
    relationships, 43
Shelov, Steven, 48, 404
Sherrard, Jain, 344
Shure, Myrna B., 277, 405
sibling rivalry, 16
sign language, 77
Singer, Naomi E., 204, 405
sleep, xvi, 52, 88, 375
Snyder, Mary, 19, 405
socialization, 234
solo sleeping, 7
spanking, xvi, 119, 279. see also *punishment*
spirituality, 10, 17, 29, 89, 101. see also *faith*
Spock, Benjamin, 47
sports injuries, 66
standards, relaxing, 91
Statman, Paula, 114, 195, 406
stepparents, 314
stereotyping, 239
stimulation, 324, 346
Stout, Maureen, 233, 406
strength training, 66
strong-willed children, 172
structure, 11
struggles, 9, 21
successes, 14, 77, 238

sugars, 73
summer camp, 56
supervision, 121, 344
support networks, 95
Sutherland, Zena, 219

teaseproofing, 229
teenagers, 2, 22, 27
    and accountability, 141
    and ADD/ADHD, 291
    and aloneness, 189
    and anger, 39
    and anxiety, 302
    and autism, 297
    challenges of parenting, 13
    and conflict, 181
    and control, 141, 164
    conversations with, 263
    and creativity, 323
    and discipline, 132, 154
    and disciplines, 160
    and divorce, 308, 314
    and encouragement, 266
    and family values, 254
    and fathers, 222
    and foundation stones, 34
    and giving, 274
    and giving thanks, 268
    good parenting of, 8, 19, 31, 197
    and gratitude, 261
    health care of, 48, 65
    intimate conversations with, 61
    letters to, 98
    listening to, 106
    and multiple intelligences, 210
    and only children, 286
    and perfect mother myth, 90
    and play, 320
    and positive memories, 271
    and power struggles, 119
    and praise, 136
    protecting, 114
    and reading, 216
    and responsibilities, 179
    and self-belief, 238
    and self-esteem, 233

and self-reliance, 242
and separations, 55
and sleep, 51
strong-willed, 172
and teasing, 228, 247
viewpoints of, 6
and weight problems, 70
and youth sports, 335
teeth, 73
television, 327, 351
temper tantrums, 156, 166
testing, 165
Teyber, Edward, 308, 407
thank-you notes, 269
thanks, giving, 261, 268
thoughtfulness, 261
threats, 166
Thurber, Christopher A., 55, 407
time-outs, 121, 279, 361
Tobias, Cynthia Ulrich, 172, 407
toddlers, 2, 22, 27, 344
    and accountability, 141
    and ADD/ADHD, 291
    and anger, 39
    and anxiety, 302
    and autism, 297
    challenges of parenting, 13
    and conflict, 181
    and control, 141, 164
    and control over food, 70
    conversations with, 263
    and creativity, 323
    and dining out, 124
    and discipline, 132, 154, 160
    and divorce, 308, 314
    and driving, 363
    and empathy, 277
    and encouragement, 266
    and family values, 254
    and fathers, 222
    and foundation stones, 34
    and giving, 274
    and giving thanks, 268
    good parenting of, 8, 19, 31, 80
    and gratitude, 261
    health care of, 48, 65

letters to, 98
listening to, 106
and multiple intelligences, 210
and only children, 286
and perfect mother myth, 90
and play, 320, 341
and positive memories, 271
and power struggles, 119
and praise, 136
protecting, 114
and reading, 216
and self-belief, 238
and self-esteem, 233
and self-reliance, 242
and separations, 55
and sharing, 129
and sleep, 51
strong-willed, 172
and teasing, 228, 247
and trust, 61
viewpoints of, 6
and youth sports, 335
toy exchanges, 348
traditions, 29. see also *rituals*
transitions, 7, 316
Trelease, Jim, 219
trust, 58, 61, 120
Turnbull, Rae, 242, 408
Twain, Mark, 216

U.S. Department of Education, 225
unconditional love, 26, 27. see also
love
united front, 149, 199

validation, of parents, 95
values, 17. see also *family values*
Vannoy, Steven W., 203
vegetables, 72
video games, 327
viewpoint, of child, 6
violence, 222, 293
visualization, 304
vitamins, 72
volunteering, 275

Waldman, Jackie, 274, 408
Wallace, Linda, 224
Warner, Penny, 354, 409
weaknesses, 99
weight training, 66
Whelchel, Lisa, 358, 410
White, Burton, 80, 410
Wiener, Valerie, 179, 410
Windell, James, 136, 410
Winnett, Azriel, 285
Wise, Nicole, 254, 411
wounds, childhood, 10

Youngs, Bettie B., 98, 411

About the Editors

Lorin Michelle Biederman

Lorin Michelle Biederman, after working in the entertainment industry for many years, now devotes her time to her writing. Along with her husband, author Jerry Biederman, she is co-author of the book *101 Ways to See the Light* (St. Martin's Press) and *Earth Angels: True Stories About Real People Who Bring Heaven to Earth* (Broadway Books, a division of Random House). *Earth Angels* was the inspiration behind Oprah Winfrey's "Oprah's Angel Network." As an outgrowth of their work on the highly successful book, the Biedermans are in the process of establishing a nonprofit organization, which will match people in need with an Earth Angel.

Lorin is also a poet and a teacher. Her poems have been published in several anthologies and have won a number of awards. She lives in Woodland Hills, California, with her husband, their 4-year-old daughter, Jennifer, their 2½-year-old son, David, and their dog, Disney.

Jerry Biederman

Jerry Biederman's popular book, *Secrets of a Small Town: The Extraordinary Confessions of Ordinary People* (Dell), was the true story of Biederman's journey to a small town "somewhere in America," where he went on "a scavenger hunt" for strangers' secrets. It was a Book-of-the-Month Club selection, and was syndicated to more than 400 newspapers. *Secrets of a Small Town* was the recipient of a prestigious international publishing award for "best representation of the English language."

Jerry authored his first book, *The Do-It-Yourself Bestseller* (Doubleday), at the age of 21. It included original story beginnings written exclusively for his book by such authors as Stephen King, Ken Follett, Isaac Asimov, Belva Plain, Erskine Caldwell, Alvin Toffler, and Irving Wallace (Jerry's uncle). *The Bestseller* promoted literacy for school children and was the focus of a national high school writing competition (the first such contest in Doubleday's 85-year history). The book received massive national media attention and outstanding reviews. In a full-page article, the *Washington Post* "Book World" dubbed Jerry Biederman a "West Coast Wunderkind."

Another Jerry Biederman collection, *My First Real Romance*, was a gathering of true stories about the first real-life romances of twenty best-selling romance authors. This award-winning book reached the Waldenbooks national bestseller list.

He's a Girl! (Price/Stern/Sloan) was a celebration of "expectant fatherhood." Jerry collaborated on the book with his cousin, best-selling author David Wallechinsky (*What Really Happened to the Class of '65, The People's Almanac, The Book of Lists*). In *He's a Girl!* fathers at a Los Angeles maternity ward were asked to share their thoughts and feelings on the day of their child's birth.

Most recently, Jerry collaborated on *Earth Angels: True Stories About Real People Who Bring Heaven to Earth* with his wife, author/poet Lorin Michelle Biederman. *Parent School* is the writing couple's third book collaboration.

Jerry has collaborated on various other literary ventures with such authors as Roald Dahl, Richard Adams, P. L. Travers, Madeleine L'Engle, Rebecca West, and Clare Boothe Luce. Jerry Biederman has garnered a reputation among New York publishers for his ability to bring together ordinary people (in the tradition of Studs Terkel), as well as prominent personalities in any given field (from Hollywood celebrities to U.S. presidents. Among his most cherished professional contacts to date is the first man to walk on the moon, Neil Armstrong). Biederman's books have been featured on *Good Morning America* and written about in the *New York Times, Los Angeles Times*, and *People* magazine, as well as many others. In addition to being an author, he is also a creator and producer of a number of reality TV series.

Extra Credit

Parent School invites you to offer *your own advice* to be shared with others in a soon-to-be published new *Parent School* book of greatest lessons from mom and dads.

Send your lesson (1,000 words or less) for possible publication to:

Parent School: *Real-life Lessons from Moms and Dads for Moms and Dads*
E-mail: ParentSchool@aol.com

Include your name, age, occupation, city of residence, and information about your children (how many, ages, genders) for publication along with your lesson. Let us know how we can contact you to let you know if your lesson has been selected.

Thank you for sharing your priceless gifts of insight, knowledge, and experience.

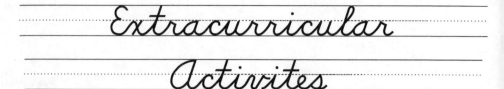
Extracurricular Activites

Never before have so many parenting experts come together under one cover for one purpose! If you would like members of the *Parent School* faculty to speak to your group or organization, they can be contacted through Jerry and Lorin Biederman at:

Parent School
E-mail: ParentSchool@aol.com

Or through:
M. Evans and Company, Inc.
216 East 49th Street
New York, New York
Phone: (212) 688-2810
E-mail: publicity@mevans.com